Edward Bouverie Pusey
and the Oxford Movement

Edward Bouverie Pusey and the Oxford Movement

Edited by Rowan Strong
and Carol Engelhardt Herringer

ANTHEM PRESS
LONDON · NEW YORK · DELHI

Anthem Press
An imprint of Wimbledon Publishing Company
www.anthempress.com

This edition first published in UK and USA 2014
by ANTHEM PRESS
75–76 Blackfriars Road, London SE1 8HA, UK
or PO Box 9779, London SW19 7ZG, UK
and
244 Madison Ave. #116, New York, NY 10016, USA

First published in hardback by Anthem Press in 2012

© 2014 Rowan Strong and Carol Engelhardt Herringer
editorial matter and selection; individual chapters © individual contributors

The moral right of the authors has been asserted.

All rights reserved. Without limiting the rights under copyright reserved above,
no part of this publication may be reproduced, stored or introduced into
a retrieval system, or transmitted, in any form or by any means
(electronic, mechanical, photocopying, recording or otherwise),
without the prior written permission of both the copyright
owner and the above publisher of this book.

British Library Cataloguing-in-Publication Data
A catalogue record for this book is available from the British Library.

Library of Congress Cataloging-in-Publication Data
The Library of Congress has catalogued the hardcover edition as follows:
Edward Bouverie Pusey and the Oxford movement / edited by Rowan Strong
and Carol Engelhardt Herringer.
p. cm.
Includes bibliographical references and index.
ISBN 978-0-85728-565-2 (hardback : alk. paper)
1. Pusey, E. B. (Edward Bouverie), 1800–1882. 2. Oxford movement.
3. Church of England–Clergy–Biogrpahy. I. Strong, Rowan.
II. Herringer, Carol Engelhardt.
BX5199.P9E39 2012
283.092–dc23
2012030102

ISBN-13: 978 1 78308 318 3 (Pbk)
ISBN-10: 1 78308 318 2 (Pbk)

This title is also available as an ebook.

CONTENTS

Acknowledgements		vii
Notes on Contributors		ix
Chapter One	Introduction *Rowan Strong and Carol Engelhardt Herringer*	1
Chapter Two	The History of the History of Pusey *Ian McCormack*	13
Chapter Three	Editing Liddon: From Biography to Hagiography? *K. E. Macnab*	31
Chapter Four	From Modern-Orthodox Protestantism to Anglo-Catholicism: An Enquiry into the Probable Causes of the Revolution of Pusey's Theology *Albrecht Geck*	49
Chapter Five	Defining the Church: Pusey's Ecclesiology and its Eighteenth-Century Antecedents *R. Barry Levis*	67
Chapter Six	Pusey's Eucharistic Doctrine *Carol Engelhardt Herringer*	91
Chapter Seven	Pusey, Alexander Forbes and the First Vatican Council *Mark Chapman*	115
Chapter Eight	Pusey and the Scottish Episcopal Church: Tractarian Diversity and Divergence *Rowan Strong*	133
Bibliography		149
Index		161

ACKNOWLEDGEMENTS

Pusey House, Oxford, has been a home from home for countless scholars, who come for its vast collection of materials on the Oxford Movement as well as on patristics and liturgy, and then happily find themselves in a community of scholars whose transience is alleviated by their frequent return visits. In many significant ways, this volume would not exist if Pusey House did not exist. The work produced in these pages is very often the product of work begun or continued in Pusey House Library, often with the guidance of the previous custodian, Fr William Davage; the previous priest librarian, Kenneth Macnab; and the current priest librarian, Fr Barry Orford. They, along with the previous and current principals, Fr Phillip Ursell and the Right Reverend Jonathan Baker, have ensured that Pusey House is a place of scholarship for scholars from around the world.

In a more practical way, this volume would not exist without Fr Davage and Fr Orford, who first proposed holding a conference to celebrate Edward Pusey, an idea that delighted Carol Engelhardt Herringer when she read about it in the Pusey House newsletter in 2007. These three declared themselves a programme committee, and arrangements were made to hold a three-day conference, 'Edward Bouverie Pusey and the Catholic Revival', at Ascot Priory, Berkshire, on 14–16 September 2009.

At the conference, ten scholars from Britain, the Continent, North America and Australia presented papers on the ideas and influence of Edward Bouverie Pusey. In addition to the papers that were expanded and developed to become the essays that make up this volume, Fr Orford, Serenhedd James, and Victoria Houseman also presented papers, which we hope will be published in the future. During the conference, Fr Ursell, now the warden of Ascot Priory, was a gracious host. We are also grateful to those who attended the conference without presenting a paper, for their comments helped the participants think through their ideas before presenting them in this volume.

Finally, we wish to express our thanks to Jill Strong and Tom Herringer, who provide us with comfort and intellectual stimulation and who have heard far more about Edward Bouverie Pusey and the Oxford Movement than they ever thought possible.

NOTES ON CONTRIBUTORS

Mark Chapman is vice-principal of Ripon College Cuddesdon, Oxford, reader in modern theology at the University of Oxford and visiting professor in church history at Oxford Brookes University. He has written widely in many different areas of theology and history. His most recent book is *Anglican Theology* (T&T Clark, 2012).

Privatdozent **Albrecht Geck** teaches church history at the University of Osnabruck and religious studies in Herne (Pestalozzi Grammar School). He completed his doctorate on the religious politics of Friedrich Schleiermacher and has also published widely on the relations between Anglican and German Lutheran theology. His most recent book is a critical edition of the correspondence between Edward Pusey and Friedrich Tholuck. He is director of the Institute of Contemporary Church History in Recklinghausen, Westphalia.

Carol Engelhardt Herringer is professor of history at Wright State University. She is the author of *Victorians and the Virgin Mary: Religion and Gender in England 1830–85* (Manchester University Press, 2008). She is currently working on a book on the cultural significance of the debates over the Eucharist in the Victorian Church of England.

R. Barry Levis is professor of history at Rollins College. His research focuses on the intersection of culture, politics and religion in eighteenth-century England. He has published a series of articles exploring the impact of the Hanoverian Succession on the Church of England as manifested in architecture, music and preaching.

Kenneth Macnab was priest librarian of Pusey House from 1993 to 1998 with particular responsibility for the archive. Subsequently he was vicar of St Barnabas, Tunbridge Wells. Since 2005 he has taught theology, history and classics at The Oratory School, John Henry Newman's foundation, in Oxfordshire. His current projects include a study of the historiography of the Oxford Movement focusing particularly on Pusey, Keble and Marriott after 1845.

Ian McCormack is the assistant curate of Horbury with Horbury Bridge in the diocese of Wakefield. He read modern history at the University of Oxford, and theology and pastoral studies at the University of Leeds. Previous research projects have included the revival of the religious life in the Church of England and the life and work of the Community of the Resurrection in Southern Africa post-1955. He trained for ordination at the College of the Resurrection, Mirfield.

Rowan Strong is associate professor of church history at Murdoch University in Perth, Australia. He has published extensively on Christianity and the British Empire, including *Anglicanism and the British Empire c.1700–1850* (Oxford University Press, 2007), and is the series editor for the forthcoming series on the history of Anglicanism with Oxford University Press. Rowan Strong is a Fellow of the Royal Historical Society.

Chapter One

INTRODUCTION

Rowan Strong and Carol Engelhardt Herringer

In an era noted for its outsized personalities and high achievers, Edward Bouverie Pusey was one of the most prominent and influential Victorians. Born into a minor aristocratic family and educated at Eton and Oxford, his early academic success culminated in his appointment as canon of Christ Church, Oxford, and Regius Professor of Hebrew at the University of Oxford at age 28. For the rest of his long life, from this prestigious academic position Pusey was at the forefront of public disputes over religion. As one of the co-leaders of the Oxford Movement, he was a staunch defender of the Catholic identity of the Church of England; he was also a very influential figure to the younger generation of Anglo-Catholics, including his biographer Henry Parry Liddon and Christina Rossetti.

Shortly after his death, Pusey's life and achievements were commemorated in the four-volume *Life of Pusey*, begun by Liddon and completed after Liddon's death by John Octavius Johnston, Robert John Wilson and William Charles Edmund Newbolt; and in Pusey House, which still houses a library, chapel, and rooms for scholars. Yet since that flurry of post-mortem recognition, Pusey has largely dropped from public memory, and from prominence among scholars of nineteenth-century British Christianity. When he is remembered, it is as a caricature. His popular image is now that of an excessively austere defender of an increasingly irrelevant and even incomprehensible way of life. Both the lack of scholarly attention and the caricature are all the more striking when contrasted with the public memories of his colleagues and close friends, John Keble and John Henry Newman, both of whom are remembered with great affection.

The stereotype of Pusey as a grim, humourless scold, more interested in the minutia of ecclesiastical rules than in the family and friends that surrounded him, does a disservice not just to him but also to Victorian religion and, more broadly, Victorian culture. To perpetuate this stereotype is also to maintain the stereotype of Victorian Christianity as a repressive, unpopular force in a culture that was happily becoming secular and progressive. In fact, however, Victorian mainstream culture was Christian, and Christians were engaged in the most pressing issues of the day, including the alleviation of poverty, the role of women, and foreign affairs.

This volume which reconsiders Pusey's life and legacy began as a three-day conference, 'Edward Bouverie Pusey and the Catholic Revival', held at Ascot Priory in September 2009. This gathering of scholars from Australia, Britain, Germany, and the United States offered new insights into the historic and theological significance of Pusey, and provided challenges to the prevalent historiography. Some of those papers serve as the basis for the essays in this collection.

An Outline of Pusey's Life

Edward Bouverie Pusey was born on 22 August 1800 to the Honourable Philip Bouverie, who had taken the Pusey surname as a condition of inheriting the Pusey estate, and the former Lady Lucy Sherard. He was the second of nine children, five of whom survived into adulthood. The elder Puseys were known as pious but somewhat severe parents. From them, Pusey learned the values that would characterize his adult life: Anglican piety, austerity, love of family, self-control, and a sense of reserve towards the larger world. His mother, who was both younger and gentler than his father, was in charge of his education until the age of seven, and Pusey retained a great affection for her throughout her long life. Pusey was particularly close to his elder brother, Philip, with whom he was educated, first at the Rev. Richard Roberts' boarding school in Mitcham, Surrey, then at Eton from 1812 to 1817 before being tutored for a year by the Rev. Edward Maltby, Vicar of Buckton and future Bishop of Durham. At Eton Pusey had the reputation of being studious and kind, as well as reserved and non-athletic.

In January 1819, Pusey went up to Christ Church, Oxford. In 1822 he received a first-class degree and met his future great friend, John Henry Newman. In 1825, Pusey was elected a fellow of Oriel College, which was then known as the most intellectually rigorous college in Oxford. As a fellow, his closest friends were Edward Hawkins, who later became provost of Oriel and an opponent of the Oxford Movement; Newman, with whom he initially lodged in the same building on the High Street; and Richard William Jelf, the future principal of King's College, London. Keble left Oxford for the life of a rural parson shortly after Pusey's election, but the two men became acquainted when Keble periodically returned to Oxford.

In June 1825, Pusey left for Germany in order to study at first-hand the rising liberal and biblically critical theology there, one of very few Englishmen to do so at the time. In Berlin, he met the leading theologians contributing to the construction of liberal Protestantism, Augustus Tholuck and Friederich Schleiermacher. After five months in Germany, Pusey returned again in June of 1826 to study first Syriac and Chaldee, and then Arabic as well as modern German theology. This time Pusey stayed for a year, returning to England in June 1827 where he was ordained in the Church of England in 1828. The culmination of Pusey's academic career came early in his life, with his appointment in 1828 as Regius Professor of Hebrew at the University of Oxford and canon of Christ Church Cathedral, Oxford. He held both posts until his death in 1882.

Pusey's young adulthood was marked by frequent periods of ill-health severe enough to make him unable to work, and by a burgeoning but difficult relationship with Maria Barker, whom he had met in 1818. Opposition to their marriage from both sets of parents ensured a lengthy courtship, and it was not until after the death of Mr Barker that Pusey and Maria became engaged in the autumn of 1827 and married in April 1828. The marriage – which lasted until Maria died in 1839 and which produced four children (three of whom died during Pusey's lifetime) – has been characterized by Pusey's biographers (even the sympathetic Liddon) as the gradual domination of Edward over Maria, as he turned her from a gay and religiously questioning young woman to an orthodox Anglican and strict parent.

As one of the prominent leaders of the Oxford Movement, Pusey's adult life was marked by the Tractarian agenda to assert the Catholic identity of the Church of England. Pusey was not one of the initial contributors to the series known as *Tracts for the Times* instigated by Newman, which marked the beginning of the Tractarian Movement, or the Catholic Revival of the Church of England. His first contribution was Tracts 67–69 in 1835, *Scriptural Views of Holy Baptism* (followed by Tract 70, an appendix to these tracts); the following year he contributed Tract 81, a catena of authorities on the Eucharist. These lengthy tracts altered the nature of the tracts from short pithy pamphlets.

The 1840s were a difficult period for Pusey. The storm of protest generated by Tract 90 (1841), in which Newman argued that the Thirty-Nine Articles were compatible with the doctrines of the Council of Trent, dismayed Pusey and led to Newman's resignation from the university church of St Mary the Virgin and his withdrawal to live in quasi-monastic retirement in the nearby village of Littlemore. In the midst of this controversy, Pusey created his own when he preached a sermon on *The Holy Eucharist a Comfort to the Penitent* at Eastertime 1843. As a result of his advocating the Eucharistic doctrine of the Real Presence in this sermon, Pusey was suspended for two years from preaching before the University of Oxford. This sentence effectively barred him from preaching in any Anglican church. However, when he returned to the pulpit, he continued to preach on the doctrine of the Real Presence and to encourage others to do so, as well. In 1845, Newman's slow withdrawal from the Church of England was completed by his conversion to Roman Catholicism. His defection meant that Pusey effectively lost one of his closest friends and had to assume leadership of the Movement, Keble having left the university in 1835, although he held the non-resident post of Professor of Poetry until 1841. Pusey and Newman continued to correspond for the next two decades, but they did not meet again until 1865 at Keble's house.

*

Pusey was one of the earliest supporters of Anglican sisterhoods, because he believed in female vocations and because he thought that the Church of England needed to provide support to women who chose not to marry. His endorsement of the vowed religious life began at home, when his eldest daughter, Lucy, expressed a desire to lead a single life dedicated to God. When she died in 1844, Pusey saw his efforts to encourage the establishment of Anglican sisterhoods as part of her legacy.[1] He encouraged the founding of the first Anglican sisterhood, the Sisterhood of the Holy Cross at Park Village, Regent's Park, in 1845. He was also significantly involved in the establishment of the Society of the Sisters of Mercy of the Holy Trinity at Devonport and Plymouth in 1848 under the direction of the formidable Priscilla Lydia Sellon. These two orders merged in 1856 under Sellon's leadership as the Society of the Most Holy Trinity, eventually based at Ascot Priory, and were dedicated to nursing and the care of children.

Pusey's support for Anglican sisterhoods stemmed from many of his concerns, including the high value he placed on chastity, the concern that Anglicans would convert to Roman Catholicism if the established church did not offer attractive options, a willingness to work outside episcopal authority, and a belief in a hierarchical society that coexisted with his view that a call to a holy life could be heard by women as well as men. However, not all Victorians shared Pusey's belief in the need for sisterhoods, and as a consequence these orders were very controversial, primarily because they seemed to encourage Roman Catholic–like practices and so lead to (in the minds of the most suspicious) the overtaking of the Church of England by Roman Catholicism. They also challenged Victorian ideals of family life, where women were expected to be under the supervision of an appropriate male. In addition, bishops tended to be sceptical of the sisterhoods because they operated to some degree outside of episcopal control.

In 1839 Maria Pusey died, and Pusey interpreted the sad event as a punishment for his sinfulness. In compensation, he became the anonymous donor for the building of a church, St Saviour's, in Leeds, a project supervised by his friend Walter Farquhar Hook, Vicar of Leeds. The first controversy associated with the church was Pusey's desire that the injunction, 'Ye who enter this holy place, pray for the sinner who built it', be placed over the entrance to the church. Although this seemed to some to imply sanctioning prayers for the dead, Charles Taylor Longley, Bishop of Ripon (and later Bishop of Durham [1856], Archbishop of York [1860] and Archbishop of Canterbury [1862]), eventually allowed it on the grounds that the donor (represented as a friend of Pusey's who wished to remain anonymous) was still alive. Given the controversies associated with Tract 90, Pusey was advised by Hook not to lay the first stone, the ritual instead being performed quietly by Hook in September 1842. The design and construction of the church – including whether to have an altar or a moveable 'holy table' and the content of some of the windows – caused controversy with the bishop, who initially refused to consecrate the church. A longer-running controversy was the association of the new church with ritualism and ensuing conversions to Roman Catholicism, an association that appeared to be validated by the two main series of conversions, one in 1847 and the other in 1851. While Pusey was never a ritualist, in the popular mind there was no distinction between 'Puseyism' and ritualism, and so he was condemned for practices he did not necessarily support. The ritualism and conversions at St Saviour's also caused a breach in the friendship between Pusey and Hook which was not healed until both were old men.

Pusey's relations with Roman Catholics were marked by ambivalence as well as by controversy. Since his involvement with the Oxford Movement he had been pilloried in the press as a secret Roman Catholic leading others to Rome. The reality, of course, was more complex. While Pusey desired and worked towards reunion, he also had deep reservations about aspects of Roman Catholicism. His involvement – indeed, his inception – of the *Eirenicon* controversy demonstrates this.[2] Even when he met Newman at Hursley Vicarage in September 1865, Pusey was working on an Anglican response to the prominent Roman Catholic convert, Henry Edward Manning, whose book, *The Workings of the Holy Spirit in the Church of England* (1864), argued that the Holy Spirit was not much in evidence in the church of Manning's birth. Pusey's response was published in 1865 as *The Church of England a Portion of Christ's One Holy Catholic Church, and a Means of Restoring Visible Unity: An Eirenicon in a Letter to the Author of 'The Christian Year'*. While his professed intent was, Pusey said, to determine the areas of agreement between Anglicans and Roman Catholics, his condemnation of Roman Catholic devotional practices was not seen as especially eirenic, even by Keble. Newman famously chided his friend that 'you discharge your olive branch as if from a catapult'.[3] Newman, who had been initially hesitant to enter the controversy, responded almost immediately, delineating doctrines from devotional practices, and Continental practices from English ones, in *A Letter Addressed to the Rev. E. B. Pusey, D.D., on Occasion of his Eirenicon* (1865). Pusey then responded directly to his old friend with his *First Letter to the Very Rev. J. H. Newman, D.D., in Explanation Chiefly in Regard to the Reverential Love due to the Ever-blessed Theotokos, and the Doctrine of her Immaculate Conception* (1869). This work focused more on the debate over Marian devotional practices, and Pusey followed it in 1870 with *Is Healthful Reunion Possible?*, a second letter to Newman.

In the latter part of his life, Pusey was involved in yet further controversies, including, in 1863, his leadership of the fight to prevent Charles Kingsley from receiving an honorary degree from Oxford, on the grounds that Kingsley's novel *Hypatia* (1853) was immoral. Longer-lasting was Pusey's outspoken support of the practice of auricular confession and his defence of the compulsory use of the Athanasian Creed in public worship by the Church of England. The optional use of the creed, which became problematic as a result of its damnatory clauses, had been recommended by the Royal Commission on Ritual established in 1867. Pusey was prominent in the battle by conservatives to retain the creed without adaptation, which was ultimately agreed to by both houses of the Convocation of Canterbury in 1873. Pusey's stand in this instance reunited him, to some extent, with the non-Anglo-Catholic High Churchmen, who had been alienated from him over the Romanist tendencies of Anglo-Catholics he was seen to lead.

Where Pusey was, ultimately, more out of step with the historical developments of the later Victorian period was in his repudiation of the methods of biblical criticism. These were moderately upheld by the contributors to *Essays and Reviews* (1860), resulting in a vociferous conservative reaction by the majority of Anglican clergy, including a number of bishops. Biblical criticism was ultimately to be accepted by the rising generation of Anglo-Catholics and younger High Churchmen in the publication of the essays from theologians of these groups known as *Lux Mundi* in 1889. But to the end of his life Pusey opposed such treatment of the Bible on the grounds that liberal criticism undermined the doctrines of the inspiration of scripture and everlasting punishment. Ultimately he saw biblical criticism as one aspect of the liberal attack on Christianity as a divinely revealed religion.

By the late 1870s Pusey's health was beginning to fail. He was increasingly deaf, and most of his own generation had already died, including Keble in 1866. His son, Philip, died in 1880. Pusey remained much concerned about the Public Worship Regulation Act, passed in 1874 to regulate the activities of the more extreme Anglo-Catholics and inspired by Archibald Campbell Tait, Archbishop of Canterbury. The Act failed when it was discovered that such Anglo-Catholics willingly went to prison for breaking the law rather than abandon or moderate their practices. Pusey was still able to issue a number of public statements in support of such priests, but by his 82nd birthday he was clearly failing. He died at Ascot Priory on 16 September 1882, and was buried in Christ Church Cathedral, Oxford, beside the bodies of his wife and two daughters.

Historiography

The Oxford Movement, initiating what is commonly called the Catholic Revival of the Church of England and of global Anglicanism more generally, has been a perennial subject of study by historians since its beginning in the 1830s. Initially, this examination was promoted by adherents of the Movement, known as Tractarians or (later) Anglo-Catholics, and a few of their Evangelical protagonists. Consequently, up until the second half of the twentieth century the predominant historiography of the Oxford Movement was either celebratory or antagonistic, depending on the ecclesiological position of the various writers. The former view is exemplified by many of the classic histories such as R. W. Church, *The Oxford Movement: Twelve Years 1833–1845* (1891), and S. L. Ollard, *The Anglo-Catholic Revival: Some Persons and Principles* (1925); while a hostile approach was adopted by the Evangelical E. A. Knox, *The Tractarian Movement 1833–1845* (1933).

Towards the latter decades of the twentieth century, the Movement began to be studied by historians less committed to it personally, or with fewer denominational axes to grind. Such studies have been often promoted by transAtlantic scholars such as Marvin R. O'Connell, *The Oxford Conspirators: A History of the Oxford Movement 1833–1845* (1969), and John Shelton Reed, *Glorious Battle: The Cultural Politics of Victorian Anglo-Catholicism* (1996). Other scholars have challenged the suppositions of the Tractarians themselves. So, for example, Peter Nockles, in his seminal *The Oxford Movement in Context: Anglican High Churchmanship 1760–1857* (1994), has drawn attention to the continuities of the Oxford Movement with earlier High Church Anglicanism, in contrast to the Tractarian disparagement of that earlier High Church theological tradition. Other scholarship has overturned the older celebratory interpretation of the Movement as rescuing a moribund High Church Anglicanism by pointing to its divisiveness. See, for instance, Rowan Strong, *Alexander Forbes of Brechin: The First Tractarian Bishop* (1995) and his *Episcopalianism in Nineteenth-Century Scotland* (2002).

Recently, the lack of intensive, critical, historical scholarship (as opposed to theological investigation) devoted to John Henry Newman has been pointed out by Simon Skinner in 'History versus Historiography: The Reception of Turner's Newman'. If this can be said of the most seminal figure of the Oxford Movement, it can, with even greater justice, be applied to the leader identified with the Movement for the longest period of time, namely Edward Bouverie Pusey. Despite the fact that Newman recognized in Pusey's adherence to the Movement a major coup for its respectability, and his prominence as Regius Professor of Hebrew at the University of Oxford which caused the Movement to be pejoratively named 'Puseyism' in the media, Pusey has long been neglected by historical studies of the Anglican Catholic Revival. This was recognized as long ago as 1983 when *Pusey Rediscovered*, a collection of essays edited by Perry Butler, was published. Attempting to pull their subject out from under the monumental weight of the four-volume Victorian biography of Pusey by Liddon[4] these studies addressed various dimensions of Pusey's historical contribution and person. However, some of the essays also contributed to the prevailing negative stereotype of Pusey (which dates from his lifetime) as a repressed, unhappy man whose impact upon the Oxford Movement was largely deleterious. Notwithstanding the importance of some of these contributions, Pusey has continued to be a figure of slight attention by historians, who have generally persisted with a largely antithetical assessment of him in the few studies that have been published since 1983.

Indicative of this modern neglect of Pusey is the fact that the only lengthy monograph devoted to Pusey since the 1983 essays has been that of David Forrester, *The Young Dr Pusey* (1989). Forrester examines a life shaped repressively by Pusey's increasing anxieties about religious liberalism, and his increasingly vehement repudiation of his earlier flirtation with German liberal Protestant scholarship. Seeing this as the motivation for Pusey's adherence to the conservative values of the Oxford Movement, Forrester argues that Pusey was a repressive influence on the Movement, largely as a consequence of his own rigorous moralism which took its toll upon his wife and children also. This negative interpretation of Pusey is still the prevalent assessment of Pusey in existing scholarship. It is echoed, for example, by Paul Avis in his book on *Anglicanism and the Christian Church*[5] and by Susan Mumm in *Stolen Daughters, Virgin Mothers*.[6] More substantially, it is largely followed by a major scholar of Victorian culture and religion, Frank Turner, in his controversial but substantial *John Henry Newman: The Challenge to Evangelical Religion* (2002). Turner finds that Pusey learned his emphasis on practical charity, but also his excessive self-denial, from his parents, who were largely without affection towards him.[7] While Turner draws passing attention to some of Pusey's tactical qualities as a Tractarian leader – being prepared to demonstrate tactical flexibility while retaining theological inflexibility, for example – he largely maintains the historiographical discourse of a life in two parts: an early liberal, not to say liberated, theological career associated with his faithful passion and courtship of Maria Barker; and a later, nearly life-long, repressive spirituality closely associated with the seriousness of post-baptismal sin. This severe religious outlook Pusey imposed on his children with the concurrence of his wife, which included excessive fasting and corporal punishment.[8] 'Pusey embodied enormous personal arrogance cloaked under a carefully crafted life of asceticism and devotional holiness'.[9] This common unattractive view of Pusey as a man, a priest, and a religious leader, will be challenged in a number of instances in the essays that follow.

In the past decade, historiographical trends have begun to shift in Pusey's favour, as scholars have begun to take his theology more seriously and, consequently, to treat him more sympathetically. In 'Pusey as Consistent and Wise: Some Comparisons with Newman', David Brown argues that the very traits that have been deemed unattractive in Pusey – such as his emphasis on human sinfulness and his consequent pessimism about human progress – make him a more realistic guide than the more optimistic Newman; while his Biblical scholarship, including his reading of discontinuities between the Old and New Testaments, is remarkably consistent with current Biblical scholarship. In a similar move, Timothy Larsen's recent essay, 'E. B. Pusey and Holy Scripture', recovers Pusey as a Biblical scholar or, as Larsen terms him, 'a Bible man who lived an exegetical life'.[10]

These works point to a re-evaluation of Pusey's life and thought by some contemporary scholars. A major dimension of this present interdisciplinary collection of essays by established and emerging scholars is a revision of the marginal place accorded by scholars to Pusey's theology and a revision of some of the very negative assessments of his religious and personal life. A number of the essays in this collection undertake a substantial study of Pusey's contribution as a theologian to the Oxford Movement. Together, these essays represent an important step towards giving a more historically accurate view of Pusey. They do not subscribe to the hagiography of Liddon's biography, but nor do they exhibit the hostility typical of more recent works. Instead, they reveal Pusey as a serious theologian who had a significant impact on the Victorian period, in the broader culture as well within the Oxford Movement, and in wider areas of church politics and theology. This revision is important not merely to rehabilitate Pusey's reputation, but also to help us understand his own contribution to the Oxford Movement, Anglicanism, and British Christianity in the nineteenth century.

Historiographical Revisions

Ian McCormack's essay establishes a cogent challenge to the normal scholarly interpretation of Pusey which has prevailed for decades. Examining Pusey's sermons, particularly those on the Holy Spirit, as well as his published and unpublished spiritual directives, McCormack rescues Pusey from a scholarly marginality in both his personality and his theology and places him in the same prominent place within the Oxford Movement that he had during his lifetime. Pusey's writings, McCormack shows, reveal a deep spiritual joy that is usually absent in characterizations of him. While McCormack would not return to the hagiography that characterized the earliest biographies and other accounts of Pusey, he does argue for a more balanced view of the man and of his theology.

The important historiographical revision evident in McCormack's essay is complemented by the work of Kenneth Macnab on the construction of the Liddon biography, which illustrates how that seminal work framed its subject. Macnab, who for many years was the priest librarian at Pusey House, Oxford, uses important and unused (and even previously unsorted) primary sources from the Pusey House Library in order to show how the editorial work of those who took over the work after Liddon's death, eliminated Pusey's early Protestant sympathies in order to make him an enduring and consistent champion of Tractarianism and Anglo-Catholicism. Incidents such as Pusey's recommending that his future wife read Luther's *Preface to the Epistle to the Romans* and the Puseys' attending a Presbyterian church in Scotland while on their honeymoon were removed in the final version of the biography as presumably too disturbing to Pusey's Anglo-Catholic friends and followers. With this essay we note again the development of Pusey's thought from sympathy towards Protestantism to a determined Catholicism. That trajectory gives us a more realistic view of the man and makes him a more sympathetic figure. Far from being an eternally austere, inflexible champion of Anglo-Catholicism, Pusey was a man whose views evolved in response to his life experiences, his friendships, and the changes in the world around him.

Pusey's openness to Continental Protestantism is examined from a different vantage point in Albrecht Geck's analysis of Pusey's second *Enquiry into the Theology of Germany* (1830). This work, about which Pusey had doubts while writing and which was ill-received when published, demonstrates Pusey's early adherence to what Geck terms 'modern orthodoxy', a mid-point between liberal Protestantism and orthodoxy. Geck makes a convincing case for the importance of Pusey's theology by demonstrating the second *Enquiry* as instrumental in the consideration of his move away from German liberal theology. In addition, this essay offers a useful reminder of the role of German theology in Pusey's intellectual development.

Peter Nockles famously challenged, in *The Oxford Movement in Context*, the Tractarians' claim of a direct intellectual lineage to the Caroline divines. R. Barry Levis addresses the question of intellectual forbears from a different angle, examining the role of cultural upheaval in encouraging high ecclesiology. He compares two periods of religious ferment – the first from the 'Glorious Revolution' to the Hanoverian Succession, and the second from the repeal of the Test and Corporation Acts to Newman's conversion – to conclude that 'high ecclesiology arose at times when the church saw itself threatened'. Besides showing the cultural context of Pusey's allegiance to the Oxford Movement, Levis's examination of Pusey's ecclesiology offers a useful reminder that Pusey was, with Keble – and unlike Newman – from a non-Evangelical or Orthodox Anglican family background.

Pusey was one of the earliest and most prominent of the Victorian Anglicans who articulated the doctrine of the Real Presence (which argued that Christ was 'really', albeit spiritually, present in the consecrated bread and wine). This understanding of the Eucharist, which nuanced High Church Anglican theology in a Rome-wards direction, was highly controversial, yet Pusey's Eucharistic theories have never been given sustained scholarly treatment. Carol Engelhardt Herringer's essay remedies that omission by describing and analyzing Pusey's Eucharistic beliefs as articulated in sermons and scholarly writings. The essay also considers the hostility Pusey's Eucharistic beliefs engendered from those who considered the Church of England Protestant and Pusey's beliefs Roman Catholic or even pagan. Herringer concludes by exploring other theological motivations for Pusey's Eucharistic beliefs, including his desire to define the Church of England as a Catholic church and his intense preoccupation with sin.

This revision of Pusey as theologically more significant and substantive than previous scholars have acknowledged is continued by Mark Chapman's essay. Chapman's examination of Pusey's involvement with Anglo-Catholic reactions to the advent of the First Vatican Council in 1871 leads him to conclude that Pusey was significant in determining early Anglo-Catholic ecumenical notions. In particular, Chapman argues that the anti-liberalism and anti-rationalism of Puseyite Anglo-Catholicism served to open up the possibility of ecumenical engagement with other anti-liberal forces in other churches both in Britain and Continental Europe. He also considers Pusey's influence on Alexander Penrose Forbes, his protégé who became the first Tractarian to be consecrated a bishop (of Brechin, Scotland), and how Forbes' reaction to the council, which he observed and communicated to Pusey, helped to discourage Anglo-Catholics from pursuing reunion with Rome and instead turn to Orthodox Christianity.

Pusey has been rarely examined by historians outside the confines of the Church of England. Rowan Strong's essay examines Pusey's long engagement with the Scottish Episcopal Church – which was precipitated by two Eucharistic issues: the accusation of heresy and subsequent trial of Forbes, and the proposed relinquishing of the Scottish Communion Office – in order to explore Pusey's engagement with the British dimension of Anglo-Catholicism. Pusey was extensively involved in defending his friend Forbes from the heresy charges, while he was more ambivalent about the proposed substitution of the English rite for the Scottish Communion Office, choosing to view this as a liturgical rather than a doctrinal matter. These episodes reveal Pusey as a warm, compassionate friend as well as a pragmatic yet principled theologian. More broadly, this aspect of Oxford Movement history suggests that the Tractarian leadership was not as unified as its adherents wished, or as scholars have continued to assume.

As a whole, these essays make a case for historians to re-examine the life, the thought, and the influence of Edward Pusey on the Oxford Movement, the Victorian Church of England, and beyond the confines of England. They argue that his influence was more profound, complex, and positive than the stereotype of a liberal Protestant spending his life regretting those theological salad days by wallowing in a reactionary and regressive churchmanship suggest.

Additionally, the essays provide evidence that Pusey was a more complex personality than previous assessments have found, and that he was both a more attractive friend and a more compassionate and joyous spiritual guide than earlier historians have thought. Consequently, it is not surprising that Pusey's influence should have spread widely in English society, and beyond into Britain, Continental Europe, and even into the Empire where one Indian Brahmin Christian found his way into Anglo-Catholicism through the reading of Pusey's writings.[11] Pusey here is resuscitated from the disparagement of both past and present writers to emerge a more vital and sympathetic person whose leadership of the Oxford Movement is, consequently, made more understandable.

Notes

1 At least 66 sisterhoods were established in England between 1845 and 1899; as many as 26 other sisterhoods, some of which were short lived, may also have been founded. For a list of these sisterhoods, see Mumm, *Stolen Daughters*, appendix 1.
2 An account of the controversy is found in Strange, 'Reflections on a Controversy'.
3 Quoted in Liddon, *Life of Pusey*, 4:136.
4 In 1933, Leonard Prestige published a breezy biography, *Pusey*, which he acknowledged to be largely derived from Liddon's biography.
5 Avis, *Anglicanism and the Christian Church*, 205–6, 212.
6 Mumm, *Stolen Daughters*, 157–8.
7 Turner, *John Henry Newman*, 92.
8 Ibid., 104–5.
9 Ibid., 91.
10 Larsen, 'E. B. Pusey', 526.
11 Nilkanth/Nehemiah Goreh, a Brahmin who became a Christian in 1848, read widely in Pusey's works as part of his transition from CMS evangelical Christianity to a greater sympathy for Anglo-Catholicism. See Gardner, *Life of Father Goreh*, 110, 115.

Chapter Two

THE HISTORY OF THE HISTORY OF PUSEY

Ian McCormack

In truth he is a grand figure of a man, and it is only the more painful to know that the four corners of the popular form of the Anglican Church could not contain him. Never dining out, never walking out, sacrificing rarely to the graces, and never, save when in chapel he shows his suspected skull-cap, to be seen out of academical dress, he passes his time in an inaccessible study in company with a crucifix and entrenched behind a confusion of Italian pictures and the heaviest works that theology has produced… He works much on University committees, in Convocation and in Council, and allows himself no other recreation than that of confessing nuns… The most astounding fact about Dr Pusey is that he did marry.[1]

I dare say he has done some good, but I feel to him as I do towards those poor Jesuit fathers that suffered in Elizabeth's reign. They are to be respected, pitied, and condemned as fighters against the light. When a man can't be at ease without a priest to bolster up his debility or nullity of conscience, it is time he went into a convent and stayed there. He isn't fit for wholesome workaday life, and his influence can't be good. It is a pity to see Liddon and such fine fellows warped by this miserable little man's teachings. He was not even a good scholar, and has never written a line worth reading.[2]

Both of these quotations give a flavour of the stereotypes and prejudices which have contributed to the reputation Edward Bouverie Pusey enjoys today. The first is from the text which accompanied the 'Ape' cartoon of Pusey in *Vanity Fair* of January 1875. The second is by Frederick York Powell, sometime Regius Professor of Modern History in the University of Oxford. The former is meant as satire, the latter is not. Only the latter is quoted in the *Journal of Theological Studies* at the end of an article on Pusey by the eminent historian Colin Matthew. According to his entry in the *Dictionary of National Biography*, Powell described himself as a 'decent heathen Aryan [sic]' in religion and 'a socialist and a jingo' in politics and was buried without religious rites at his own request.[3] He was, therefore, hardly likely to be well disposed to Pusey; yet Matthew nonetheless saw fit to conclude a serious piece of academic work with this finely honed rant.

To be fair to Matthew, the argument of his essay is that in a self-conscious change of direction from the liberalism of his early days as an academic, Pusey erected a vast anti-modernist edifice against the perceived dangers of liberalism and rationalism in church and state and so should be seen not as a theologian but as a Christ Church statesman.[4] Now this is an interesting idea that is worthy of serious discussion, but it does not justify the inclusion, in semi-approving tones, of York Powell's invective, nor Matthew's own assertions that 'we cannot see Pusey as a scholar',[5] and that 'intellectually and theologically he led Anglo-Catholicism…into a dead end'.[6]

The argument of this chapter is that most modern scholarship on Pusey is circular and self-referencing, based on a limited selection of material from the archive at Pusey House, which has found its way into the secondary material and has thereafter been quoted – and mis-quoted – *ad infinitum* without people bothering to go back to the archive material and study the man properly for themselves. I will argue that this willingness to accept what is in effect a caricature of Pusey at face value goes hand in hand with a refusal to consider him as a theologian proper in his mature years. Finally, I will point to some sermons and just a few letters and other material from the archive material which might start the process of rescuing Pusey from the history of Pusey.

In the introduction to *Pusey Rediscovered*, the collection of essays on Pusey published in 1983, Perry Butler wrote, 'For many people today their picture of Pusey is still either that of scholar and saint, heroic leader of the Anglo-Catholic movement, confessor and spiritual writer, or that of a man whose scholarship and teaching were marred by his lack of a free intelligence, a life-denying joyless man whose austere piety bordered upon the pathological.'[7] It is a sad fact that, 29 years later, this statement is if anything more true now than it was then. Modern scholarship has not been kind to Pusey, but nor in many cases has it been fair. No doubt this has often been a reaction to the hagiographical early treatment of Pusey. Liddon's *magnum opus* is famously uncritical of his master. Maria Trench's *The Story of Dr Pusey's Life* (1890) was intended to highlight areas of Pusey's personal life ignored or avoided by Liddon. Trench quotes Pusey's only surviving daughter to do this to some extent, but there is still little in the book that is not in Liddon, and even less that is critical of Pusey. The other intention of the book was to make Pusey's biography more accessible – but it still runs to 570 pages. After Trench came

G. L. Prestige's 1982 biography, which is genuinely short and readable, but inevitably therefore not original. Moreover, what Liddon and Trench implied, Prestige stated explicitly: 'In one word, [Pusey] was a saint.'[8]

If this early material is bordering on the hagiographical, then the contemporary response to it was just as patently hatchet-job material: Protestant propaganda such as Walter Walsh's *Secret History of the Oxford Movement* (1897). There was very little in between, however, and no full-length and serious academic reappraisal of Pusey until the 1980s, although Yngve Brilioth's treatment of Pusey in *The Anglican Revival: Studies in the Oxford Movement* (1925) is still worthy of close attention. Like more modern scholars, Brilioth highlights Pusey's emphasis on Judgement and Hell,[9] but unlike his successors he also places this emphasis firmly in the context of Pusey's overarching theological makeup. Specifically, Brilioth sees Pusey as a mystic, the *doctor mysticus* of the Oxford Movement, imbued with an almost Evangelical doctrine of assurance, certain that the Everlasting Arms will catch all those who want to be caught.[10] 'Here as elsewhere the chief aim of mystic piety is to lose itself in God, to let itself be carried away by the strong flood of the Divine, to sink in its sea.'[11]

In 1983 *Pusey Rediscovered* was published to coincide with the 150th anniversary of the Oxford Movement, and then in 1989 David Forrester's doctoral thesis of 1967 on Pusey's early life and work was published as *Young Doctor Pusey*. The latter work is better on Pusey's theology than it is on his personal life. At this point I want to finish the broad-brush historiography that I have just been painting, and delve into *Young Doctor Pusey* in some detail to explain why I think it is indirectly responsible for much of the lazy caricaturing of Pusey that has occurred since.

The first thing to say about *Young Doctor Pusey* is that it stops in 1845, so it is not a full biography. It is a fine study of Pusey's early theological development. Where it is at fault is in its portrayal of Pusey's personal life and in particular his relationship with his wife Maria and their children. Forrester deals here with the Puseys' treatment of their children, some of the details of which are, undoubtedly, shocking to twenty-first century sensibilities. Maria wrote to Pusey informing him that 'for kicking I had [Mary, aged five] tied to the bedpost; for naughtiness I...have just whipped her'.[12] Pusey himself left Lucy tied up for 'obstinacy', and Philip was whipped for the same offence.[13] This disobedience was often for minor things such as refusing to say a certain word of spelling.[14] These are examples which I myself have found in the archive, and so Forrester is right to draw attention to the issue – he was, so far as I know, the first to do so. However, Forrester's account leaves a lot to be desired. There is, for example, at least one misquotation from the transcripts at Pusey House. Forrester writes that, 'As a boy of five and a half, Pusey's son, Philip, was not regarded with much favour by his father. "One thing to be guarded against in him", Pusey told his wife, "is display and other forms of self.""[15] This is a misquotation taken out of context. Pusey was describing how he thought Philip 'decidedly improved during my absence... One thing *now* to be guarded against in him is display and other forms of self.'[16] By omitting the word 'now' from his quotation (without indicating its omission), and by failing to acknowledge the battle against 'self' which pervades Pusey's spiritual letters,[17] Forrester takes an incidental remark occasioned by praise for Philip, and turns it into an all-encompassing repression of the boy's personality. I will return to Pusey's notion of 'self' and denial of self since it is a recurring and generally misunderstood theme.

Forrester also writes that 'as a remedy for Philip's lack of progress, Pusey was in the habit of beating him with bundles of rods; when he was considered to have improved, an equivalent amount of birches was destroyed by way of reward'.[18] Now this is a curiosity. In *Young Doctor Pusey*, it is not footnoted. In Forrester's thesis, it is footnoted, but incorrectly. It refers to a letter that does not exist. What does exist, in the letter nearest to the date given by Forrester, is a message from Pusey to Maria saying that

> you may tell Philip if he is a good boy, as I hope, that I fetched the hearth broom out of the schoolroom, and swept up all the pieces which there were lying about in the little room, and burnt one of the bundles which were there, and hope, that when he comes back again there will be no need of any such things and if I hear a good account of him at the end of the week, I will burn the one which remains.[19]

The implications of this are indeed that Pusey had beaten Philip – or at least threatened to do so – at least once in the past. It is not an unambiguous statement to that effect however, as Forrester seems to suggest, nor does it imply a 'habit' on Pusey's part.

Similarly, Forrester highlights the fact that Pusey's brother Philip prohibited Pusey from looking after his children in his will.[20] This was indeed the case, but it is strange that Forrester makes no reference to the six happy months which Philip's children spent with Pusey before the terms of the will were enforced, nor of the testimony of one of his nieces about him: 'from the moment [of Philip's death] and ever since, he was a father to us, and such a father as falls to the lot of few.' Moreover, this information is not hidden away in a box deep inside the bowels of Pusey House; it is in Liddon's biography.[21]

Forrester concludes that 'perhaps the saddest result of Pusey's and Maria's methods of education was the heartless indifference it bred in them towards the physical suffering of children'.[22] I think that this statement is simply untrue, and that a fairly cursory examination of other material in the Pusey House archive makes that clear. I will discuss some of this material at the end of this essay, but it is worth bearing in mind for the moment that Pusey served an unpaid curacy in Spitalfields in the middle of a cholera epidemic and gave most of the legacy from his mother to purchase the grounds on which was built Ascot Priory, and from which were built, among other things, an orphanage and a school.

Forrester's account of Pusey's family life is, in other words, partial and one-sided. Yet it has been taken by subsequent historians as incontrovertible fact. Colin Matthew, for example, in the essay already quoted, writes that Pusey 'began to crush his family under a tyrannical order of religious discipline',[23] and uses as evidence for this the story about birches being removed one by one as Philip showed improvement. Matthew references this back to Forrester – which as we have already seen is at best a dubious source. Similarly, in a brief description of Pusey's development from radical to conservative, Paul Avis refers to him as 'the guilt-mongering penitent who made Maria as obsessive as himself and scarred his children's minds with the wrath of God and the rod of chastisement in their father's hand.' Once again, the only quoted authority for this is Forrester's thesis.[24] These are the most explicit examples of the circular and self-referencing nature of too much modern academic writing on Pusey. Too often things are simply taken for granted without reference back to the original sources.

It is also likely, although impossible to prove, that Owen Chadwick's stark, almost poetic description of the depth of Pusey's mourning in the years following Maria's death has become too influential.[25] That is to say, it has been passed on from one historian to the next, and along the way the limitations and qualifications with which Chadwick surrounded his description have been lost. So, for example, Chadwick's statement that Pusey 'made Keble his confessor and asked to be allowed not to smile except with young children or in a matter of love',[26] becomes, over time, the bald statement that Pusey adopted a rule never to smile.[27] In the case of the latter, there is no longer any questioning of whether the wish was granted, and if so the length of time Pusey stuck to his rule. As we will see, there is a substantial amount of evidence which points to the fact that over time Pusey recovered from the depths of his despair and modified his behaviour accordingly; whilst the behaviour of Queen Victoria after the death of Prince Albert would suggest that there was nothing unique about the extent of Pusey's mourning for his wife.

Pusey tends to fare particularly badly when he is mentioned in passing in the context of a piece of work about somebody or something else. An example of this is Frank M. Turner's massive study of John Henry Newman, in which the author writes that 'possibly having wrestled unsuccessfully with his own sexuality after his wife's death, Pusey applied to himself the same language of personal uncleanness that he used when writing of the sexual temptations confronting young men in the public schools and universities'.[28] It is very likely that Pusey did struggle with his sexuality after Maria's death, but if so then this is a topic which deserves serious and dispassionate examination, not simply a passing reference in a book about somebody else. The evidence available does not justify the significance given to it and the conclusions which are implied by Turner as a consequence. Yet this is not the only sweeping statement on Pusey in Turner's book. So, for example, 'Pusey embodied enormous personal arrogance cloaked under a carefully crafted life of asceticism and devotional holiness.'[29] 'The years immediately following Pusey's marriage, his appointment to the Hebrew Chair, and the controversy over the *Enquiry* were the only period of his life associated with scholarly activity… Thereafter a deeply depressive strain came to the fore.'[30] 'Even by what often appear the austere practices of Victorian childrearing, the Pusey household was extreme and abusive.'[31] Turner's value judgements may or may not be true, in whole or partly, but they are certainly not based on a complete view of the evidence available, nor are they explained by him in detail sufficient to justify the severity of his language. We may say that this is even more true of John Webster, who in his inaugural lecture as Lady Margaret Professor of Divinity in the University of Oxford summarily and entirely gratuitously condemned Pusey as a 'crackpot…who can safely be dismissed',[32] before moving on to more palatable pastures.

In short, it is as if recent scholarship has made a collective decision to accept the caricature of Pusey as the morbid, sin-obsessed ascetic who effectively killed off his wife and several of his children in his pursuit of purity. In case the current author is thought guilty of exaggeration at this point, a brief extract from the editorial introduction to an essay by David Forrester in the *Ampleforth Journal* should help to set the record straight. According to A. J. Stacpoole, O.S.B., Pusey's marriage was

> a paradigm of dim religious gloom subduing the vital creative forces as they respond to life – it is itself an instance of spiritual constriction forcing physical collapse. Pusey's wife knew what it was to love life and to bring life to others, even for a while to her own strange husband; but she could not ultimately withstand those crippling habits of Pusey which had throttled his own nature before marriage, and which went on in the end to kill the marriage and then the wife… Deep in Pusey's character was a cold refusal to rejoice.[33]

As will be seen, I believe this last sentence to be entirely incorrect, whilst the rest of the passage reads more like the back cover of a Mills & Boon novel than the introduction to a serious piece of academic writing.

It would be foolish to deny that there was a severely ascetic side to Pusey and that at times he did not appreciate the extent to which his own ascetic practices would influence others.[34] But plenty of other material exists which shows a different side to him, and it is this which scholars have failed to find or use, being happy instead to use Forrester's *Young Doctor Pusey* and its forerunners as a convenient way of justifying the lazy way in which Pusey is portrayed in too many academic works today.

I want to argue that there are two ways out of this situation. The first is to give Pusey the respect he deserves as a serious theologian. The second is to give proper prominence to the wide variety of material in the Pusey House archive which shows a very different side to Pusey than that which most of the modern material chooses to portray.

Let us examine the question of Pusey as a theologian first. His early academic career has been well surveyed by modern historians, not least by Forrester himself and by several of the contributors to *Pusey Rediscovered*.[35] Most of his later adult life, though, from about the time when he became publicly associated with the Oxford Movement, has been of much more interest to historians than to theologians. Indeed, the whole argument of Colin Matthew's controversial essay is that Pusey effectively sacrificed his scholarly career to concentrate on his work at the forefront of the Tractarian Movement. In the words of A. M. Allchin, 'Pusey's writings have been shamefully neglected by Anglicans this century.'[36] It is only necessary to add that the admonition applies to those in the academy as well as in the assembly.

Owen Chadwick argues that Pusey 'was not a speculative theologian', and that 'Newman did not recognize that Pusey had made any intellectual contribution to the Movement; or, if he recognized it, he was silent upon the subject.'[37] Much of Pusey's published work was in the form of catenas of the early fathers, and in this sense Chadwick is correct to say that he was not a speculative theologian. However, Pusey was himself responsible for the rediscovery and translation of many of the works which he published and quoted, an important fact which should not be overlooked. Furthermore, Pusey's vast number of sermons – published and unpublished – comprise (when considered as a whole) a wide library of theological thinking which have not been given anything like the attention they deserve.[38] There is much among Pusey's published work that is worthy of study, but the sermons are of particular interest, since taken together they provide a body of material which is indicative of systematic theological thought. I want to look briefly at two areas: Pusey's treatment of pneumatology, which is based on a theology of indwelling; and his treatment of 'joy' in his sermons. The intention is both to illustrate that the claim of systematic theological thought can be sustained, and also to show that the process of doing so throws more light on the real Pusey, as opposed to the Pusey of caricature.

Pusey's published beliefs on the Holy Spirit are spread widely. His 1876 book *On the Clause 'and The Son'* is still one of the best expositions of the history and value of the *Filioque* from an Anglican pen. Tracts 67–69: *Scriptural Views of Holy Baptism*, and his sermons on 'The Entire Absolution of the Penitent' and *The Presence of Christ in the Holy Eucharist* also contain material on the nature and work of the Holy Spirit. Yet by a huge margin the bulk of Pusey's treatment of the Spirit is to be found in the shorter sermons, such as those published in *Parochial Sermons*.[39] Put together, the result is something approaching a systematic theology of the Holy Spirit which in many areas foreshadows the work of twentieth-century theologians such as Rowan Williams and Yves Congar.[40]

Pusey's pneumatology is based on the notion of 'indwelling', which he explains thus:

> To dwell in God must be by His Dwelling in us. He takes us out of our state of nature, in which we were, fallen, estranged, in a far country, out of and away from Him, and takes us up into Himself. He cometh to us, and if we will receive Him, He dwelleth in us, and maketh His Abode in us. He enlargeth our hearts by his Sanctifying Spirit which He giveth us... By dwelling in us, He makes us parts of Himself, so that in the Ancient Church they could boldly say, "He Deifieth Me"; that is, He makes me part of Him, of His Body, Who is God.[41]

This indwelling required an emptying of self: that much-maligned concept which caused Forrester so much anxiety in the context of Pusey's son Philip. At this point we may develop Brilioth's point about mystic piety (quoted above) and say that an essential part of such piety is the sweeping up of *self* into the Godhead.[42] But this is an upward, expansive movement, not a downward, suppressive one. So in Pusey's thought the emptying of self is not a negative thing but a positive one, not a dismal but a joyous thing, because it makes possible the indwelling of God and the resulting deification.

Matthew wrote that if Newman lacked holy joy, Pusey was the 'apotheosis of its antithesis'.[43] Yet Pusey preached: 'The windows of Heaven are open; close we up our hearts no more. Empty we our hearts before Him, and He will cleanse them anew with His Spirit, and fill them with the Wine of His love.'[44] If we are to receive the Spirit, we must first empty ourselves of everything within us that is contrary to it.

In another sermon, Pusey insisted that it is the Holy Spirit himself who is given to us:

> Not the grace only of the Spirit, not any created gift or quality, or power, or habit of grace, but the Holy Spirit Itself... Thenceforth He is the life of our soul, the author, in-worker, perfecter... He knits our souls into one, and knits them in Himself to God. And thenceforth man is the

dwelling-place of the Holy Trinity. For where one Person of the Ever-Blessed Trinity dwells, there dwelleth the Undivided Trinity; and our Lord has said, 'My Father will love him, and We will come unto him, and make our abode in him.'[45]

This is not the language either of a man who did not know joy, nor of a man who 'has never written a line worth reading'. For Pusey the consequences of sin were real and total since they led to the damnation of souls – 'Satan ensnares mankind, alike through false hopes or through hopelessness', he preached[46] – so to deny the severity of sin would be in itself a grave sin. But the reverse of that is a joyous, ecstatic conviction in the love and mercy of God through the work of the Spirit, if only we will let Him in.[47]

Allchin has written perceptively of the sermons Pusey gave in the week following the consecration of the church for which he had paid in Leeds in 1845 – and the same may be said of the corpus of his sermons as a whole – that 'There is, on the one side, a darkness, an austerity and a rigour when he speaks of the dangers of eternal loss, which may trouble us. But on the other side there is a tone of ecstatic joy when he comes to speak of the end of the Christian life, our union with God in heaven, a joy which may also disturb us, though in a different way.'[48] There is, in fact, a consistent undercurrent of joy in many of Pusey's sermons, though it is admittedly the joy of a man who has been blessed with the vision of the glory of the life to come as opposed to that of a man who is looking forward to a jolly weekend. Not for nothing did Owen Chadwick observe that 'It should rightly have been said of Pusey, what was later said of Christopher Wordsworth, that he had one foot in heaven and the other foot in the third century A.D.'[49]

An entire book could – and should – be written on this theme, but here I will quote briefly from just two sermons. In a sermon entitled 'The Ascension our Glory and Joy', Pusey begins by saying: 'Truly, if we could ever live in this day, all were joy. It is the crown of all joys, the joy of all creation, the wonder of the blessed angels, the union of all being, the finishing of the earthly course of the Son of God, His entrance into glory.'[50] He goes on to describe this joy in more detail:

> Well might our hearts die within us for joy, could we hear or picture to our souls the faintest echoes of that everlasting harmony, in which the Church of the First-born, men and angels, on this day first blended, each separate voice singing, with its own special sweetness of thanksgiving for His mercies to itself, some distinct notes of that unceasing, unwearying, undying, ever renewed, ever new, song, whose compass none can reach, for it is of the Infinite love and mercy of our God, Whose love hath been,

is and shall be, from everlasting to everlasting, without beginning and without end.[51]

And in a sermon for Trinity Sunday, Pusey argues that the love we have for others in this life will not cease in the next. 'Rather, it shall be part of our joy, to love all which we loved here; only how much more, because every infirmity which in ourselves or in others, ever checked for an instant the flow of love, shall then have been absorbed into the love of God, and God shall fill all with Himself.' Indeed,

Holy Scripture hath not said, that we should so love God, as to shut out any other love, or any other joy, which does not shut Him out…[in Heaven] all will love all… All will be transparent with His Glory and His love. His beauty (as it does here in a manner) shall make all beautiful. His love shall make all lovely. His joy will beam in every countenance… All shall be full of Him; all shall joy in Him; the joy in Him shall vibrate from soul to soul.[52]

This emphasis on joy was not restricted to Pusey's sermons: it is found in his spiritual direction as well. Here, as in the sermons, Pusey made an explicit distinction between simple merriment and joy. While the former is not in itself a bad thing, only the latter is a specifically Christian emotion. Pusey was for many years the spiritual director of Sister Clara of the Society of the Most Holy Trinity. He began advising her before she joined the community, while she was still Miss Clarissa Powell. Among the letters he wrote to her at this time was a series of instructions not to suppress joy in the full and proper sense of the term. 'Meantime you should be cheerful, (not frivolous or merely gay-hearted)',[53] he told her on one occasion. A few months later he wrote, 'Do not, as I have often said, be dejected at any thing. Let nothing interfere with a childlike trust in God.'[54] And, in a passage which rather makes one wish that the other half of the correspondence had survived, he says: 'I do not mean to say that you may not be cheerful, even playful (but this "burlesque or whatever it was" is too much)… Even in Convents, they now mostly look for cheerfulness, and the gay gladness of a pure heart… J K [John Keble?], between 50 and 60, has still the playfulness (they say) of a child.'[55]

To highlight the ecstatic element in Pusey's sermons[56] and the repeated injunctions against depression in his spiritual letters is not to deny the other, more familiar depressive side of his nature. It is, however, to insist that both sides of that nature should be revealed in academic discussions about Pusey; otherwise the result is merely half the true picture of the man (or the true picture of half the man). Once again, it is Allchin who has most clearly expressed how it is that the apparently contradictory elements of Pusey's nature could reside together in one person. Allchin points out that although in the pulpit Pusey always went to great lengths to support his statements with references from the church fathers, it is also true to say that he had made the teaching his own, through his own bitter experience of life:

> That he has made this teaching his own in the depths and heights of his own experience is…clear from these sermons. The painful experiences of self-reproach, the agonised depths of penitence through which he passed in this decade, are surely only the other side of the brilliance of the vision of the divine glory which shines out in these pages. The great saints are full of what seem to us exaggerated acknowledgements of their sin. The light and clarity of God which they have glimpsed show up the distress and misery of man in ways which are unfamiliar to us.[57]

This may be the place to acknowledge a methodological problem: to call Pusey a saint is to open oneself to the charge of partiality. But to refuse to acknowledge the particularly heightened religious awareness (for want of a better phrase) with which Pusey lived on a daily basis is to refuse even to attempt to understand why Pusey acted and wrote as he did, and that in itself is as important a duty of the historian as impartiality. That being as it may, and returning to the point, we can safely conclude that Pusey's sermons hold within them material which is indicative of systematic theological thought, and that that theological thought when studied for its own merit goes a long way to disproving many of the caricatures which still prevail about Pusey.

I will conclude with a deeper study of the archival material. Here again, there is so much that should at the very least make us reconsider the picture of Pusey with which we are presented by most modern writers. It is a bit difficult to know where to begin, since most of the material is fragmentary and scattered across the archive. One major source is the material connected to Pusey's involvement with the religious communities. Here again, Pusey has too often been carelessly accused of an ascetic extremism damaging to all around him. Turner wrote that in the sisterhoods with which Pusey was involved, he 'either cultivated or permitted extravagant fasting and other forms of self-denial criticized by physicians and other onlookers'.[58] Susan Mumm, who portrays the early sisterhoods as proto-feminist institutions in her book *Stolen Daughters, Virgin Mothers*, wrote that 'Pusey had a consistently detrimental effect on any community with which he got involved. Given his insistence on a morbidly penitential spirituality, combined with his love of interfering…it should not surprise us that any community he had much to do with remained chaotic and weak'.[59] Both Turner's and Mumm's criticisms are true of the first sisterhood at Park Village, where the sisters followed a gruelling pattern of daily prayer in addition to their works of mercy, and where one of the sisters died, seemingly in part as a result of the ascetic practices encouraged by Pusey.[60] But in starting a version of the religious life from scratch, this community was attempting to do something which had not been done in England for hundreds of years, and Pusey learned from his mistakes, to the extent that he was subsequently to warn against extravagant fasting or asceticism.[61] Once again, a claim which may justly be made of one particular moment in Pusey's life has been allowed to become a blanket condemnation of him. Furthermore, the Society of the Most Holy Trinity (SMHT), which Pusey did so much to found, whose first warden he became, and in whose grounds at Ascot he died in 1882, thrived throughout the last decades of the nineteenth century and most of the twentieth, finally coming to the end of its life in the early years of the twenty-first century. At one stage – within Pusey's lifetime – the Sisterhood had three separate congregations within it adhering to the enclosed, the mixed, and the active forms of the religious life respectively. This is hardly the history of a 'chaotic and weak' community.

The archive at Pusey House contains a lot of material on Pusey and the religious life which has never been published. There is the *Rule* for the Ascot sisters, for example, which was almost entirely written by Pusey, and which shows the ecstatic quality of his writing:

> Those who lodge Jesus in their heart as their invisible Spouse, have need to live a hidden and retired and lonely life, cherishing diligently within them every spark of grace, until at length they like the Angels, become enwrapped in the rays of Divine Love, through which may be discerned the Beauty of the Image of God, which is impressed on the children of Light in the Kingdom of Life. It is thus, Beloved Daughters, that ye shall resemble the wise Virgins who never left their lamps of Love untrimmed.[62]

And again, more briefly, in a later part of the rule, 'Let the Nuns of the Love of Jesus [the most enclosed of the Ascot sisters] be as the Cherubim described by Ezekiel, suspended between heaven and earth, covered with eyes and with great wings, to express the light of their thoughts and the sublimity of their love.'[63] In both these passages, Pusey is describing an ecstatic vision of love which hardly accords with the standard portrayal of him.

Pusey's involvement in founding and supporting the early sisterhoods raises other important questions about the nature of his personality, not least through his close relationship with Priscilla Lydia Sellon, the foundress and first superior of the SMHT. It is almost certain that Pusey's early biographers stayed clear of this topic because the relationship was seen as controversial in some quarters: primarily among those who were suspicious of Pusey and the sisterhoods, but nonetheless to such an extent that Keble thought it prudent to warn his friend of the public perceptions of the relationship.[64] There is no evidence that these perceptions were anything other than groundless. What they do show which is of relevance here is that into middle age and beyond Pusey was capable of forming warm, intimate friendships with women as well as men. Allchin has written of the depth of Pusey's affection for Sellon, and 'the importance of her friendship for him. In the lonely and intensely difficult years after 1845, Pusey's extremely warm and human personality looked for someone who would enter into his position, and in Miss Sellon he found such a person.'[65] It is in summarizing these events that Allchin makes a vitally important, and criminally neglected, summary of Pusey's character: 'The harsh and unremitting asceticism of [Pusey's] later years, was the product not of a cold and unattractive nature, but of a warm and intensely emotional one. Under the authoritative and apparently unfeeling exterior of the leader of the High Church Movement, the sensitive and feeling nature lived on.[66]

We have already encountered Miss Clarissa Powell, who became Sister Clara when she joined the SMHT. Her correspondence with Pusey continued and is included in the Liddon Bound Volumes at Pusey House. She also wrote some 'Reminiscenses' of Pusey, which are included in the last volume of correspondence. In these reminiscences, Sister Clara recalled the two Hawaiian children who were raised by the sisters at Ascot after the foundation of a daughter house in Hawaii. 'To these children, Dr Pusey became devotedly attached and they returned his love by the sweetest affection. He was a father to them… [H]e used to take the little Palemo (4 years old) in his arms and stand at the window to show her the "Pretty mu cows[?]"… The children called him "Dear Papa".'[67]

Another sister wrote of her surprise at hearing Pusey use words a child could understand as he spoke to them about the Old Testament while having his lunch, 'and the joy it seemed to bring him when he saw that she understood and asked him questions. Sometimes he would have two or three children with him when he took his walk, and then he always talked to them in the most delightful way about general things, and always would end with speaking of the Love and Goodness of God.'[68] Miss Milner, in her unpublished (and unpaginated) 'Reminiscences of Dr Pusey', recalls Pusey shaking with laughter on one occasion. She also describes Pusey visiting her one day whilst she happened to be holding his grandson:

> I remember how his face beamed with the sweetest tenderest smile, as he came across the room to where I was and said, 'so you have turned nurse, have you!' and then he looked down at his little grandson as I held him up

for him to see – and he said in his own dear way 'God bless you' and then turned to ask Mary [his daughter] about her plans for the afternoon.[69]

Another unpublished source is a letter written to Pusey's daughter Mary Brine by a friend of hers shortly after the death of her father. The writer recalls staying with the Pusey family at the time that Lucy Pusey was dying.

> I remember so well on Christmas morning we had been to the Holy Communion, and when I came into the breakfast-room (Miss Rogers's room) afterwards Lucy and you were standing on either side of your dear Father, looking so bright & happy, and the contrast between that and my own loneliness came across me with a sharp pain which I suppose made itself visible, for Dr Pusey took his hand off Lucy's shoulder and greeted me with that peculiarly beautiful smile of his, which seemed to take away all the sadness at once – this seems but a small thing to mention now, and yet the quick sympathy which [one] will feel even for a child's small troubles as well as for the wider and deeper ones of human nature must be very near akin to that Divine Love which encompasses everything. I can never forget your Father's kindness to me that morning when I had looked my last upon dear Lucy; he was coming part of my way that morning and came in the same carriage with me, and his words of comfort and counsel have been with me ever since – it was so self-forgetting too, for by that time Lucy's recovery had been quite given up and you know what a trial her loss was to him.[70]

Liddon's biography includes a passage where he describes Pusey reading stories to the children on Hayling Island. 'Little children were more at home with him than the rest of the world', he quotes one observer as saying.[71] The unpublished material which we have quoted here would seem to go some way to supporting that claim, whilst simultaneously throwing serious doubt on Forrester's claim that Pusey showed a 'heartless indifference' towards the suffering of children.

Now it may be thought at this stage that like a certain type of Anglo-Catholic clergyman, Pusey had a special way with nuns and old ladies that caused them to view him through rose-tinted glasses. Should the reader be thinking that, then a 'paper written [in] 1891 for [Charles] Gore' in the Acland Papers at Pusey House should dispel the notion that Pusey's appeal was limited to such people. Sir Henry Wentworth Acland was the Regius Professor of Medicine in the University of Oxford, a fellow of All Souls, and one of the key players in the founding of the University Museum, and so unlikely to be a soft touch for an ageing Tractarian cleric.[72] But nevertheless, he recalls paying Pusey a visit and observed that 'Dr Pusey, as most great men, had a certain – even keen – sense of humour... He threw himself back in his chair in a fit of laughter. Soon he recovered himself, and sitting straight upright, he slowly said in the solemn and almost stern way, which to many seemed his chief expression'. Acland concludes his paper by saying that 'this whole story must be one of the most remarkable illustrations of the manliness of a great religious teacher, on record in history'.[73] Manliness aside, I think it speaks for itself in terms of the argument I have advanced in this chapter.

By way of conclusion, there is the fascinating question of John Octavius Johnston and William Charles Edmund Newbolt's *Spiritual Letters* of Pusey. Many of these letters were in fact written to Sister Clara, and the chapter at the end of the book entitled 'Fragments of Conversations and Letters' is similarly drawn from a section of her reminiscences in the Pusey House archive. What is intriguing is the difference between the transcripts of Sister Clara's reminiscences and the version published by Johnston and Newbolt. For example, various High Church sentiments are omitted: 'Ask God for the Prayers of the Saints';[74] 'The miracle of the Holy Communion is greater than that of raising Lazarus from the dead.'[75] Also omitted, however, are certain phrases which, if more widely known, would help to dispel the caricature of Pusey as defined by the history of Pusey. In the section 'On Recreation in a Sisterhood', Johnston and Newbolt kept in the bits about self-restraint and not laughing or talking loudly on a Friday,[76] but omitted the phrase: 'Laughter is not wrong: smiling one would rather have.'[77] Even more telling is a passage where Sister Clara recalls Pusey teaching the sisters:

> And his own beautiful countenance would irradiate with love [in the printed *Letters*, this is edited to read: 'and his own face would lighten up with love'] while he would pour out, 'Oh that boundless, shoreless, ocean of the Divine Love. If we had not been told, we could never have imagined it, that God should unite Himself to us, the least of all his rational creation and dwell in our hearts. Oh the wondrous, marvellous intensity of that love!!!'[78]

The *Letters* give an edited version of that passage up to that point. But they omit what follows in the Liddon Bound Volumes transcripts: 'And this radiation each time we saw him seemed to increase, so that he could only be looked upon as *a very apostle of love.*'[79] So it would appear, that for reasons of Tractarian reserve, or whatever else it may have been, phrases and passages which gave a hint as to the depth and warmth of Pusey's personality were deliberately omitted from the *Spiritual Letters*, and have been lost ever since. This would suggest that the editorial activities discussed by Kenneth Macnab continued throughout

Johnston and Newbolt's work. It also indicates that the caricature of Pusey so beloved of modern historians has its roots in the very earliest publications about him.

In 1933, Geoffrey Faber described the depths of Pusey's mourning following the death of his wife, and memorably concluded that 'Whether, in his exploration of these depths, he is to be called a pervert or a saint is a matter for every reader's private judgement.'[80] At least Faber gave his readers the choice. For if the early historians of Pusey implied – and then finally stated – that he was a saint, their modern successors are equally guilty of implying that he was, if not a pervert, then at least a man in whom recognisable Christian virtues such as joy and gentleness were completely absent. Perhaps the greatest mystery is why those historians who have had need of a brief description of Pusey, or passing reference to him in a work whose main focus lies elsewhere, have almost uniformly adopted the Forrester image, without reference to scholars such as Allchin who have consistently given a more rounded, but much neglected, picture of Pusey.[81] More importantly, they have also ignored the abundant primary material which would help to augment and flesh out that picture of Pusey as both theologian and man. While it is far beyond the scope of this essay to paint such a picture in any kind of fullness, I hope that I have at least shown that the material with which to do so exists, and that it is a task waiting, and indeed needing, to be done.

Notes

1. Anon., text to accompany 'Ape' cartoon, *Vanity Fair*, 2 January 1875.
2. Oliver Elton, *Frederick York Powell: A Life and a Selection from his Letters and Occasional Writings* (Oxford: Clarendon Press, 1906), 1:66–7, quoted in Matthew, 'Edward Bouverie Pusey', 123–4.
3. *Oxford Dictionary of National Biography*, s.v. 'Frederick York Powell'.
4. Matthew, 'Edward Bouverie Pusey', 124.
5. Ibid., 124.
6. Ibid., 123.
7. Butler, 'Introduction', in Butler, *Pusey Rediscovered*, x.
8. Prestige, *Pusey*, 54.
9. Brilioth, *Anglican Revival*, 17, 227n.
10. Ibid., 242f.; 296.
11. Ibid., 301.
12. Mrs Pusey to Edward Bouverie Pusey, 9 June 1838, Liddon Bound Volumes 22.
13. Edward Bouverie Pusey to Mrs Pusey, 29 and 30 April 1838, Liddon Bound Volumes 25.
14. E.g., Mrs Pusey to Edward Bouverie Pusey, 14 June 1838, Liddon Bound Volumes 22.
15. Forrester, *Young Doctor Pusey*, 70.
16. Edward Bouverie Pusey to Mrs Pusey, 4 November 1835, Liddon Bound Volumes 25, emphasis added.

17 See, for example, Edward Bouverie Pusey to Sister Clara I, passim, Liddon Bound Volumes 76.
18 Forrester, *Young Doctor Pusey*, 70.
19 Edward Bouverie Pusey to Mrs Pusey, 22 May 1837 (*not* 20 May, as footnoted in Forrester's thesis), Liddon Bound Volumes 25. See Forrester, *Young Doctor Pusey*, 70; Forrester, 'The Intellectual Development', 138.
20 Forrester, *Young Doctor Pusey*, 70.
21 Liddon, *Life of Pusey*, 3:414–15.
22 Forrester, *Young Doctor Pusey*, 70.
23 Matthew, 'Edward Bouverie Pusey', 116.
24 Avis, *Anglicanism and the Christian Church*, 206.
25 Chadwick, *Victorian Church* (1966–70), 1:198.
26 Ibid., 198.
27 As in, for example, Matthew, 'Edward Bouverie Pusey', 116.
28 Turner, *John Henry Newman*, 107–8.
29 Ibid., 91.
30 Ibid., 103.
31 Ibid., 105.
32 Webster, *Theological Theology*, 20. My thanks to Fr Thomas Seville, C.R., for directing me to this.
33 Stacpoole, editorial introduction to Forrester, 'Dr Pusey's Marriage', 33.
34 See the discussion of the earliest sisterhoods below.
35 E.g., Forrester, *Young Doctor Pusey*; and the following essays from *Pusey Rediscovered*, ed. Butler: Frappell, 'Science'; Jasper, 'Pusey's *Lectures*'; Livesley, 'Regius Professor of Hebrew'.
36 Allchin, *Participation in God*, 53.
37 Chadwick, 'Mind of the Oxford Movement', 37.
38 Exceptions include work by Geoffrey Rowell, A. M. Allchin and Owen Chadwick. See, for example, Rowell, *Vision Glorious*, 71–98; Allchin, 'Pusey the Servant of God'; Allchin, *Participation in God*, 48–63; Chadwick, *Spirit of the Oxford Movement*, 1–54.
39 See, for example, Pusey, *Parochial Sermons* 2.
40 I am thinking in particular of Congar's discussion of the indwelling of the Spirit in his monumental *I Believe in the Holy Spirit*, esp. 2:79–99, and Rowan Williams's essay 'Word and Spirit', in *On Christian Theology*, 107–27.
41 Pusey, *Sermons during the Season*, 233.
42 Brilioth, *Anglican Revival*, 301.
43 Matthew, 'Edward Bouverie Pusey', 116.
44 Pusey, *Parochial Sermons*, 2:258.
45 Pusey, 'Our Being in God', *Parochial Sermons*, 2:380.
46 Pusey, 'Hope', *Parochial Sermons*, 2:21.
47 McCormack, 'Glory of the Indwelling God', 16.
48 Allchin, *Participation in God*, 54.
49 Chadwick, *Victorian Church* (1966–70), 1:198.
50 Pusey, The Ascension our Glory and Joy', *Parochial Sermons*, 2:216.
51 Ibid., 2:236–7.
52 Pusey, 'The Rest of Love and Praise', *Parochial Sermons* 2:262.
53 Edward Bouverie Pusey to Sister Clara I, August 1845, Liddon Bound Volumes 76/226f.

54 Edward Bouverie Pusey to Sister Clara I, 24 Jan 1846, Liddon Bound Volumes 76/239f.
55 Edward Bouverie Pusey to Sister Clara I, Advent 1846, Liddon Bound Volumes 76/280f.
56 Owen Chadwick uses the term 'ecstatic' to describe Pusey's sermons. See Chadwick, *Spirit of the Oxford Movement*, 39.
57 Allchin, *Participation in God*, 54. He is referring specifically to the St Saviour's sermons of 1845.
58 Turner, *John Henry Newman*, 107. There is no reference in support of this assertion.
59 Mumm, *Stolen Daughters*, 157–8.
60 See Gill, *Women and the Church of England*, 151.
61 There are several examples of this in the correspondence with Sister Clara, including letters sent at about the time the Park Village Sisterhood was going through its difficult early days. See, for example, Pusey to Sister Clara, letter dated Saturday after Ascension Day 1846, and letter undated but sent during Advent 1846, Liddon Bound Volumes 76.
62 Chapter 13, Statutes, Society of the Most Holy Trinity, 1861, Ascot Priory Archive, Ascot.
63 Ibid., chapter 34.
64 Allchin, *Silent Rebellion*, 128.
65 Ibid. See 128–30 for a more detailed discussion of the nature of the relationship between Pusey and Sellon.
66 Ibid., 128–9.
67 Sister Clara III, 'Reminiscences of Dr Pusey by Sister Clara', Liddon Bound Volumes 78/38–40. On the children, Palemo and Manoannoa, see Williams, *Priscilla Lydia Sellon*, 244n and 262–8. These children came to Ascot in 1865, and others in 1867.
68 Sister Clara III, 'Reminiscences of Dr Pusey – sent by one of the Devenport Society', Liddon Bound Volumes 78. This is likely to be Sister Georgiana Louisa.
69 Milner, Miss [Maud], 'Reminiscences of Dr Pusey', Pusey House Library, Oxford. I am grateful to Fr Barry Orford, whois currently working on an edition of this volume, for pointing me to this document during the course of other research in 2003–04.
70 Edward Bouverie Pusey and Miss Rogers, 16 October, 1882, Liddon Bound Volumes 124.
71 Liddon, *Life of Pusey*, 3:187.
72 *Oxford Dictionary of National Biography*, s.v. 'Sir Henry Wentworth Acland'.
73 Acland, 'Paper written Christmas 1891 for Canon Gore', Acland Papers, Pusey House Library, Oxford.
74 Sister Clara III, Liddon Bound Volumes 78/914.
75 Ibid., 837.
76 [Pusey], *Spiritual Letters*, 339.
77 Sister Clara III, Liddon Bound Volumes 78/946.
78 Sister Clara III, Liddon Bound Volumes 78/832.
79 Ibid., emphasis added.
80 Faber, *Oxford Apostles*, 376.
81 For example, Avis, *Anglicanism and the Christian Church*, lists *Young Doctor Pusey* in the bibliography, but nothing by Allchin.

Chapter Three

EDITING LIDDON: FROM BIOGRAPHY TO HAGIOGRAPHY?

K. E. Macnab

The cellars of academic institutions can be fascinating places. The cellar of Pusey House is no exception. Fifteen years ago it contained a large amount of unsorted material, some of which dated to the earliest days of the house. There were trunks, boxes of various vintages and, in one corner, a battered old suitcase. Opening it revealed thousands of small blue pieces of paper in the hands of Dr Henry Parry Liddon and his North Oxford amanuenses. Clearly here was the manuscript of Liddon's four-volume *Life of Edward Bouverie Pusey*, for the most part still sitting inside the grubby envelopes in which it passed back and forth, chapter by chapter, between J. O. Johnston's house at 9 Keble Road and Horace Hart, the Printer to the University.[1] As with the manuscripts of Pusey's sermons in a nearby chest, it seemed a relatively straightforward task to put these pieces of paper in order using the four blue-bound volumes of Liddon's *Life*. An incentive to do this came from the fact that Liddon had provided detailed references for the letters from which he quoted, references which are often missing from the printed volumes. The daunting prospect of cross-referencing the many letters quoted on the printed page with the well-used and well-loved Liddon Bound Volumes seemed to have been removed at a stroke. Of particular interest were the footnotes which give the dates of private conversations between Liddon and Pusey, other footnotes which refer the reader to documents such as 'The Hon. P. Pusey's account book' for details in the narrative which can appear to be hearsay, and others again which cite documents available to Liddon but lost in the intervening 120 years.

However, it soon became clear that there was a considerable discrepancy between what lay on the paper in Liddon's hand and what was on the page of the posthumously published biography. The more one read the original manuscript, the more one realized that the process of editing Liddon's enormous work undertaken by his friends and followers, John Octavius Johnston, Robert John Wilson and William Charles Edmund Newbolt, had played a part in producing the picture of Pusey which we read from its pages, one which we instinctively attribute to Liddon himself.[2] One could not avoid asking some linked questions. Did the editorial process in the 1880s and 1890s materially alter, tinker with or, at the worst, even obscure the picture of Pusey which Liddon had committed to paper? If it did, why might that have been the case? Was the 'quest for the historical Pusey' which has been the concern of historians in the last forty years, particularly with regard to the changes in Pusey's thought up to c.1835, in fact present to a greater or lesser extent in Liddon's original version? This essay tries to ask those questions of that early period in Pusey's theological career. It relies exclusively on what we find in the manuscript of the *Life* and does not stray into the correspondence of Liddon, let alone Johnston, Wilson or Newbolt. That essential task remains to be tackled.[3]

Liddon's *Life* has been, from the first moment of its publication, the indispensable starting point for any study of the career and influence of Pusey, but scholars have not been blind to its shortcomings. Owen Chadwick made an often-quoted observation:

> It was tragic that [Pusey's] biography should have been entrusted to the obvious author, the most intimate of his immediate disciples, H. P. Liddon. For Liddon treated Pusey's letters and papers with reverence, the reverence due to a great man (but not due to a great mind, for the mind is not that kind of mind), and the reiteration at inordinate length of detailed information, succeeded in concealing Pusey's stature behind a pile of paper, and rendered the biography readable only by the student.[4]

Johnston and Wilson, in their Preface to the first published volume, dated August 1893, were clear as to the task that had faced them on Liddon's death.

> With such expedition as has been possible amid the pressure of their ordinary duties, the present editors have done their best to carry out what they knew of Dr Liddon's intentions. Dr Liddon had expressly stated that what he had written was not in his judgement at all in a state for publication; at the same time it of course indicated the scale on which he intended the 'Life' to be published.
>
> The editors therefore, though compelled carefully to examine and revise the whole of the manuscript, did not feel themselves in any way at liberty materially to alter the character, the scale, or the plan of the work. This would have involved writing a new Life of Dr Pusey, instead

of editing Dr Liddon's projected work, and would have entailed, as they think, a grave loss to all readers.[5]

In his biography of Liddon, which appeared in 1904, Johnston went further in expressing his reservations about a project which became close to a religious duty in Liddon's eyes.

> The preparations were indeed most lengthy and elaborate, and some of them he allowed others to do for him; but the work of writing which fell on himself alone, was a burden, lovingly borne indeed, but a very heavy burden, until the end. Every fact had to be stated most exactly and minutely in order to satisfy his scrupulous sense of what was due to his subject; and the length of his analyses of Pusey's works and early Sermons was beyond all possible proportions for a biography... [W]e may well wish that the burden of the work had been entrusted to some other hand... Beyond all other one cause, the attempt to write Pusey's *Life* led to Liddon's comparatively early death.[6]

That Liddon's manuscript required editing is beyond doubt, and it is clear that Liddon knew that as well as anyone. The chapter on Pusey's *Theology of Germany*[7] alone runs to 36,000 words, in part because Liddon quoted long letters in German between Friedrich August Gottreu Tholuck[8] and Pusey. Similarly, the long genealogical chapter on the Pusey and Bouverie families was left by Liddon as the first chapter of the biography proper. One wonders how many readers would have ploughed through that long account of over 1000 years had it been printed, as Liddon intended, as chapter one. It was also clear that Liddon's manuscript required considerable work to pass muster under the strict scrutiny of the guardians of *Hart's Rules*.

Johnston was one of Liddon's literary executors with Francis Paget and, more controversially, Charles Gore. Wilson and Newbolt knew Liddon equally well. There are relatively few passages of any significant length on the printed page, certainly in the first volume, which we may attribute directly to their editorial pencil – perhaps we might say 'freely composed in the style of Dr Liddon' – although there are many paragraphs and sentences which they re-cast, often to condense several pages of Liddon's manuscript into a few pithy phrases. They did, however, consider themselves free to quote extensively from Newman's *Letters and Correspondence*, published just after Liddon's death.[9]

To recast the question which we have asked already, did the editors, consciously or subconsciously, fail in the task which they set themselves, namely 'not...to alter the character, the scale, or the plan of the work'? If that was their guiding principle, why was it that the book-buying public of

1893 did not have the opportunity to read the account which Liddon had put into his manuscript about Pusey worshipping in a succession of Presbyterian congregations in Scotland or about his seeing nothing wrong with priests getting married? Why was the Anglo-Catholic world of the 1890s not told, in the way in which Liddon had first committed to paper, that there was a time when Pusey did not believe in prayers for the dead or the invocation of saints? Why was a considerable portion of Pusey's correspondence in the 1820s with his future wife about the church, apostolic order and the nature of schism not found on the printed page? Above all, was it in line with Liddon's intentions to remove a quotation which still has the power to shock: namely that there was a time in his life when Pusey considered the Church of England's Eucharistic doctrine to be Calvinistic?

We must be careful not to construct a melodramatic conspiracy theory claiming that Liddon's honesty was deliberately perverted by Anglo-Catholic plotters, but equally we may ask the question, 'What may have been the forces at work behind the editing process which contributed to these omissions?' We shall conclude this paper with a number of tentative suggestions for future consideration. Hence this paper is principally a study of the historiography of the 1890s rather than a doctrinal history of the 1820s.

In *Young Dr Pusey*, David Forrester acknowledged that Liddon's *Life* was 'a remarkable achievement' before arguing persuasively that

> the deep respect which Liddon rightly earned for his labours has mesmerized later historians into an uncritical acceptance of his portrayal of Pusey and his times… Up to the early 1830s there is almost no evidence to suggest that Pusey was ever likely to sympathize with the ideals which the Tractarians made their own and much to the contrary.[10]

Although nothing in Liddon's manuscript argues for a theological *volte face* on the part of Pusey in the early 1830s in such explicit terms, a combination of factors leads us to wonder whether Liddon might not have accepted, at least in part, Forrester's argument. Forrester claimed that 'no account is given of the evolution of Pusey's theology'.[11] That may be true of the printed *Life of Pusey*. It is certainly true that Liddon's manuscript does not give detailed descriptions of particular moments, let alone 'road to Damascus' moments, where Pusey's opinions changed decisively. However, had Liddon's original words reached the printed page intact, we would have a far clearer story of Pusey's theological and spiritual development than the one which finally emerged.[12]

Johnston and Wilson moved Liddon's historical and genealogical first chapter to the appendix of volume one in a reduced point size, but they left the manuscript's description of Pusey's childhood in Berkshire and his education at Clapham, Eton and Buckden relatively untouched. Similarly, relatively little was removed by the editors' pencils from chapter two where Liddon describes Pusey and Sheffield Neave's tour of Switzerland in considerable detail.[13] One thing which was excised, however, was the simple sentence from the young Pusey commenting on the interior of a Roman Catholic Church they came across. 'Though as a Protestant, I should have wished the decorations of those chapels different, there was something most striking in the blending of exultation for their country's redemption with religious gratitude.'[14] That Pusey should claim the title 'Protestant' for himself in such a matter-of-fact way may well have made later eyebrows rise. If Pusey, a self-professed Protestant, could see any good in the church furnishings of a little Catholic country church, it was for reasons of liberal politics, not theology: he rejoiced to see the natural way in which the people's thanksgiving for Swiss independence was expressed in the decoration of the chapel built at William Tell's supposed birthplace.

Chapter three poses a number of problems for the modern reader of the manuscript as Johnston and Wilson chose to replace a large section of Liddon's manuscript (which reproduced Newman's memories of first meeting Pusey at Oriel College) with the account given in Anne Mozley's first volume of Newman's Anglican letters.[15] The substance of Liddon's version of the story, however, was untouched, and what is most striking is the similarity between Liddon's account of his conversations with Newman, footnoted as taking place on 27 September 1882 and 5 June 1883 and the version of the same events Mozley published nine years later.[16]

If these early chapters are relatively uninteresting for our purposes, the editorial process becomes more prominent with the published chapter four describing Pusey's first visit to Germany and his early years at Oriel. Liddon had no qualms about writing about 'the Lutheran Church', but the published version consistently talks about the Lutheran 'body' or 'attending the Lutheran service'.[17] Liddon's perhaps surprisingly sympathetic depiction of Friedrich Daniel Ernst Schleiermacher[18] was hardly touched although one or two elements of hyperbole were removed: '[Schleiermacher's] lectures were… lighted up by a fire and eloquence of great distinction…[which] added to the brilliant effect of his language'.[19]

The published chapter five describes Pusey's second visit to Germany, again at considerable length. Johnston and Wilson abbreviated some of the technical elements of learning Arabic with Johann Gottfried Ludwig Kosegarten[20] and Georg Wilhelm Freytag.[21] Perhaps this would have been of more interest to a retired professor of New Testament, as Liddon was by the time he drafted the chapter, than it would have been to the general reader. One thing which strikes the modern reader of the manuscript, however, is the extent to which Liddon's descriptions of Pusey's friendly relations with, and admiration of, some of the prominent names of contemporary Lutheran theology were also removed. Liddon's manuscript also mentions the possibility, first raised by Christian August Brandis (1790–1867)[22] and Karl Immanuel Nitzsch (1787–1868),[23] that Pusey and Maria should settle at Bonn after their marriage.[24] Liddon does not speculate what might have happened had Pusey taken his bride abroad rather than to Christ Church. Had the young Pusey chosen that path, how different things may have been.

If there is an implied reference to ecclesiology in the consistent refusal on the part of the editors to use the word 'church' for German Lutherans, the subject becomes more of an issue in chapter six. The first time this occurs is with regard to the Catholic teaching that the Bible is the church's book. The printed edition comments, 'The question what the Universal Church might have to say about the meaning of the books of which it is the witness and keeper would have appeared to Pusey much more pressing and important in 1835 than it did in 1827.'[25] However, an unpublished passage adds, 'even if it at all distinctly presented itself to him at the earlier date. And thus it was, in after years, he only looked at his early work to feel regret and pain at it.'[26] A little later Liddon's manuscript returns to an increasingly familiar theme: 'As to supposed contradictions in respects of matters of fact in Holy Scripture, Pusey would have expressed himself in later years with much more caution and knowledge. The influence of some of his German friends was strong upon him.'[27] Only the first clause was retained by Johnston and Wilson.

The section in which Liddon describes Pusey and Maria's correspondence about the preaching of Francis Close, Rector of Cheltenham,[28] was similarly pruned by the editors. Ecclesiology is the principal theme again. At the beginning of a long section, all of which was to be omitted from the printed chapter, Liddon's judgement was succinct:

> Edward Pusey's reply [to Miss Barker] shows that at that time the idea of the Church, with her Divinely ordered and historical structure, and with a definite Creed independent of the eccentricities of sects or individuals, had not clearly presented itself to his mind.[29]

He quotes an undated letter to Maria, probably written on 9 October 1827:

> Take, for instance, the different sects in England...[and] you will find that the difference can in no case, except the Socinians, by any mind well read in Scripture, be assumed to be of vital importance. In the Independents and Presbyterians the question is merely one of Church Governments, which however important some may think it for keeping out untruth, is not the truth *itself*.[30]

After several more examples and four pages of quotations, Liddon's unpublished conclusion is again clear: 'Ten years later [Pusey] would have eagerly disavowed such language... But to quote it is a matter of historical justice.'[31]

In a later chapter, Johnston and Wilson removed a passage rich in unstated irony in which Charles James Blomfield, Bishop of London, accused Pusey in 1830, not without justification, of giving insufficient importance to episcopacy and creeds.

> Pusey had said that articles of faith are useful, but not necessary to the existence of a Church. If they are not necessary, replies the bishop, it will be hard to show that they are lawful. But in principle they existed in Apostolic times: and to dispense with them would be to authorise 'an arbitrary, and licentious exposition of Scripture truth'. Pusey had, unconsciously, taken the ground of 'the Socinian petitioners against Subscription in 1771'.[32]

Quite how an Anglo-Catholic of the 1890s would have reacted to the thought that Dr Pusey had, at one point, considered that Nonconformists basically differed from episcopally ordered Churches only in subordinate theological points is ours to speculate. These passages were never printed.

Another omission on the part of the editors was the comment that in recommending books to read when studying the New Testament, Pusey referred his future wife to Martin Luther's *Preface to the Epistle to the Romans*. Maria asked Pusey's advice about how she might keep Lent. Liddon's comment, once again removed from the printed version, stresses how unlikely it would have been for the young Pusey to use the words 'the church teaches' concerning a matter of devotion.

> Pusey was not yet [in 1828] in a position to help her, except by telling her what he and his Oxford friends thought about it. That which they thought came very much out of their more general sense of the fitness of things, and not from the teaching of Church authority.[33]

We find ourselves asking yet again how that sentence would that have read to Anglo-Catholics in 1893. A little further on, Liddon comments, seemingly to himself, in a footnote, 'it is simply honest not to omit anything which enables us to follow the history and growth of his religious mind'.[34]

The rest of Liddon's chapter six was cut significantly by Johnston and Wilson. The manuscript contains 18,000 words against the published edition of 14,000. One passage which survived the editing process more or less intact is found in the final few pages about the repeal of the Test and Corporation Acts and Roman Catholic Emancipation.[35] However, Johnston and Wilson removed a comment which is now almost tediously familiar. Talking of the government changes in the spring of 1828, Liddon wrote, 'Edward Pusey permits himself to adopt a tone which in later years he would have condemned as scornful, and which reads as if inspired by Whately.'[36] Even on the very last page of the chapter, Johnston and Wilson removed the bald statement, 'Miss Barker was evidently republican in her sympathies.'[37]

With the published chapter seven, Liddon returned to domestic affairs starting with the 1828 election to the provostship of Oriel and Pusey's reaction to the sudden death of his father a few weeks later, on 13 April. Although this chapter does not set out to explore theological issues in the same style as the chapters on Pusey's journeys to Germany, theological controversies are never far from the surface. Anglican battlegrounds which would have been only too familiar to the readers of the 1890s come to the fore. Liddon has no reticence in pointing out that Pusey at this time had no concept of praying for the dead. His manuscript quotes a letter from Pusey to his brother William (omitted from the printed *Life*) written as late as 1833. 'Our sainted father's departure dwelt much on my mind when I heard of the happy leave which Lord Carnarvon was allowed to take of his children.'[38] There is no hint of the possibility that his father's soul – or indeed that of Lord Carnarvon, his relative by marriage – might be assisted by the prayers of the faithful, let alone the prayers of the saints. Liddon's manuscript adds:

> In Edward Pusey's language at this date there is a noteworthy indefiniteness about the state of the dead in Christ. One expression possibly seems to point to belief in an intermediate state: but the general tenor of what he writes implies the popular Protestant idea that those who die in a state of grace go straight to heaven. A clearer knowledge was yet to come. Pusey's sense of his father's happiness was qualified by the presence of natural sorrow; and there is no trace of his relieving this, as in later years, by intercession for the departed.[39]

Once again, not a word of this verdict was included in Johnston and Wilson's final version.

The next part of chapter seven brings the reader up against the question of ordination, marriage and celibacy. By the 1890s debates were frequent in Anglo-Catholic clerical circles about the desirability of celibacy. The Society of the Holy Cross (SSC), not the most numerous but perhaps the most prominent and abiding Anglo-Catholic organization for priests (and one to which Pusey had briefly belonged), had elected a married priest as its Master in the 1860s.

By the 1890s there were regular debates in SSC chapters and synods, which were to continue far into the twentieth century, proposing that membership of the society should be restricted to celibates.[40]

When Pusey was ordained deacon on 1 June 1828, he was still engaged to be married to Miss Barker. It would not have occurred to the vast majority of nineteenth-century Anglicans that there was anything odd or improper in this. Liddon, however, clearly second-guessed some of the objections which might be raised and felt the need to add an explanatory paragraph which was later to be excised.

> In later years Pusey would have taken care to postpone his ordination as deacon until after his marriage; since the Ancient Church, which undoubtedly allowed married men to be ordained, affords no example of marriage after ordination. But the authority of Christian Antiquity was not yet a practical question for him.[41]

Why might this have been removed? Is it possible that it was felt to draw attention unnecessarily to an Achilles' heel in Pusey's biography from the point of view of a later generation?

There was to be a final sting in the tail of chapter seven. This concerned Edward and Maria's honeymoon following their marriage 11 days after his ordination as deacon. Their tour was largely spent in Scotland. Once again Liddon's account of those weeks was almost entirely removed by his editors. Most of it is a picturesque travelogue. However, one detail is particularly striking. Throughout their time in Scotland Edward and Maria worshipped with Presbyterian congregations[42] where, for example, they kept – or, one may suppose, did *not* keep – St Peter's Day 1828 at Lanark. The following Sunday they worshipped at the Presbyterian service in Tobermory; two Sundays later found them at a service in Skye which was almost entirely conducted in Gaelic and the following Sunday in the parish church in Callender. It was not to be until 10 August that they worshipped in what we would today call the Episcopal Church (referred to by Liddon as the 'Church of Scotland') when they reached Edinburgh.[43]

As Queen Victoria attended the local parish church whenever she was in Scotland, especially at her beloved Balmoral, Liddon could have been on thin ice if he had been overly critical of Anglican communicants worshipping with Presbyterians. Liddon's manuscript, however, could not let the fact of the newlyweds' Sunday pattern of worship go unremarked.

> This [attending Presbyterian worship] they constantly did when in Scotland. It does not seem to have been due to curiosity, or to any theory

that an established religion must as such have claims upon the conscience; but simply to a wish to share in the fuller worship of God where it was provided. Pusey's letters to Miss Barker show that at this time he did not yet understand what he afterwards believed to be the Divinely ordered structure of the Church of Christ; and considered the questions of Church Government, as they were called, which divided Christian from Christian, matters of no serious moment.[44]

That paragraph was omitted from the published account. Whether the Puseys received Holy Communion in a Presbyterian church – an act which would have shocked 1890s Anglo-Catholics to the core – is unclear and unlikely, not least given the timing of their visit and the complicated and lengthy preparations for the Lord's Supper which were standard among Presbyterians at the time. Liddon describes their receiving Holy Communion together on 31 August at Marchwiel when staying with Pusey's friend from Eton, J. Montague Luxmoore, as, 'it would seem, the first time since their wedding'.[45] However, there is a tantalizing unpublished comment from Liddon which means that we may not be entirely certain. '[Pusey] would not have repeated an act which might seem to treat the apostolic structure of the Church of Christ, or the validity of the sacraments, as matters of indifference.'[46] The use of the word 'act' in the singular and the reference to 'the validity of the sacraments' may just hint that the Puseys did, in fact, attend and receive Communion at the Presbyterian Lord's Supper.

And so we come to the final chapter under discussion: the gargantuan piece of work, swollen to a vast and unwieldy size, entitled simply 'Controversy with the Rev. H. J. Rose on the Theology of Germany'. Suitably edited, this was published as chapter eight in volume one at a length of 11,500 words. As we have seen, at 36,000 words this chapter as drafted by Liddon approaches half the length of a modern doctoral thesis. It quotes the two volumes entitled *Theology of Germany* with almost slavish devotion. Many of the letters which Liddon had been able to collect from Pusey's German friends, especially those from Tholuck,[47] were quoted in full or in part, in German as well as in translation. The chapter certainly could not have been published in its original form. But, yet again, some of the excisions are striking. It must be remembered that the initial print runs of both of Pusey's books on the *Theology of Germany* had been small, and Pusey had done his level best in later years to recall and suppress them. Liddon's manuscript quotes another letter, omitted from the published version, in which he tells George Williams in 1863, 'What I said myself I retracted a few years after I wrote it… The two books on Germany I withdrew. Of Part II, only 250 were ever printed. There were only two or three copies left. Of Part I, of which 750 were printed, I bought of Rivington what remained on hand.'[48] Therefore, in quoting the books extensively Liddon was putting this material before most of his readers seemingly in defiance of Pusey's later ideas.

Liddon is honest about Pusey's high estimate of Luther.

> The fruitless attempts to satisfy an uneasy and active conscience by the meritorious performances of a Romish convent, had opened his eyes to the right understanding of Scripture in whose doctrines alone it could find rest: and the clear and discerning faith which this correspondence of Scripture with his own experience strengthened in him gave him that intuitive insight into the nature of Christianity which enabled him for the most part unfailingly to discriminate between the essential and non-essentials, and raised him not only above the assumed authority of the Church, and above the might of tradition, but above the influence of hereditary scholastic opinions, the power of prejudices, and the dominion of the letter.[49]

The very fact that this glowing assessment of Luther was removed by the editors from the middle of a section of the manuscript which was otherwise little touched suggests that it was deemed to be too explosive for the printed version. A little later we find another significant passage from Liddon's pen which was also removed.

> In this, Pusey's first book, there are many features both of thought and language which he subsequently outgrew or repudiated... For the German Reformation, and its leading author, he cherished, at this time, almost unbounded admiration.[50]

Similar comments are a common refrain. Talking of the creeds of the church, Liddon writes, 'We miss any perception of the profound distinction upon which Pusey would have insisted in later years, between the national or provincial formulae which were drawn up at or after the Reformation, and those great authoritative Creeds which had been recognized for centuries by the Universal Church.'[51] There are also other passages in which Liddon acknowledges Pusey's profound 'attraction' to the work of Spener as well as to that of Luther himself. All this is, of course, available to the modern reader who has access to the two volumes of *Theology of Germany* in either a library or through the modern-day magic of the internet. What surprises us is the candour with which Liddon's manuscript addresses the contents of the two books, not least in view of Pusey's severe misgivings later in life. The fact that this chapter was finally published without many of these quotations says more about the editing process than it does about Liddon's mind at the time when he penned this relatively early chapter. He gives a lengthy account of the mixed reception which the books received among not only friends such as Keble and Newman but also establishment figures such as Bishop Blomfield. Yet again, much of this section was to be omitted.

There is much more in a similar vein. What might later readers, for example, have made of the section in chapter eight where Pusey plans a sympathetic work on the history and theology of Islam? Would they have expected a more trenchant comment from Pusey reflecting the formula, 'no salvation outside the church'? Perhaps they would have been surprised to read Pusey's rather tolerant assessment:

> I cannot but think that the exclusively polemical position which has been taken up against Mohammedanism has been injurious. The habits of my own mind have rather inclined me to look for what there is of good, and what calculated to promote God's great design for man, where others seem to see an unmixed manifestation of evil.[52]

However, the biggest thunderbolt for the pious Anglo-Catholic reader, a thunderbolt which Liddon's original does not shy from hurling but which Johnston and Wilson removed, comes at the reader relatively unannounced. It is the quotation from the preface to the first book of *Theology of Germany* which states very simply that Pusey – in the 1820s – considered the Church of England to hold a Calvinistic view of the Eucharist. Liddon's manuscript admits says quite openly,

> How little Pusey had as yet studied on subjects on which he was to become so great an authority in later life, will appear from the statement that the Calvinists 'agree in the devotion of the Lord's Supper with ourselves'.[53]

It remains to make a number of suggestions rather than firm conclusions. In the first place, the idea that Pusey's thought developed significantly over the course of the 1820s and 1830s, a process charted by Forrester's *Young Dr Pusey* and others, is not a new one. Forrester's conclusion runs thus:

> In the late 1820s and early 1830s, and before he experienced a considerable revolution in his outlook, Pusey's own views on such things as the Articles, the Reformation and individual reformers, the role of 'feeling' in religion, the value of the Episcopate, the nature of Inspiration in the Bible, the meaning of schism and the future of the Church in Germany, were all evidence of how greatly he had been influenced by his contact with German theology. The overall picture of Pusey in these years is vastly different from that of a later time.[54]

Access to the manuscript proves that Liddon acknowledged this and committed much of it to paper. Gentle hints at a story of development survive in a number of places in the published *Life*, but the story of development is present in the early chapters of Liddon's manuscript on page after page. What might explain such a change in emphasis? Locating and investigating the correspondence of the men involved is a task for the future as well as continuing this analysis of the changes between manuscript and published form beyond chapter eight. However, a number of tentative theories spring to mind.

The first consideration is the psychological one that had Liddon's *Life* been published as it was left on the day he died, it would have caused a sensation. To put it crudely, Liddon had drafted a biography. Was his readership expecting a hagiography? Pusey had been the figurehead for the developing phases of the Catholic Revival for nearly four decades. He was the grand old man of the Tractarian Movement. He had founded Anglo-Catholic parishes; he had been responsible, in tandem with remarkable women such as Marian Hughes and Priscilla Lydia Sellon, for the restoration of the religious life for women in the Church of England; he had given practical help to the work of slum parishes in the industrial cities. His involvement in the East End of London during the cholera outbreaks of the 1860s was, by the 1880s, no longer a simple memory but part of the mythology of the Catholic Revival. The world of 1890s Anglo-Catholicism was a different world with different practices and language from the world of the 1850s, let alone the 1830s. Can we picture in our mind's eye that mythical creature, the typical Anglo-Catholic priest of 1893, sitting down in the study of a clergy house in his cassock, having returned from celebrating a requiem mass with incense, unbleached candles, black vestments and prayers in Latin, picking up the long-awaited biography of the great Dr Pusey of whom he had heard so much, only to be told by Dr Liddon, no less, that his hero had at one time believed that the Anglican Eucharist was Calvinistic, that episcopal structure was not part of God's plan for his Church, or that praying for the dead was superfluous?

There may be some mileage in this, however fanciful the picture. But why should such a story cause undue upset? The history of the Oxford Movement was full of stories of men who had received Evangelical upbringings before their ideas had developed in a Catholic direction. Newman was and is, of course, only the most famous example among many. Why should 1890s Anglo-Catholics have worried about the prospect of reading a tale in which Pusey's beliefs developed in a similar direction although, of course, with a different ecclesiastical terminus to the journey? Perhaps the timing of Newman's death on 11 August 1890, barely a month before Liddon's on 9 September, was critical. The cardinal's death was accompanied by a great deal of what our age would call media attention. This renewed concentration on Newman was the inevitable theological and literary background to Johnston and Wilson's editorial work over the next three years. Did it, consciously or unconsciously, affect them? If re-telling the story of Newman's development reminded 1890s England of a journey from a Calvinistic childhood to the arms of Rome, was there a need when writing the biography of the Tractarian who stayed in the Church of England to play down a similar story of development, albeit one which did not go so far? To put it crudely, could the inevitable comparisons between Newman's development and Pusey's lead to awkward questions being asked about the logic of the Anglo-Catholic position and Anglo-Catholicism's loyalty to the Church of England?

A more general historiographical consideration, however, may stem from the way in which the historians of the Catholic Revival were looking to highlight a degree of continuity between the Oxford Movement of the twelve years 1833–45 and the generation which preceded it.[55] These pre-Tractarian High Churchmen, brought back to prominence in recent decades by Peter Nockles,[56] are discussed in some detail in the published chapter 11 of Liddon's *Life of Pusey*. But long before we reach chapter 11, Liddon's first published chapter quotes Pusey saying,

> All I know about religious truth, I learned, at least in principle, from my dear mother. But then, he would add, behind my mother, though of course I did not know it at the time, was the Catholic Church.[57]

An important section in James Pereiro's book *'Ethos' and the Oxford Movement* provides food for thought. Was the picture which Johnston and Wilson give us of Pusey, shorn of dramatic personal development, important for claiming an intrinsic Anglo-Catholic loyalty to the whole post-Reformation Anglican tradition?

> The Oxford Movement, although not immune to other influences, had been born within a High Church intellectual context. The Tractarians shared much doctrine and practice with High Churchmen; they also shared with some of them a critical view of the pre-Tractarian condition of the Church of England. It was therefore, natural for many High Churchmen to consider the Oxford Movement as rejuvenated High Churchmanship.[58]

Discussing a certain approach to writing the history of the years 1833–45, Pereiro continues,

> Overton, in 1897, thought that High Church principles could hardly fail to have their supporters while men had the Prayer Book in their

hands. He and others claimed that the Oxford Movement was part of an Anglo-Catholic revival which could be traced back to the reign of Queen Elizabeth I.[59]

Hence there was one school of Anglo-Catholic historical writing, contemporaneous with Liddon's posthumous editors, which sought to stress continuity at all costs and play down the degree of radical change which was experienced by many of the protagonists. This view would have sat ill, for example, with the admission from Pusey's own pen, reiterated by his disciple Liddon, that he had once not hesitated to claim the word 'Protestant' for himself.

Finally, there is another hunch which may be worth exploring. Liddon began compiling the mass of papers which was to be the raw material for the *Life* in the 1870s. The manuscript's footnotes meticulously record conversations with Pusey as early as 1874, eight years before his death. By the time the manuscript was left unfinished almost sixteen years later the controversy over *Lux Mundi* (1890) had blighted the final year of Liddon's life and set him at loggerheads with Gore and the newly founded Pusey House. Could it be the case that drawing attention to Pusey's early enthusiasm for some of the German theologians of the 1820s ran the risk of undermining Liddon's part in that dispute? Liddon's manuscript writes in relatively constructive terms not only of the Orientalists Tholuck and Freytag but also of far more radical theologians including Schleiermacher. Consciously or unconsciously, could it be argued that the origin of the biblical criticism which bitterly upset Liddon and other conservative academic Anglo-Catholics was perceived to lie precisely in the work of those German theologians whom Pusey had once known, read and admired? Was it possible that the long-dead Germans whom Pusey had met in the 1820s were, with the gift of theological hindsight, the forerunners of the scholars who, in the eyes of Liddon and his followers, seemed to attack everything that Pusey had defended later in life? If that is the case, then it is hardly surprising that the essential task of preparing Liddon's near-unpublishable manuscript for publication reflected, even unconsciously, tensions within Anglicanism, particularly Anglicanism in Oxford and, indeed, Anglicanism at Pusey House, precisely at the time when the manuscript was in the printers' hands half a mile away at Oxford University Press in Walton Street.

Notes

1 The manuscript was numbered and divided into sections, presumably by someone at Oxford University Press, and labelled with the names of the typesetters to whom each section was apportioned. This would seem to indicate that galley proofs of Liddon's version existed from which Johnston and Wilson worked. There are almost no alterations in either Johnston or Wilson's hand on the manuscript itself. Given that the

printed version is significantly shorter than the manuscript, one can only marvel at the amount of hard work on the part of the typesetters which did not see the light of day. It is unknown whether these proofs survive. They are not part of the Liddon Papers at Pusey House. Although published by Longmans, Green and Company, each volume contains the printers' details: 'Oxford[:] Horace Hart, printer to the University'.
2 Johnston and Wilson were among the most prominent Anglo-Catholics in Oxford during the 1880s and 1890s. Johnston (1852–1923) was chaplain of Merton College 1883–95, principal of Cuddesdon Theological College 1895–1913, and chancellor of Lincoln Cathedral 1913–23. Wilson (d. 1897) was a fellow of Merton College 1867–89, warden of Radley College 1879–88, and warden of Keble College 1894–97. Newbolt (1844–1930) was principal of Ely Theological College 1887–90; he succeeded Liddon as a canon of St Paul's Cathedral in 1890. Newbolt worked only on the final volume and hence does not figure in this paper which discusses material from the first published volume. It is interesting to note that that all three men combined theological orthodoxy with a liturgical and devotional restraint characteristic of one tradition of late nineteenth-century Anglo-Catholicism.
3 I am grateful to the principal and chapter of Pusey House for giving me the opportunity to revisit this project, as too the headmaster of The Oratory School. I am also very grateful for conversations with Dr James Pererio, Dr Peter Nockles and participants in the conference on 'Edward Bouverie Pusey and the Catholic Revival', among them Dr Albrecht Geck, whose recently published edition of the Pusey–Tholuck correspondence has proved indispensable.
4 Chadwick, *Mind of the Oxford Movement*, 48.
5 Liddon, *Life of Pusey*, 1:ix.
6 Johnston, *Life and Letters of Liddon*, 300f.
7 Liddon, *Life of Pusey* 1:chapter 8; Liddon, manuscript of *Life of Edward Bouverie Pusey* (hereafter referred to as MS), chapter 9, 1375–1789. The full title of Pusey's work was *An Historical Enquiry into the Probable Causes of the Rationalist Character Lately Predominant in the Theology of Germany*.
8 Geck, ed., *Autorität und Glaube*, passim. Tholuck signed his letters with the Christian name 'August'.
9 Anne Mozley started work on this project in 1884 at Newman's request and returned the papers which the Cardinal had lent her in 1887. However, her preface is dated November 1890 and makes explicit mention of the death of Liddon which had taken place on 9 September.
10 Forrester, *Young Doctor Pusey*, xiiif.
11 Ibid.
12 Forrester's hunch that Liddon exercised a self-denying ordinance not to use Maria Pusey's private correspondence, letters which Forrester used a century later to such good effect, was correct. Johnston and Wilson retained Liddon's sentence, '[Maria] becomes for the time a depository of his theological confidences; and indeed no other source of information exists which tells us so much about his mind as a young man' (Liddon, *Life of Pusey* 1:123). However, they omitted Liddon's next sentence: 'Letters of the kind could not be published in their entirety; but they may be largely drawn on without disrespect either to the living or the dead' (MS 1010v). Liddon never quotes directly from Maria's side of the correspondence, but he quotes so extensively from Pusey's letters to her that it is not difficult to infer the nature of Maria's letters to him.
13 Liddon, *Life of Pusey*, 1:33–41; cf. MS 286–349.

14 MS 330.
15 The principal sections in the *Life of Pusey* where Johnston and Wilson rely on Mozley's work rather than Liddon's manuscript are 1:55 (quoting [Newman], *Letters and Correspondence*, 1:115–16, inserted between MS 462 and 463) and 1:60–62 (quoting [Newman], *Letters and Correspondence*, 1:116–18, inserted between MS 505 and 506). Johnston and Wilson's source for 1:62–4 in the *Life of Pusey* is unclear.
16 MS 461f.
17 This change is explicitly made at MS 588, 840 and 1460. Other references to 'the Lutheran Church' in the MS are simply omitted from the *Life of Pusey* altogether.
18 1768–1834. Geck, ed., *Autorität und Glaube*, 361.
19 MS 607.
20 1792–1860. Geck, ed., *Autorität und Glaube*, 350.
21 1788–1861. Geck, ed., *Autorität und Glaube*, 341f.
22 Geck, ed., *Autorität und Glaube*, 335.
23 Geck, ed., *Autorität und Glaube*, 356.
24 MS 845.
25 Liddon, *Life of Pusey*, 1:121.
26 MS 981f.
27 MS 1027.
28 Close (1797–1882) was Rector of Cheltenham 1826–56 and Dean of Carlisle 1856–81. In both places he was famous for his trenchant Evangelical preaching.
29 MS 1033.
30 MS 1034f., quoting E. B. Pusey to M. C. Barker, n.d. [?9 October 1827], Liddon Bound Volumes 23/2.
31 MS 1040.
32 MS 1639, quoting C. J. Blomfield to E. B. Pusey, 4 January 1830, Liddon Bound Volumes 40/1.
33 MS 1150.
34 MS 1166n.
35 Liddon, *Life of Pusey*, 1:131–4.
36 MS 1239.
37 MS 1244.
38 MS 1291.
39 MS 1302–4.
40 See Davage, *In This Sign Conquer*, chapters 5, 7.
41 MS 1332.
42 It is misleading to use the term 'Church of Scotland' in its modern sense. The Disruption of 1843 which has shaped Scottish Presbyterianism to this day was yet to come. Liddon consistently uses the phrase 'Church of Scotland' to describe that part of the Anglican Communion in Scotland now known as the Episcopal Church.
43 For the whole tour, see MS 1339–66.
44 MS 1344f.
45 MS 1366. Liddon does not comment that this event took place two and a half months after their marriage. How might the Pusey who celebrated the Eucharist every morning in later life have looked back on this period?
46 MS 1346.
47 Liddon Bound Volumes 139, 145. Geck provides a critical edition of this correspondence in Geck, ed., *Autorität und Glaube*.

48 MS 1754f., quoting Pusey to George Williams, 22 January 1863, Liddon Bound Volumes 133/23.
49 MS 1341f., quoting Pusey, *Historical Enquiry*, 1:8.
50 MS 1473–7.
51 MS 1696f.
52 MS 1581f., quoting E. B. Pusey to A. Tholuck, 29 June 1829, Liddon Bound Volumes 127/2. Cf. Geck, ed., *Autorität und Glaube*, 130.
53 MS 1480, quoting Pusey, *Historical Enquiry*, xiv.
54 Forrester, *Young Dr Pusey*, 231.
55 We do well to remember that almost the last thing that Richard William Church, dean of St Paul's Cathedral and author of *The Oxford Movement*, did was to bury Liddon.
56 Nockles, *Oxford Movement*.
57 Liddon, *Life of Pusey*, 1:7; cf. MS, 144.
58 Pereiro, *'Ethos'*, 72.
59 Ibid., 75f., citing Overton, *The Anglican Revival*. John Henry Overton (1835–1903) was an important and sympathetic historian of eighteenth century Anglicanism. Cf. *Oxford Dictionary of National Biography*, s.v. 'John Henry Overton'.

Chapter Four

FROM MODERN-ORTHODOX PROTESTANTISM TO ANGLO-CATHOLICISM: AN ENQUIRY INTO THE PROBABLE CAUSES OF THE REVOLUTION OF PUSEY'S THEOLOGY[1]

Albrecht Geck

In 1828 Edward Bouverie Pusey published his very first book, the *Enquiry into the Probable Causes of the Rationalist Character Lately Predominant in the Theology of Germany* – quite a title, but typical of book-titles at the time; not snappy or eye-catching, but summarizing the content of the book. One hundred and seventy-five years later H. C. G. Matthew wrote that the *Enquiry* had been Pusey's best book ever[2] – but he probably said this to annoy Anglo-Catholics.

However, the young Pusey would have disagreed with Matthew. The reception of the book in England was a disaster. Some thought, as Pusey wrote in a letter to Friedrich August Gottreu Tholuck, that he was a 'Rationalist', some a 'rash innovator', some a 'mystic', some a 'Methodist'.[3] So he came to have doubts about what he had written. In November 1835 he wrote to his wife Maria that 'I was dazzled with the then rare acquaintance with German theology, and over-excited by it; I thought to do great things, and concealed self under the mask of activity.'[4] That came after his inward revolution, of course, and after his turn towards the Anglo-Catholicism of the Oxford Movement. From then on Pusey could be seen searching the antiquarian bookshops for copies of the *Enquiry* to buy in order to eliminate them. He even forbade the *Enquiry* from ever being reprinted. Ironically enough, the book is now available on the internet on open-access library.

Pusey's verdict also included the second *Enquiry*, as it is called, which he published in 1830.[5] The reception of this book, a massive volume of 435 pages, was even more unfortunate. Pusey had been reluctant to write it in the first place. He kept asking his friends from Oriel College, Oxford what he should include and what he should leave out. He sent the manuscript to Richard Bagot, the Bishop of Oxford, asking for his opinion. Then Pusey fell ill and found it hard to go back to work on the book again. He wrote to Tholuck almost in despair: 'Controversy is so irksome and painful a task that I have gladly turned aside from it, when I could, so that I fear that my new book will be rather heterogeneous.'[6] When it was eventually published, he was not happy with it at all and indeed called it 'a heterogeneous & disproportionate mass', which lacked 'every thing but like order'.[7] Nobody seemed ever to have taken any particular notice of the book. Even though Charles Pourtales Golightly once mentioned 'Pusey's Germany, Parts I and II', what he really meant was 'Part I'.[8] As far as I can tell there were no contemporary reactions at all. Pusey, who had already begun to have doubts about his liberal Protestantism, was not at all disappointed.

So what is it about Pusey's second *Enquiry into the Theology of Germany*? In his biography of John Henry Newman, Frank M. Turner argues to the effect that the second *Enquiry* was but a revision of the first.[9] This, I think, is clearly wrong. Matthew argues that the book was only written with 'faint resolve'.[10] In a sense this is true. Pusey would have preferred doing something else: for example, finishing his predecessor Alexander Nicoll's catalogue of the Arabic manuscripts in the Bodleian Library, publishing some of the Oriental manuscripts in the Bodleian, writing an introduction to the Old Testament, starting the revision of the Authorized Version of the Bible, preparing his lectures, or writing an account of the rise of Islam. He had become Regius Professor of Hebrew at Oxford University in the meantime, and the first *Enquiry* had not been much of a recommendation. So why should he write another volume? And yet Matthew is wrong when he suggests that the theology of the second *Enquiry* was less developed. On the contrary, nothing was withdrawn. The second *Enquiry* provided but an illustration of the conceptual background of the first volume. It is generally believed that the two 'Enquiries' represent liberal Protestantism and there is some truth to that. Here, however, I want to suggest the term 'modern orthodoxy' is more appropriate. This term is used by Tholuck in his later writings to characterize his position as a *via media* between liberalism on the one side and orthodoxy on the other.[11]

How, why and when exactly did Pusey's change from Protestant 'modern orthodoxy' to Anglo-Catholicism come about? This is the question the present essay endeavours to answer. I will begin with an analysis of the first *Enquiry* and then show how its principles are maintained and defended in the second. I will then analyse Pusey's report on 'The present state of English theology', which he wrote for Tholuck's theological journal, the *Litterarischer Anzeiger*, in May 1830,[12] and I want to show that this report, which has as yet been completely neglected, provides some clues as to the how, when and why of Pusey's inner revolution. The last parts of my paper then deal with Pusey's revised attitude towards Continental Protestantism. However negative he had become in the end, my conclusion is that any critical biography of Pusey has to pay due attention to his persistent interest in Germany in general and in Lutheran theology in particular.

Modern-Orthodox Protestantism in Pusey's First *Enquiry into German Theology* (1828)

After the Napoleonic Wars the rich cultural exchange between England and Germany quickly resumed. Ever since the Reformation era the cultural transfer between the two countries had reflected the general history of church and theology. It must be said, however, that Cambridge had played a more important role than Oxford. As early as 1521 Thomas Cranmer, Hugh Latimer, Robert Barnes and other eminent English reformers discussed Lutheran ideas in the White Horse Tavern, Cambridge, which was henceforth called 'Germany'.[13]

In the eighteenth century the most prominent German influence in English theology was 'higher criticism', which attempted to investigate the 'setting in life' (*Sitz im Leben*) of the biblical text without 'theological prejudice'. From 1793 to 1801 the English translation of Johann David Michaelis's *Introduction to the New Testament* appeared. The translator was Herbert Marsh, a Cambridge man. Around the turn of the nineteenth century Cambridge still seemed like 'Little Germany'. In 1788 the notorious rationalist from Heidelberg, Heinrich Eberhard Gottlob Paulus, visited the Unitarian community at Cambridge.[14] Julius Hare was born in Germany and grew up among the Germans. At the age of ten he met Goethe. His library contained hundreds of German books. It was perhaps the biggest private library of German theology in England after Pusey's.[15] Hare admired Schleiermacher, 'whose dialectic development of fundamental thought is almost always exquisite'.[16] And one generation later he was to defend Luther against Tractarian condemnation and confessed that to Luther 'I owe such a debt of gratitude and love as can never be paid.'[17] Connop Thirlwall, later bishop of St David's, translated Friedrich Schleiermacher's *A Critical Essay on the Gospel of St Luke* into English in 1825. When Thirlwall heard about Schleiermacher's presence in London in 1829 he hastened to see him, inviting him to preach at Cambridge. In a letter to his brother he called him 'a very distinguished foreigner…of Berlin, a person who of all others in the world I had always been most desirous of seeing and knowing'.[18]

In contrast Oxford seemed less absorbed by the Germans. Pusey's biographer Henry Parry Liddon remarks that there was only a certain 'Mr Mill of Magdalen College' who could speak the language.[19] This may be an exaggeration to highlight Pusey's position as a person who knew German and the Germans well. And yet it remains true that higher criticism was received with more reserve at Oxford than at Cambridge. Charles Lloyd sent Pusey to Germany to study higher criticism, not to bring it to England, but to be better prepared to refute it. In 1824 John Josias Conybeare apparently expressed his fervent hope 'that all your German theology might be buried at the bottom of the German Ocean'.[20] However, Conybeare could not read German, and so he based his statement on German books written in Latin, which Thirlwall thought was unfortunate, because in recent times German theologians had started to write and publish in the vernacular almost exclusively. To put it in a nutshell: where Thirlwall, the Cambridge man, admired Schleiermacher immensely, Newman, the Oxford man, coldly accused him of an inclination for 'private judgment'. For Newman, it was no wonder that Schleiermacher, the champion of the 'religion, (so called) of the heart and feelings', should have such meagre views of the Trinity. Newman believed that Protestantism had turned revealed truth into an opinion based on 'a reflection [of the theologians] upon their own feelings and belief, and the genius of their system'.[21]

At the same time, however, the troops were beginning to gather at Cambridge, too. One year after Conybeare's Bampton Lecture from the university pulpit at Oxford, Hugh James Rose climbed the pulpit of Cambridge University Church to preach against the influence of German Protestant theology at his university and in the country. His sermons were published in the same year under the title *The State of the Protestant Religion in Germany*. Referring to Newman's later recollection that this was an outstanding event at the outset of the Oxford Movement. As Jörg Mosig ironically asked: 'Did [then] the Oxford Movement start at Cambridge?'[22]

It did not, of course. Rose's call for orthodoxy was rather in line with traditional high-and-dry churchmanship. Although he had been to Germany, there is no evidence about his sources. He was sympathetic to the conservative church government of the Prussian king Frederick William III, and this perhaps suggests that he had friends in the Ministry of Culture, Education and Church Affairs. But this is pure speculation. Evidently there were similarities between Rose's church-and-king orthodoxy and the Prussian state-church system. These included the appreciation of state intervention to safeguard the unity and soundness of doctrine.

The motto of Rose's sermons was Isaiah 47:10: 'Thy wisdom and thy knowledge, it hath perverted thee.' He described contemporary German theology as 'a dreadful pest', 'an evil seed and poisonous crop' and 'a wretched mass of abomination'.²³ Rose subdivided the history of German Protestantism into a glorious age of uniformity and a dark age of diversity. He praised the age of Lutheran orthodoxy in which soundness of doctrine was safeguarded by binding and reliable confessions of faith such as the Lutheran Formula and Book of Concord of 1577/80. When, however, the church and the people became tired of the endless scholastic controversies, pietism based religion on feeling. According to Rose this marked the beginning of the age of diversity or, as we would say, plurality. The process was modified and accelerated during the Enlightenment when Johann Salomo Semler used the notorious Theory of Accommodation to adjust Christian tradition to the cultural level of his age. As Rose saw it, 'private judgment' became the vehicle of theology.

Against the historico-cultural approach to theology Rose reminded his audience that

> The great safeguards which must be requisite for the *preservation* of any church, are obviously the possession of a clear and distinct declaration of faith, to which strict adherence must be required, of a liturgy which shall practically apply the doctrines of that declaration to men's wants and infirmities, and of a government which shall diligently repress every tendency to carelessness and every attempt at innovation.²⁴

The word 'preservation' suggests that the 'safeguards' mentioned were indeed means to maintain 'the very *existence* of the church'.²⁵ Perhaps the word 'existence' just slipped out, but it infuriated Rose's German readers as they diagnosed a deviation from Protestantism. Pusey also was scandalized by this elevation of what he saw as 'human means' only. It is therefore remarkable that in the completely revised second edition of the *State of the Protestant Religion* of 1829, Rose left out the word 'existence' and replaced the word 'preservation' with 'well-being'.²⁶ Pusey wrote with great satisfaction to Tholuck: 'Mr Rose has published a very enlarged 2nd edition of his book on Germany, altering its form. He has left out the offensive parts which seem to make "human *means* [i.e., devices or instruments]" every thing.'²⁷ We should note the fact that at this time neither Rose nor Pusey considered episcopacy to be of the *esse* ('the being') of the church, but of the *beneesse* ('the well-being') of the church. Rose certainly regretted that episcopacy had been given up at the time of the Reformation in Germany, but apparently he did not believe this fact to be church-dividing. Pusey even explicitly equated Anglican bishops and Prussian general-superintendents (*Generalsuperintendenten*).²⁸ This shows that around 1830 he had no misgivings about the validity of Lutheran orders.

There was, however, a fundamental difference between Rose and Pusey as to the description of the causes of the rise of rationalism in Germany. And this leads us to the core of the controversy. Rose had described the state of Protestantism, but he had given only a very scant history. Pusey's first *Enquiry*, inspired by his German friends Tholuck, Karl Heinrich Sack and August Neander, provided this very history. The concept of the book was complex indeed.[29] The history of Protestantism was seen as a process, in which after the downfall of rationalism faith had prevailed through dialectical development. Whereas Rose considered the age of Lutheran orthodoxy as a model, Pusey used the word 'orthodoxism' to express his view that the petty confessionalism and dry intellectualism of this age unintentionally caused the rise of unbelief in Protestant Germany. This verdict was the *leitmotif* of the first – and indeed the second – *Enquiry*, and it much upset and irritated Pusey's High Church colleagues at Oxford University. Pietism, Pusey continued, revitalized faith, but without sound science it quickly turned into a 'dream of bewildered imagination...oppressive to the intellectual powers'.[30] As a reaction the enlightenment cultivated the relation to the sciences. It made up for the intellectual defects of orthodoxism and pietism, but it also transformed theology into an 'exclusively intellectual conviction'.[31] Thus, however, it demonstrated that the human intellect was unable to fathom the unfathomable character of revealed religion. The 'new era in theology',[32] which was ushered in by Schleiermacher, the mediation theology, and some representatives of revival theology, such as Tholuck and Neander, sought to reconcile faith and science. This represented a synthesis of 'faith' and 'understanding'. Tholuck used the phrase 'intelligent faith' and, as I found in his later writings, 'modern orthodoxy'.[33] Pusey called it an 'animated science', science 'poured forth from the fullness of the heart'.[34] From this point of view the history of Protestantism in Germany presented itself as a history of recovery, not of decline.

Again Rose gave way. In the revised second edition of the *State of the Protestant Religion*, he added a chapter about the 'present state of things' in Protestant Germany diagnosing 'a more healthy spirit of religion'.[35] He mentioned Schleiermacher and the rest, but he remained sceptical. He clearly identified with Ernst Wilhelm Hengstenberg's neo-orthodox theology, which sought to return to the orthodoxism of the seventeenth century.[36] This shows that Rose did not see history historically, as it were, but dogmatically. While Pusey diagnosed a fruitful development which sprang from 'free enquiry', Rose simply stated a somewhat belated return to the old orthodox system. He even favoured state intervention in matters of faith. For example, he approved the state's commissioning the Synod of Berlin to censure theological tracts. He mentioned that Schleiermacher was a member – in fact he was its president – but he did not mention that Schleiermacher had violently protested against such a commission.[37]

In Pusey's eyes, going back to the old orthodoxism merely meant that history was going to repeat itself. Pusey wrote almost with resignation about

Hengstenberg's *Christology of the Old Testament* (*Christologie des Alten Testaments*), which indulged intransigently in Messianic exegesis: 'The returning to the theology of the 17th century seems like wilfully throwing away our experience.'[38]

The Defence of Modern-Orthodox Protestantism in Pusey's Second *Enquiry into German Theology* (1830)

Rose was infuriated with Pusey's Germanic plea for 'free enquiry', particularly as he had to acknowledge his opponent's 'far superior knowledge of the subject'.[39] But he was determined to make the young man see sense, and in a private letter charged him with plagiarizing from his German friends. Indeed Pusey had used a lecture of Tholuck's on the *Theology of the Eighteenth Century*. Tholuck seems to have been aware of this borrowing, for he wrote to Pusey that 'Some passages from my booklet are imperfectly copied (*abgeschrieben*).' He then replaced 'copied' by the less reproachful 'paraphrased' (*nachgeschrieben*).[40]

Rose was quick to publish against the *Enquiry*. In a pugnacious *Letter to the Lord Bishop of London* (1829), he polemicized against Pusey's alleged liberalism. Why had he not, a member of an episcopal church, mentioned episcopacy? What did he mean by the phrase 'new era in theology'? Did he mean the invention of new doctrines? In response, the second *Enquiry* was subtitled 'An explanation of the views misconceived by Mr Rose'.

Newman assisted Pusey in his defence against Rose. His diary entries note when he was 'With Pusey the whole day at his answer to Mr Rose' or when he 'Hunted in old divines for Pusey and wrote to him'. Partly because Charles James Blomfield, the Bishop of London, had questioned 'the soundness of your [Pusey's] ecclesiastical views', Newman advised him to disapprove explicitly of schism and to say 'some sharp things against Dissenters'.[41] Pusey was so irritated by the altogether unfavourable reception of the first *Enquiry* that he sent the manuscript to Blomfield and asked for his opinion. The bishop found it 'too latitudinarian in tone'. In particular he regretted the use of the word 'orthodoxism' and criticized the distinction Pusey had made between essentials and non-essentials. For the sake of the integrity of 'a right system of belief' and 'uniformity of doctrine' Blomfield was quite prepared to accept 'some possible errors on points not fundamental'.[42] Pusey only reluctantly referred to this in the second *Enquiry*. He did so, but he conscientiously added that '*possible* errors...should be corrected as soon as discovered'.[43]

As Pusey found it hard to write a coherent essay on this topic, the second *Enquiry* eventually contained eleven separate chapters. There is a great variety of themes, but the crucial point is that Pusey defended his Protestant, modern orthodox identity that blended faith and science without compromise.

He renewed his criticism of 'orthodoxism' and positively said that faith was 'not...a mere adherence to a certain sum of credenda, but a practical habit of mind'.[44] He even went as far as to claim certain 'latitude' in using tradition.[45] Bearing in mind that Blomfield had called the *Enquiry* 'too latitudinarian in tone', this seemed quite self-confident. Pusey insisted that confessions of faith should determine only essentials and leave non-essentials free.

Pusey did not quite understand that Rose had urged him to put episcopacy at the centre of his approach. He was, he said, 'thoroughly sensible of the blessings of Episcopacy in our own Church, and that it is better adapted than any other form for all the purposes of Church Government'.[46] Yet this seemed to say that episcopacy was *de jure humano* – or, as said above, of the *beneesse* and not of the *esse* of the church. This was similar to Hooker's understanding of matters of order:

> The church hath authority to establish that for an order at one time, which at another time it may abolish, and in both may do well... Laws touching matters of order are changeable, by the power of the church, articles concerning doctrine not so.[47]

Hooker's view was shared by other eminent High Church theologians such as Archbishop Laud, who inferred from this the validity of Lutheran orders: 'Luther, since he would change the name, yet did very wisely that he would leave the thing, and make choice of such a name as was not altogether unknown in the ancient church.'[48]

Pusey also saw no practical reason to glorify episcopacy. For example, he did not believe that it would necessarily have prevented the rise of rationalism in Germany. He took episcopal Denmark, which was struck by rationalism, as an example and Presbyterian Scotland, which was spared. Bishops were after all children of their time, so that it was wiser to have no other authority in the church than Scripture itself. It was quite daring to quote Juvenal in this context: 'Quis custodiet ipsos custodies?'[49]

Secondly, Pusey believed that the use of human authority in matters of faith was counterproductive: 'The utmost which human authority can avail in opposition to unbelief, is to repress its outward appearance.'[50] Pusey here rejected Rose's neo-orthodox approach which looked for, let me quote this again, 'a government which shall diligently repress' – rather than discuss – alternative views.

Finally, Pusey could not understand Rose's reservations about the use of the phrase 'new era in theology'. Apparently it was a phrase used in the Berlin of Pusey's days. When Schleiermacher died in 1834, Neander interrupted his lecture and said: 'This man ushered in a new era in theology.'[51]

Neander's opinion was based not only on his speeches *Ueber die Religion* (*On Religion*), because they liberated religion from metaphysics and morality, but also on Schleiermacher's *Der Christliche Glaube* (*The Christian Faith*), which made 'feeling' the basis and foundation of theology. Pusey was also quite impressed by Schleiermacher's *Kurze Darstellung des Theologischen Studiums*, published in 1811 and translated into English as late as 1850, because it offered an encyclopaedic and new systematic architecture of theology in the broader context of philosophy, history and culture. Friedrich Lücke later asked him to translate this book into English, but Pusey declined the offer.[52]

Rose had criticized the use of the phrase 'new era in theology' as a *carte blanche* for innovation and for making up new doctrines. Was this a mere playing on the word 'new' and a wilful misinterpretation? Pusey explained that Schleiermacher's achievement was the restoration of the possibility of developing an up-to-date version of Christianity that kept the essence and was yet directed to the needs of the present age. In this sense Pusey asked for a 'Re-translation of Scripture'.[53] Its aim was 'to influence the heart by the occupation of the understanding'.[54] Modern German theology, he explained, sought to present truth 'blended with the circumstances of life' and 'in the language of our own day'.[55]

It is obvious that compared with the subsequent development of his thought, Pusey's language was quite extraordinary. And yet he complained about Rose's 'heavy charge of "liberalism" upon theological subjects'.[56] In what sense might we say that Pusey was a liberal at the time? In 1790 Edmund Burke had published his *Reflections on the Revolution in France*, in which he warned that 'Rage and phrensy will pull down more in half an hour than prudence, deliberation, and foresight can build up in a hundred years.'[57] Pusey agreed and quoted from the book in the second *Enquiry*. There is a lengthy passage in which Burke draws the distinction between the obstinate, who reject all improvement, and the thoughtless, who are tired of everything they own.[58] This distinction Pusey applied to theology. The orthodoxistic are the obstinate who stick to the letter of faith. The liberals are the thoughtless who replace tradition by their own ideas. Modern orthodoxy represents the happy medium, as it were, because it balances tradition and modernity. The concept was liberal in the sense that it appreciated and respected all contributions, even unbelief. Again there is an interesting quote from Burke in the *Enquiry*: 'Our antagonist is our helper.'[59] Tholuck used the same idea in a dialogue he wrote almost 40 years later. The first speaker there said: 'Certainly modern orthodoxy is not a reactionary system.' 'No', answered the second speaker. 'It is a scientific reform and your rationalism under God's providence helped to bring it about.'[60]

Doubts about Modern-Orthodox Protestantism in Pusey's Report on 'The Present State of English Theology' (1830)

Pusey's modern-orthodox Protestantism was not to last very much longer. His letters to Tholuck and his report on the 'The Present State of English Theology'[61] indicate that even before the publication of the second *Enquiry* he had begun to have doubts about his 'modern-orthodox' approach. For instance, Pusey's letter to Tholuck of August 1829 has an interesting passage about the doctrine of inspiration. In the original version of the text, Pusey writes, 'I think the Bible is the "writing of inspired men" rather than an inspired book.' He then corrects the text a few times by crossing out words and phrases and by adding others in between the lines, so that the final version runs as follows: 'I think the Bible is "an inspired book" [notice the quotation marks here] because it is the "writing of inspired men".'[62] One can virtually feel Pusey struggling for orthodoxy here.

In his essay on the 'The Present State of English theology', translated into German by Tholuck and published in his *Litterarischer Anzeiger* in July 1831, Pusey mentions some 75 books, which he classifies into four fields of theological study: 'Ecclesiastical history',[63] 'Evidences',[64] 'Scriptural interpretation & criticism'[65] and 'Doctrinal theology'.[66] His report provides an intriguing insight into English theology between the outbreak of the French Revolution in 1789 and the beginning of the Oxford Movement in 1833. It describes the influence of German higher criticism in some detail. Pusey defends the Reformation in England against the German prejudice that it was 'a work in which state-policy was the principal agent'.[67] He also seems fascinated by recent enquiries into the theology of the fathers, including Edward Burton's *Testimonies of the Ante-Nicene Fathers to the Divinity of Christ* (1826). Pusey expressed a wish that 'We may I hope expect much more, and especially some improved editions of the earlier Fathers, within the next few years. The stimulus has been given; our Church's need pointed out.'[68]

The majority of theological books Pusey mentioned were categorized as 'Evidences'. John Davison's *Discourses on Prophecy* (1824), the future archbishop John Bird Sumner's *The Evidence of Christianity* (1824), Thomas Chalmers's *The Evidence and Authority of the Christian Revelation* (1814), and William Paley's two-volume *A View of the Evidences of Christianity* (1794) and his *Natural Theology: or, Evidences of the Existence and Attributes of the Deity, Collected from the Appearance of Nature* (1802) had already gone through, respectively, 2, 5, 7, 15 and 20 editions. Butler's classic *Analogy of Religion* had only recently been re-published. Of course, Paley's rationalism did not appeal to Pusey. In the English draft of his essay, he writes: 'On Evidences the older books are generally used, especially the immortal *Butler*, and Paley's works.'[69]

Tholuck's translation left out the comma in front of 'and Paley', and thus ironically obliterated Pusey's preference for Butler. Of contemporary writers it was Davison and Sumner who represented Pusey's ideal of Evidence literature. Davison's book 'interests the affections, while it produces the proof'.[70] In his mind 'Evidences' should not be written for unbelievers, but 'for those who already believe on other grounds, & wish to know, "the order & tenour of that Revelation which they believe".'[71] Sumner's work he describes as 'pious, candid, mild'.[72]

However, the 'modern-orthodox' approach began to lose its appeal. This becomes clear when we read Pusey's comment on Henry Hart Milman's *History of the Jews* (1829). Milman was Professor of Poetry at Oxford University, and in his *History* he wanted to present a thoroughly scientific – historical, not theological – approach. The exodus from Egypt he explained without the supernatural. Passages that seemed morally, intellectually and scientifically incompatible with the modern mind, he freely attributed to some divine accommodation: 'The Deity did not yet think it time to correct the savage.'[73] Pusey was irritated, because he had known Milman as a 'sincere believer in the Old Testament Revelation'.[74] He rejected Milman's description of Abraham and Moses as religious and political leaders rather than as 'the inspired agent[s] of God'.[75] Apparently he asked himself whether the pious Milman, in the effort to convince the sceptic, had not lost his own faith.

Milman's book caused much controversy in Oxford. In 1830 the Lady Margaret Professor of Divinity, Godfrey Faussett, preached against it from the university pulpit. His sermon was published as *Jewish History Vindicated from the Unscriptural View of It Displayed in 'The History of the Jews' (by Henry Hart Milman)* and quickly went through three editions. Much to Pusey's horror, Faussett made abundant use of language from Rose's *State of the Protestant Religion* and thus threatened him with the continuation of this much-hated controversy, now even at his own doorstep.

People have always wondered when and why Pusey's inner revolution came about. I think it is here that we stand by the deathbed of his 'modern-orthodox' views. He had fears that the discourse with the sceptic might eventually undermine his own faith and that even for others it might blur the distinction between religion and opinion, as he saw it. That he should now fight against Faussett and again dwell on the dialectical use of unbelief in history, which the country had once understood as but a justification of unbelief, was by no means an exciting prospect. Instead Pusey remained silent for a while. Liddon's bibliography in his *Life of Pusey* records only two publications between the second *Enquiry* and Tract 18, *On the Benefits of the System of Fasting*, in December 1833.

The Abandonment of Modern-Orthodox Protestantism and the Shaping of the Anglo-Catholic Position in Pusey's Tracts *On the Benefits of the System of Fasting* (1833) and on *Scriptural Views of Holy Baptism* (1835)

Tract 18, *On the Benefits of the System of Fasting*, shows that Pusey had undergone a fundamental change in perspective. The very choice of his theme indicates that he was no longer interested in theory, but in practice; not in understanding, but in action. Theology was no longer to convince the intellect, but to aid the submission of the will. 'We are', Pusey said, 'reluctant to yield to unreasoning authority and to submit our wills, where our reason has not first been convinced.'[76] 'Man', he later wrote, 'cannot escape from authority; the question only, in religious truth as in civil society, or in private life, is, whose authority he will follow.'[77] According to Tract 18, authority was not established by an act of understanding on the part of the believer. 'Truth', he said, 'must become objective, and as such accepted by an act of submission of the entire person.'[78] Writing to Tholuck in 1837 about the Evangelicals, he claimed: 'Many idolize indeed the Reformers, & make them the Church; but still the appeal lies *out* of themselves.'[79] This choice of words shows that Pusey disapproved of setting up the reformers as a 'standard of faith', but the very fact that people longed for such standards 'out of themselves' made him optimistic.

In Pusey's eyes, however, not the reformers but antiquity represented the longed-for authority. In the preface to the 1836 edition of the *Tract on Baptism*, he argued that the Protestant theology of faith and the rationalism of the day were in fact related to each other.[80] Both were mind-orientated and put the private person at the centre of theology. In the same year this view was also expounded in Newman's tract *On the Introduction of Rationalistic Principles into Religion*, which criticized Schleiermacher harshly.[81] The Tractarians looked for an alternative view that did not compromise with the philosophy of the day. As Pusey put it:

> Our daily habits, our philosophy, our morals, our politics, our theories of education, or national improvement, are founded upon a low and carnal basis, and are at direct variance with the principles of faith: one must give way; a more vivid faith must penetrate our social, domestic, intellectual system, or it must itself be stifled.[82]

From this point of view 'Evidence-Theology', which sought to convince the sceptic, seemed like a false compromise which brought faith 'down to our tastes & feelings'.[83] The Tractarian project was extremely ambitious, and was far from confined simply to church and theology.

Pusey's departure from his modern-orthodox views implied a different concept of theology as a science. Matthew described this somewhat sarcastically as his development from scholar to Tractarian.[84] Pusey's understanding might instead be viewed as far closer to the medieval ideal of 'scholarship and devotion'.[85] It must be said, however, that the interaction with alternative theological concepts became increasingly difficult. Pusey took great pains to explain this new ethos to Tholuck.[86] He gave an exhaustive account of the Hampden controversy, because he feared that Tholuck might hear about it from others and take the side of the 'persecuted' Hampden. He justified his and his friends' action by the example of Vincent of Lerins, who said 'when a heresy first appears, put it down, if you can; [only] afterwards, if it gains head and you must, enter into arguments.'[87] In this statement the modern-orthodox approach was turned upside-down. The antagonist was no longer the helper, but an opponent who had to be silenced. There was no room for argument. Pusey expressly wrote: 'One has done more good by scaring people away from it [heresy], than by any conviction of the understanding.'[88] The modern-orthodox approach had been religious and *intellectual*; the Tractarian approach clearly was religious and *moral*.

It is quite characteristic that when Pusey wrote to Tholuck about the 'Library of the Fathers' project, Tholuck warned him against the moralizing tendencies of the Nicene Age. 'Don't you ever', he wrote, 'lose the Christian freedom which Luther has won back for us.'[89] He impressed upon Pusey the need to treat his opponents – Evangelicals and Dissenters alike – charitably. 'On your side there is just as much danger as on theirs.'[90] He expressed his love for the 'venerable Episcopal church [of England]', but was certain that, should its present constitution collapse, God would give to it another form as healthy as it had been previously.[91] Clearly Tholuck tried to mitigate the objectivity of Pusey's approach and to win him back for 'modern orthodoxy'.

Pusey's change had far-reaching repercussions for the relationship to the Continental churches. In the first *Enquiry*, Pusey had exalted Luther as one of the 'mighty heroes of your [German] Reformation'. He called him a 'master-mover', a 'pure and rich fountain'. He admired his 'commanding spirit' and his 'pious and discriminating mind'.[92] In the second *Enquiry*, this positive attitude persisted, and he again described him as 'this great instrument of God'.[93] In his letters to Tholuck he had freely spoken of the 'German Church', the 'Jewish Church', the 'Lutheran Church', the 'Reformed Church', the 'German Reformed Church', or the 'Church in Germany'.[94] Then in 1836 he used the phrase 'the Lutherans & English Church'.[95] Strictly speaking this was grammatically wrong and probably a correction from 'the Lutheran & English Church'. These findings are supported by Rune Imberg's observation that in his wife's copy of the *Tract on Baptism* Pusey systematically replaced the word 'church' with the ecclesiologically indifferent word 'body'.[96] For example, the print version's 'At the time of the Reformation the English and the Lutheran branches retained the ancient doctrine' Pusey changed into 'At the time of the Reformation the English Church and the Lutheran bodies retained the ancient doctrine.'[97]

In the *Letter to the Lord Bishop of London* (1839), Pusey rejected the term 'Protestant' on the grounds that 'it does not belong historically to our Church, but to the Lutherans'. Lutheran orders, he now argued, were invalid, as Luther had lacked the authority to ordain: 'So those ordained by them have *received no Commission* to administer the Sacraments.' And: 'Mere length of time cannot mend the original invalidity.'[98] Any union with parts of the 'Lutheran Church', he wrote in 1836 – and the word 'Church' here obviously slipped through – 'must not be…by our giving up Episcopacy or counting it indifferent, but by your receiving it, – not from us but from the Apostles'.[99] In 1845 the tone became slightly more jarring: 'To give Episcopacy to Prussia now…is like arraying a corpse or whitening a sepulchre.'[100] He wrote this in a private letter to Gladstone. Tholuck would have been astonished to have read these words.

It is no wonder that after 1835–36 the interaction between Tholuck and Pusey had become increasingly strained. Tholuck criticized the Tractarians for disparaging Luther's doctrine of justification, and Pusey, in turn, answered: 'I wish the Sacraments entered more into your doctrines.'[101] Pusey's enthusiasm for Luther and the Lutherans had clearly weakened, but he retained some respect for Luther, precisely because Luther had 'prized his Baptism as the source of his spiritual life in CHRIST'.[102] So in 1836 he wrote to his brother Philip: 'I respect Lutheranism for having retained the high doctrine of the Sacraments, although one error therein, falsified their theology and so led to its corruption and destruction.'[103] I will not dwell on what Pusey deemed erroneous in the Lutheran doctrine of the sacraments. Suffice it to say that he trusted that 'GOD may make His own Sacraments efficacious, even when irregularly administered' and he added, probably with reference to himself: 'We should trust it might be so: some of us are bound up by ties of affection to those very Protestant bodies.'[104] These sentences show that Pusey's turn towards Anglo-Catholicism was no orthodox*istic* turn, but it allowed for lenience and compassion. In practice, however, Pusey could be very harsh, and in 1854 he refused communion to Max Müller, Taylor Professor of Modern European Languages at Oxford, because, as he told him, he was confirmed in a Lutheran, that is, a non-episcopalian, church.[105] This was undoubtedly a very disturbing and embarrassing experience for Müller.

Conclusion

This essay presents an account of Pusey's life and work from a German, Lutheran perspective. Pusey's biography is intriguing because he was not a two-dimensional but a three-dimensional character, so to speak, who changed throughout the course of his life. My discussion has concentrated on Pusey's inner development through a detailed analysis of key passages from the first *Enquiry* (1828), the second *Enquiry* (1830) and the hitherto almost-unknown essay on 'The Present State of English Theology' (1830). These works reveal a coherent picture of the nature of the revolution of Pusey's theology. Pusey developed from modern-orthodox Protestantism to Anglo-Catholicism because he feared that the intimate intercourse with science might eventually weaken his faith and thus endanger his personal salvation.

From an Anglo-German point of view this story is of great interest, and there is still much more to be discovered, particularly as Liddon systematically played down Pusey's continuing interest in German theology. After all, Pusey continued to correspond not only with Tholuck, but also with Karl Heinrich Sack, Friedrich Lücke, August Neander, Isaak August Dorner, Karl Immanuel Nitzsch, Ignaz Döllinger and many others.[106] The relationship between authority and faith is further pursued in these letters and eventually came to focus on the question of papal infallibility. These letters also merit a critical edition. It becomes obvious that any critical biography of Pusey would have to pay due attention to his Germanophilia. As late as 1854, Pusey wrote in his *Collegiate and Professorial Teaching and Discipline*: 'I myself love the Germans and respect them.'[107] The statement shows that also the history of Pusey's thoughts on education, if not of those of the Oxford Movement, may require some additional illustration and perhaps illumination from a German perspective.

Pusey may not have been, nor did he aspire to be, an original theological thinker; nor was he a spellbinding preacher or writer. And yet, his long-term influence as contributor to the *Tracts for the Times*, as leader of the Oxford Movement following Newman's departure to Rome and, last but not least, as Regius Professor of Hebrew at Oxford University until his death in 1882 make him one of the foremost English theologians in modern times, even if the answers he eventually gave were essentially, if not exclusively, conservative.

As I have argued elsewhere,[108] the development of Pusey's thought in the 1830s shows that modern Anglo-Catholicism in great measure is the product of historical circumstances, an effort to answer the struggle for certainty in the face of theological, cultural and religious diversity. Following the Enlightenment and Enlightenment theology, theologians had to make up their minds which course they wanted to follow. Pusey's revolution from modern-orthodox Protestantism to Anglo-Catholicism is but one example of this. As Pusey put it, 'Man cannot escape from authority.'[109] It remains to be discussed, however, but is not the issue of the present chapter, whether the deliberate exclusion of cultural and general history from theological discourse does justice to the complexity of modern life, or, indeed, to the complexity of theology itself.

Notes

1. Much of the following paper is based on my critical edition of Pusey's correspondence with Tholuck; see Geck, ed., *Autorität und Glaube*. I am grateful to Mark D. Chapman for polishing my English.
2. See Matthew, 'Edward Bouverie Pusey', 108.
3. Pusey to Tholuck, Oxford, 7 December 1829, in Geck, ed., *Autorität und Glaube*, 137–40, 137.
4. Pusey to Maria Pusey, November 1835; quoted in Liddon, *Life of Pusey*, 1:87.
5. See Pusey, *Historical Enquiry: Part II*.
6. Pusey to Tholuck, Oxford, 13 August 1829, in Geck, ed., *Autorität und Glaube*, 132–5, 132.
7. Pusey to Tholuck, Oxford, 24 May 1830, in Geck, ed., *Autorität und Glaube*, 140–41, 141.
8. Golightly to Newman, 18 October 1830; in: [Newman,] *Letters and Diaries*, 2:295.
9. Turner, *John Henry Newman*, 101.
10. Matthew, 'Edward Bouverie Pusey', 111.
11. Tholuck, 'Gespräche über die Vornehmsten Glaubensfragen der Zeit', 258.
12. Pusey's report on 'The Present State of English Theology' is an appendix ('Beilage') to his letter to Tholuck from 30 May 1830. It was first published in Liddon, *Life of Pusey*, 1:238–48. As there are minor, but meaningful alterations in Liddon's transcription, I will quote from my edition of this text in Geck, ed., *Autorität und Glaube*, 141–52. In the *Litterarischer Anzeiger* Tholuck published his translation of Pusey's essay into German; cf. [Pusey,] 'Ueber den Zustand der Neuern Englischen Theologie'.
13. See Tjernagel, *Henry VIII and the Lutherans*, 38.
14. See Rogerson, *Old Testament Criticism*, 159.
15. For detailed information about Hare's library, see Paulin, 'Julius Hare's German Books'.
16. Hare to Whewell, 12 November 1843, quoted in Lubenow, *Cambridge Apostles*, 111.
17. Hare, *Vindication of Luther*, 75.
18. Thirlwall to John Thirlwall, 23 July 1829, in Thirlwall, *Letters Literary and Theological*, 95.
19. See Liddon, *Life of Pusey*, 1:72.
20. This is a statement attributed to Conybeare by Thirlwall. I was, however, unable to find it in Conybeare, *An Attempt to Trace the History*; see also Thompson, *Cambridge Theology*, 75.
21. [Newman,] *Tract 3*, 54.
22. Mosig, *Birthpangs of Neo-Protestantism*, 102.
23. Rose, *State of the Protestant Religion*, 58–9, 84.
24. Ibid., 14; emphasis added.
25. Ibid., 12; emphasis added.
26. Rose, *State of the Protestant Religion* (2nd ed.), 8.
27. Pusey to Tholuck, Oxford, 13 August 1829, in Geck, ed., *Autorität und Glaube*, 132–5, 134.
28. Pusey, *Historical Enquiry: Part II*, 15.
29. See Geck, 'Concept of History', 387–408.
30. Pusey, *Historical Enquiry*, 110.
31. Ibid., 148.
32. Ibid., 115n.
33. Tholuck, 'Gespräche über die vornehmsten Glaubensfragen der Zeit', 258.
34. Pusey to Tholuck, 30 May 1830, Oxford (Appendix on the History of English Theology), in Geck, ed., *Autorität und Glaube*, 141–52, 150.
35. Rose, *State of the Protestant Religion*, 228–9.

36 For a detailed analysis of Hengstenberg's repristination of the theology of Lutheran orthodoxy see ibid., 231 and Mosig, *Birthpangs of Neo-Protestantism*.
37 See Geck, *Schleiermacher als Kirchenpolitiker*, 282.
38 Pusey to Tholuck, Oxford, 29 June 1829, in Geck, ed., *Autorität und Glaube*, 129–31, 131.
39 Rose to Pusey, 14 March 1838; quoted in Liddon, *Life of Pusey*, 1:176.
40 Tholuck to Pusey, Rome, 23 March 1829, in Geck, ed., *Autorität und Glaube*, 123–4, 124.
41 Newman to Pusey, 31 August 1829, in: [Newman,] *Letters and Diaries*, 2:160.
42 Blomfield to Pusey, 4 January 1830, Liddon Bound Volumes 40.
43 Pusey, *Historical Enquiry: Part II*, 34.
44 Ibid., 98.
45 Ibid., 31.
46 Ibid., 15.
47 Hooker, *Works of That Learned and Judicious Divine*, 446.
48 W. Laud, *Works* (Library of Anglo-Catholic Theology), vol. 3, (Oxford 1853), 386; cited in Chapman, 'Bischofsamt und Politik', 449.
49 Pusey, *Historical Enquiry: Part II*, 17; English translation: 'Who Supervises the Supervisors?'
50 Ibid., 16.
51 See Lücke, 'Erinnerungen an Dr. Friedrich Schleiermacher', 750.
52 Lücke to Pusey, 22 February 1827; Liddon Bound Volumes 142.
53 Pusey, *Historical Enquiry, Part II*, 39–40. Pusey remarked, however, that any such 're-translating' along with its 'extensive usefulness' might carry 'extensive danger', so that 'more or less a "human system" is introduced into theology'.
54 Ibid., 38.
55 Ibid., 36, 39.
56 Ibid., 88.
57 Burke, *Reflections on the Revolution*, 164.
58 Ibid., 164–5.
59 Pusey, *Historical Enquiry, Part II*, 105; see also Burke, *Reflections on the Revolution*, 163.
60 Tholuck, 'Gespräche über die Vornehmsten Glaubensfragen der Zeit', 258 [my translation].
61 See Pusey to Tholuck, 30 May 1830, Oxford (Appendix on the History of English Theology), in Geck, ed., *Autorität und Glaube*, 141–52. For details on Pusey's report, see note 12.
62 Pusey to Tholuck, Oxford, 13 August 1829, in Geck, ed., *Autorität und Glaube*, 132–5, 132.
63 Pusey to Tholuck, 30 May 1830, Oxford (Appendix on the History of English Theology), in Geck, ed., *Autorität und Glaube*, 141–52, 143–6.
64 Ibid., 146–8.
65 Ibid., 148–50.
66 Ibid., 150–52.
67 Ibid., 143.
68 Ibid., 144.
69 Ibid., 146.
70 Ibid.
71 Ibid., 146–8.
72 Ibid., 152.
73 Thus Milman in the preface to the third volume of the fourth edition from 1866 of *The History of the Jews*, v.

74 Pusey to Tholuck, 30 May 1830, Oxford (Appendix on the History of English Theology), in Geck, ed., *Autorität und Glaube*, 141–52, 145.
75 Ibid.
76 [Pusey,] *Tract 18*, n.p.
77 [Pusey,] *Tracts 67–69*, 9.
78 Pusey to Tholuck, Oxford, 19 November 1839, in Geck, ed., *Autorität und Glaube*, 175–8, 177.
79 Pusey to Tholuck, Oxford, 6 March 1837, in Geck, ed., *Autorität und Glaube*, 168–71, 169.
80 Pusey, *Tracts 67–69* (2nd ed.), ix–x.
81 See [Newman], *On the Introduction of Rationalistic Principles into Religion*, 54–5.
82 Pusey, *Tracts 67–69* (2nd ed.), ix.
83 Pusey to Tholuck, 30 May 1830, Oxford (Appendix on the History of English Theology), in Geck, ed., *Autorität und Glaube*, 141–52, 145.
84 See Matthew, 'Edward Bouverie Pusey', passim.
85 See Rowell, *Vision Glorious*, 71.
86 See Pusey to Tholuck, Oxford, 6 March 1837, in Geck, ed., *Autorität und Glaube*, 168–71, 170; Pusey to Tholuck, Oxford, 19 November 1839, in Geck, ed., *Autorität und Glaube*, 175–8, 176–7.
87 Pusey to Tholuck, Oxford, 6 March 1837, in Geck, ed., *Autorität und Glaube*, 168–71, 169.
88 Ibid.
89 Tholuck to Pusey, Berlin, 4 April 1837, in Geck, ed., *Autorität und Glaube*, 171–3, 172.
90 Tholuck to Pusey, Berlin, 4 April 1837, in Geck, ed., *Autorität und Glaube*, 171–3, 172–3.
91 Tholuck to Pusey, Halle, 19 July 1836, in Geck, ed., *Autorität und Glaube*, 161–2.
92 Pusey, *Historical Enquiry*, 9, 102, 50.
93 Pusey, *Historical Enquiry: Part II*, 363.
94 See Pusey to Tholuck, Oxford, 13 August 1829 and 30 July 1836, in Geck, ed., *Autorität und Glaube*, 133, 134, 165.
95 Pusey to Tholuck, Oxford, 30 July 1836, in Geck, ed., *Autorität und Glaube*, 162–8, 164.
96 Imberg, *In Quest of Authority*, 159–77, 171.
97 Pusey, *Tracts 67–69* (2nd ed.), 89.
98 Pusey, *Letter to the Bishop of Oxford*, 12, 151.
99 Pusey to Tholuck, Oxford, 30 July 1836, in Geck, ed., *Autorität und Glaube*, 162–8, 165.
100 Pusey to Gladstone, 9 September 1846; quoted in Liddon, *Life of Pusey*, 3:71.
101 Pusey to Tholuck, Oxford, 19 November 1839, in Geck, ed., *Autorität und Glaube*, 175–8, 178.
102 Pusey, *Tracts 67–69* (2nd ed.), 28.
103 Pusey to Philip Pusey, 1 July 1836; Liddon Bound Volumes 26.
104 Pusey, *Letter to the Bishop of Oxford*, 152.
105 Müller, *Life and Letters*, 164.
106 See Geck, ed., *Autorität und Glaube*, 17.
107 Pusey, *Collegiate and Professorial Teaching*, 56.
108 See Geck, ed., *Autorität und Glaube*.
109 [Pusey,] *Tracts 67–69* (2nd ed.), 9.

Chapter Five

DEFINING THE CHURCH: PUSEY'S ECCLESIOLOGY AND ITS EIGHTEENTH-CENTURY ANTECEDENTS

R. Barry Levis

Theories about the true character of the church presented a major challenge to the Tractarians. They wanted to determine the church's nature, its authority and its relationship to secular powers. Yet they were not the first to attempt this: this concern cropped up often within the Church of England, looking at itself in connection to other branches of Christianity and at its unique position as the established church in England in relation to the dissenting sects. This apprehension especially arose during the period from the Glorious Revolution to the accession of the Hanoverians. Here too debates over ecclesiology raged in the pamphlet press. In many respects, these two periods – from the Glorious Revolution to the Hanoverian Succession, and from the repeal of the Test and Corporation Acts to the departure of Newman to Rome – exhibit a number of interesting parallels. Specifically, these periods show that high ecclesiology arose at times when the church saw itself threatened.[1]

In his excellent work, *The Oxford Movement in Context*, Peter B. Nockles presents a portrait of the relationship between the High Churchmen and the Tractarians. While he demonstrates the continuity between the High Church tradition in the eighteenth century and the Tractarians, he focused on the period after 1760, a relatively quiescent period. As Owen Chadwick has pointed out, however, questions about the nature of the church escalate when its defenders perceive outside or internal threats.[2] In fact, 'The Church is in Danger' served as a High Church rallying cry producing a high ecclesiology both among the Tractarians, especially Edward Bouverie Pusey, and in the reign of Queen Anne.

From the publication of the William Warburton's *Alliance of Church and State* in 1736, which effectively ended the ecclesiological controversies of the early Hanoverian period, until the tensions over the repeal of the Test and Corporation Act and Catholic Emancipation, the warmth of ecclesiastical debates remained low. These later events, however, outraged many in the church, especially those gathered in the common room at Oriel College, Oxford. Rising concerns about threats to the church agitated the future Tractarians. Apprehension about the well-being of the church initially arose because of the passage through Parliament of the Catholic Emancipation Bill in 1829. Although some churchmen, such as Thomas Arnold and Bishop Henry Bathurst of Norwich,[3] candidly supported the bill, the vast majority of bishops voted against the legislation, including the most senior members of the bench.[4] Nevertheless, the Duke of Wellington thought that he had no choice but to forge ahead with the bill even though it split the Tory party and lost Sir Robert Peel his parliamentary seat at Oxford. Although the government added securities to the bill to protect the church and the new oath required Catholics to swear that they would undertake no steps in Parliament against the established church in England and Ireland, many churchmen nevertheless feared for the future of the church, especially from Irish radicals who would regard the oath as illegitimate and not binding.[5]

The election following the accession of William IV resulted in a Whig majority under Lord Grey who proceeded with the Whig determination to reform Parliament. This action also posed problems for churchmen who feared that any redistribution of seats in the House of Commons might threaten their position. Many shared an unstated dread that the church might face disestablishment as a result.[6] Increased attacks on the establishment from Dissenters and others opposed to the church only exacerbated these fears. In particular *The Extraordinary Black Book* (1831), which sold more than 14,000 copies, assailed the church with false accusations, especially on the size of bishops' salaries.[7] As a result, Lord Henley proposed the removal of the bishops from the House of Lords. The Church Temporalities (Ireland) Act in 1833, which reduced the number of archbishops by two and bishops by ten, only confirmed the worst fears about the Whig government's intentions for the church. Yet even the Tories proved unreliable. Peel, seeing the need for church reform, appointed an Ecclesiastical Commission composed of clerical and lay representatives to examine church finances.[8] Although Peel's ministry lasted only three months, the effects of the Ecclesiastical Commission rippled through the church for the next several decades. Lord Melbourne, a man widely suspected of casual religious opinions, replaced Peel as prime minister and was immediately confronted with the vacancy of the Regius Professor of Divinity at the University of Oxford. Passing over a list of recommendations compiled by Archbishop Howley, including Edward Bouverie Pusey, John Henry Newman and John Keble, he selected Renn Dickson Hampden, a man with equally objectionable religious views, at least to the High Churchmen gathered at Oxford.[9] Following the publication of Richard Hurrell Froude's *Remains* (1838), Charles Pourtales Golightly urged the defence of the Reformation by soliciting contributions for the Martyrs' Memorial, to be placed strategically next to the church of St Mary Magdalen. Newman, Keble and eventually Pusey all refused to subscribe.[10] Some churchmen even recalled the 1830 French Revolution and the spectre of the guillotine.

Pusey, like the other Tractarians, feared the intentions of the Whig politicians. Initially he did not exhibit the immediate distress that some others did. He applauded the repeal of the Test and Corporation Acts, which he regarded as 'a disgrace and deterrent to religion'.[11] When Peel ran for Parliament in 1829, after initially resigning his seat because of his support for Catholic Emancipation, Pusey opposed most of his colleagues, including Keble, Newman and Froude, in supporting Peel's re-election.[12] Not until the Irish Temporalities Bill did Pusey take alarm.[13] 'One can have but little hope', he wrote, 'from politicians who know so little either of the Church's needs or of the mode of relieving them.'[14] His apprehension increased even more with Hampden's appointment as Regius Professor. He wrote to William Ewart Gladstone, 'we are under great anxiety as to our new professor'[15] and quickly produced a pamphlet, *Dr Hampden's Theological Statements and the Thirty-Nine Articles Compared*, which challenged Hampden's orthodoxy. In particular, Pusey objected to Hampden's indifference to the Apostolic Fathers:[16] 'I cannot refrain from protesting earnestly against the harsh and often bitter and sarcastic language employed by Dr Hampden towards the Fathers of the Christian Church, and whole classes of God's departed servants.' One might have expected such language from 'the infidel Gibbon' but not from a Christian theologian.[17] After matters had calmed and the university had shunned Hampden, Pusey smugly observed that 'the Ministry are apparently alarmed at the rising energy of the Church'.[18]

Two later incidents confirmed Pusey's anxiety about threats to the church. Pusey's response to the appointment in 1841 of a joint Anglican–Prussian bishop of Jerusalem had been muted in comparison to that of Newman and others.[19] Yet when the original Anglican incumbent, Dr Michael Solomon Alexander, died and was replaced by a Prussian candidate, Pusey's opinion changed radically. 'What a misery it would be if the ultimate object of the Prussian government were attained, and they were to receive Episcopacy from us, and we were to become the authors of an heretical Succession. I think it would split the English Church at once… To give Episcopacy to Prussia now, or even to prepare for it, is like arraying a corpse or whitening a sepulchre.'[20]

The other crisis arose when the Reverend George Gorham appealed the Court of Arches' decision against him to the Privy Council. This affair followed hard on the heels of Hampden's elevation to the see of Hereford in 1846; both actions called into question the notion of the royal supremacy. Pusey's first reaction was muted: 'A judicial decision on a doctrinal question, reversing an ecclesiastical judgment and deciding against the Creeds, would be a miserable thing, though one must, if God avert it not, make the best of it, and sit down by the waters of Babylon, toiling on under bondage.' He thought it would have been better had Bishop Henry Phillpotts of Exeter instituted Gorham to avoid such a calamity.[21] However, Pusey's alarm increased significantly when a number of clergy used the Gorham debacle as an excuse to convert to Rome, and his tone changed accordingly:

> This is clear to me…that the same authority which imposes upon us the oath of supremacy, and gives the Queen power to judge in ecclesiastical causes, forbids any one, acting under those powers, to declare anything to be heresy which has not been so declared, or shall hereafter be declared by Parliament *with the assent of the clergy in their Convocation*. It plainly follows that it was not intended to give any judicial body the power to settle what is the doctrine of the Church of England.[22]

Pusey feared that the Privy Council in effect would define doctrine for the church. To Keble he wondered, 'But the real question seems, "Is the doctrine of the Church of England sufficiently defined or no?" or, in any case in which it is not defined, has the Civil Power the right to conceded to it, to define it?'[23] Each of these events demonstrated the danger of state intervention in church affairs. One should also note that except for the initial appointment of the Jerusalem bishop (which did not raise much concern in Pusey), all of the threats that Pusey did take seriously came from Whig administrations, whom he regarded having indifferent support for the establishment.

Pusey, however, saw the problems of the church stemming not only from these events; the beginnings of current troubles stretched back to the previous century. Pusey, as well as other Tractarians, maintained that the eighteenth-century church had 'suffered deeply, both in lukewarmness of life and degeneracy of faith, until the horrors of the French Revolution awoke us as out of a death-sleep'.[24] In Tract 66, he wrote

> while not deciding as to the whole extent of their allegations, the eighteenth century was comparatively a stagnant period of the Church, – in England, owing to the violent revolution, whereby so many of her best members, the Non-Juring Clergy, were ejected, and that, at one time,

the State set itself to corrupt and degrade her, and her writers looked for strength in foreign alliances; – abroad, through the development of the principles of the ultra-reformation, and the influence of degraded England and corrupted France.[25]

Latitudinarianism had weakened the authority of the church,[26] and the clergy now needed to organize against these threats. '[T]he peril is not of some miserable temporal endowment, but of men's souls'.[27] His concern, however, focused not only on attacks by government; he equally feared Roman Catholic encroachments among Anglicans.[28]

In seeking answers to these challenges, Pusey concentrated on the writings of the Apostolic Fathers. ''Tis in this way that I have received everything which I have received. Whatever I have received, I received on the authority of the Ancient Church.'[29] From the fathers, Pusey came to his definition of the church. One of his characterizations seems almost like a catechism answer. 'The Church is the Body of Christ, as Scripture saith, "the Temple of Christ…" but thereby are we brought nearer to Him… [T]o be in the Church is to be *in* Christ, a member of Christ'.[30] Pusey's description of the church resembled that of the other Tractarians, but he posed it in a mystical sense[31] that also imbued his sermons.[32] The church, he proclaimed, had but one guide: 'All from Abel to the end…belong to that one City of God, that one Body, whereof [Christ] is the Head.'[33]

Pusey repeatedly emphasized the patristic inspiration of Anglicanism: 'Our Church, both by the declarations of the Reformers, by her Canons, and by the combined teaching of approved divines, refers to Antiquity, the early Church.'[34] In response to a query about the meaning of Puseyism, he listed 'High estimate of the Episcopacy, as God's ordinance', a 'High estimate of the visible Church as the Body wherein we are made and continue to be members of Christ' and 'the authority of the Universal Church as the channel of truth to us'.[35] As he wrote in the preface of the *Library of the Fathers*: 'Clergy shall be careful never to teach anything from the pulpit, to be religiously held and believed by the people, but what is agreeable to the doctrines of the Old and New Testament, and collected out of that same doctrine by the Catholic Fathers and ancient Bishops.' He also argued that the church appealed 'not to the Fathers individually, or as individuals, but as witnesses; not to this or that Father, but to the whole body, and agreement of Catholic Fathers and ancient Bishops'.[36]

Pusey vigorously defended the Church of England as part of Universal Church, along with Rome and the Orthodox churches.[37] Significantly, Pusey referred to clergy of the Church of England as 'Ministers of the Apostolic Church of this land'.[38] As he wrote Walter Farquhar Hook, who defended the Protestant aspects of the Church of England in *Call to Union on the Principles of the English Reformation*: 'we urge what is Catholic, and that we are agreed what is Catholic... This struggle *is* about the Catholic faith.'[39] Yet he did not question the authenticity of the Roman Church and scolded those who denigrated Rome. 'I am frightened at your calling Rome Antichrist, or a forerunner of it', he wrote Hook. 'I believe Antichrist will be infidel and arise out of what calls itself Protestantism, and that Rome and England will be united in one then to oppose it. Protestantism is infidel, or verging towards it.'[40] On another occasion he wrote to Newman, 'I am no nearer thinking that the English Church is no true Church, or that inter-communion with Rome is essential... I earnestly desire the restoration of unity, but I cannot throw myself into the practical Roman system, nor renounce what I believe our gracious Lord acknowledges.'[41] Although one might regret the division, '[t]here is then no ground to assume that suspensions of inter-communion (sad and mournful as they are) in themselves hinder either body from being a portion of the Body of Christ.'[42]

Pusey shared the High Church apostolic notions of the later eighteenth century.[43] Nevertheless, he approached that concept from a much narrower perspective, which in his view limited the freedom of the church to wander beyond fifth-century conventions. Pusey insisted authority resided solely with the hierarchy and uniquely in the first four councils: 'The Bishops therein assembled bear witness to the faith which they had received from their predecessors, and so from the Apostles.'[44] An ecumenical council cannot go astray because of Christ's promise of his abiding presence. 'The Romanists have erred in applying this promise to particular Councils or Councils held in conjunction with the Pope... To say that we are bound by them *because* they declare the faith which *we* acknowledge, would plainly be to say that we are not bound by them at all; for we should then accept [them] on our own authority, because they fell in with our views.'[45] On the other hand, the church at the time of the ecumenical councils stood in its purest form, as he noted in Tract 18: 'Its ministers derived their commission not of man, but of God.'[46]

Although Pusey granted that the lower clergy might influence provincial synods, only bishops as the direct descendants of the apostles held authority in general councils to determine matters of doctrine and discipline.[47] The laity, if present, only observed 'not even as Jury, much less as Judge'.[48] He foresaw grave dangers if any other than bishops held authority.[49]

> Accordingly, until the unhappy precedent, made in a very evil time by the Church in the United States, when struggling for life, the question of lay-representation was consistently confined to bodies which rejected the Apostolic succession, the Continental reformers, and the dissenters in Great Britain. It must be said plainly, that the precedent set in the

> United States is radically wrong, and in fact, is so far, the adoption of a principle belonging to bodies who reject the Apostolic succession and the whole principle of a deposit of faith, and of a commission, transmitted from the Apostles and part of the mind of Christ. Yet, in so saying, I do not mean (God forbid!) that she thereby forfeited her claim to be a part of the Church. She has abandoned a bulwark of the faith, a function of the office inherited by her Bishops, not the faith itself nor the Apostolic succession.[50]

He privately expressed horror at the prospect of lay participation in synods: 'It at once invests them with an ecclesiastical office, which will develop itself sooner or later, I believe, to the destruction of the Faith.'[51] At the same time, he warned of the dangers that might arise since the Scottish church had permitted laity into their synod.

> The deposit of the faith, the form of sound words, was committed by the Apostles to the Bishops...with the charge that they should commit it to others also. If the Church of the United States [note his designation] has admitted the laity to a voice in deciding on matters of faith, I believe that her Bishops have abandoned a trust committed to them, and, sooner or later, they must suffer by it. God only knows how much heresy this many not let in upon them.[52]

Even when the emperor attended a council, he served only as a witness;[53] 'it is a known fact that while laity were admitted to be present at Councils on the faith, they were never (whether Emperors or others) admitted to have a voice as to the decisions of faith... The Bishops exclusively laid down every principle.'[54] In England, too, councils had always exercised control over the church, even in the face of the royal supremacy.[55] This power had been usurped and required restoration, Pusey believed, especially considering the presence of Dissenters in Parliament determining church matters.

> What concerns us, is, that if the State withdraws the protection which it gives us, it should give us power to protect ourselves. Shepherd's dogs are safer guardians than wolf's cubs... Why should politicians fear entrusting the Bishops with declaring what is the faith of the Church, more than they fear trust in eminent lawyers with declaring what is the law of the Realm?[56]

Despite a growing fear of rationalism and liberalism within the church and state intervention from without,[57] Pusey did not regard royal supremacy a fatal threat,[58] nor did he consider bolting from the church's bosom. During the controversy he stirred over baptismal regeneration, he observed that '[a] wrong decision, even in a supreme court, cannot alter the faith of the Church. No wrong interpretation put upon it by a Court, nor any wrong judgment passed in neglect of it, can alter the sense in which the Church received it from the Apostles, and still receives it.'[59] Pusey regarded emperors and kings primarily as watchdogs; neither they nor their secular ministers held any right to determine church doctrine.[60]

> In acknowledging the Queen's Supremacy, we wholly deny to the 'civil magistrate' that authority which we have acknowledged to belong to the Church only...; that we wholly deny to the Crown, directly or indirectly... through delegated Judges, or in any other way, a power so foreign to its office as that of judging or defining in the smallest jot or tittle the doctrine or discipline of the Church.[61]

The Christian Church had ceded to the emperor certain authority: 'when not abused, it was cheerfully submitted to by the Church; and that even anomalies were borne with for a time, and amended when they could.'[62] The converse also remained true: if kings had no spiritual mandate, neither did the church have temporal power. 'The Ecclesiastical Authorities of the Church have nothing to do, by virtue of their office, with any civil legislation, or any civil sanction or authority for their acts.'[63] He further argued that

> the acts of the Church, as a spiritual body, affect only the court of conscience, and are binding only on her members. She declares, for instance, what is the law of God as to marriage; her exposition of that law is binding upon her children, But whether that law shall involve any temporal consequences to children, born contrary to the law of God and of the Church, is a matter, not of the Church to decide, but for the civil authorities.[64]

Nevertheless, considering those contemporary threats facing the church, it must defend its spiritual authority and apostolic heritage vigilantly.[65]

Although Pusey himself denied that political upheavals had a bearing on his religious thinking, the turmoil of the 1830s undoubtedly had a major impact. Certainly, most of the Tractarians – almost all from high Tory families – regarded the new Whig regime in 1830 as a threat to the church. Nockles argues that Pusey definitely reacted to political turbulence.[66] As discussed above, Pusey did not initially find the new Whig regime troublesome. Chadwick also saw that the movement had a 'political impetus'.[67] Seemingly every time the cry of the 'Church in Danger' arose, the Whigs had gained political ascendancy, thereby menacing the Tory High Churchmen.

One cannot confine this observation, however, only to the Tractarians. Striking parallels exist, in particular, between the 1830s and the reign of Queen Anne. In the early eighteenth century, many members of the church also feared that enemies – primarily Whigs – had launched a concerted attack. During both periods, Anglican traditionalists dreaded the rise of heterodox thought and irreligion.[68] In both instances, writers turned their minds to ecclesiological debates. Therefore, a comparison of these two periods provides useful insights into the disputes that centred on ecclesiology. Francis Atterbury, Benjamin Hoadly and to a lesser extent William Warburton appear here because they generated as much heat on these issues in the eighteenth century as Newman, Froude and Pusey did in their generation.

In 1689, the Church of England had barely withstood the challenge of a Roman Catholic monarch, only to be confronted by a new Calvinist king with questionable sympathies towards the establishment. Although a few Tories perceived the handiwork of God in the Glorious Revolution,[69] some High Churchmen refused to accept the new monarch and became Non-Jurors. Those conservative clergy who remained in the church became increasingly alarmed by what they witnessed. The king spurned a plan for comprehension, instead supporting the Toleration Act, and appointed several suspect bishops. The church also resisted growing irreligion, which seemed a menace to its stability. From threats of Socinianism and Arianism to downright scepticism, the church surely did appear in danger.[70] The creation of an exclusively Whig ministry in 1695 only exacerbated these fears.

The publication of Socinian pamphlets provided the immediate cause of the controversy that led to assembling convocation. Worried churchmen urged the bishops to counteract these challenges to true religion, but some regarded the matter as so serious that only convocation could address the crisis.[71] Francis Atterbury, later Bishop of Rochester and traitor, expressed this anxiety and in the process provided a definition of the church that reflected the High Church standard. 'The infidelity of the Age has forced me', he wrote, 'to dwell often on the great Articles and Mysteries of our Faith, and to explain them largely... The *Faith* I have deliver'd to you, the Faith of the Church of *England*, into which we were *all* baptized, is, I am entirely satisfied, the same that *was once delivered to the Saints.*'[72] The Church of England, he asserted, 'is without doubt, the purest and soundest, the most reasonable and moderate Church upon Earth, the nearest to the primitive Pattern of any, and the most serviceable to our Improvement in Virtue and Godliness'.[73] The emergency arose because of 'open looseness of Men's Principles and Practices'; and scepticism, Socinianism, Deism and atheism 'overflow us like a Deluge'.[74]

While it might be suggested that the bishops had the power to act or the universities to strike down heresy within their midst, the current situation demanded far more radical action.[75]

In his *Letter to a Convocation Man*, Atterbury argued that the clergy had a constitutional right to assemble in convocation and not solely at the crown's whim.[76] Within this context he indirectly began an argument about defining the church and its relationship to the state, which raged for the next several decades. Once attacked by Whig clergy, he responded with a second book, *The Rights, Powers and Privileges of an English Convocation*, in which he elaborated on what he regarded as orthodoxy.

Atterbury defined the church as 'a Society instituted in order to a supernatural End; and, as such, must have an inherent Power in it, of governing it self [sic]...for a Society without a Power of Government, is a Bull in Polity'.[77] He admitted that questions existed about the origins of temporal power, but no one would deny that the authority of the church descends directly from God.[78] He acknowledged two powers: All nations could implement the secular; the spiritual, however, 'can Rightly be exercised among Christians only...as Members of a Spiritual Society, of which Christ Jesus is the Head, who has also given our Laws, and appointed a standing Succession of Officers under himself for the Government of this Society'.[79] Here Atterbury alludes to the Apostolic succession, although rarely in his writings does he use that expression. None of the eighteenth-century thinkers, even Atterbury, emphasized the apostolic origins of the church to the extent that Pusey and the other Tractarians did.[80] '[T]hese Ministers of his did actually govern it... From whence it follows, that such Spiritual Jurisdictions cannot be in its own Nature necessarily dependent on the Temporal.'[81] The power of the church to govern itself existed before 'Kings, States, and Potentates became Christian'.[82] The church is, therefore, a divinely created independent institution that (more vaguely) derived its authority from the Apostolic Fathers.

Not focusing on the early councils to the same extent Pusey later did, Atterbury reached quite different conclusions from Pusey about the relative powers of bishops and presbyters. The power of governance for the church, Atterbury stressed, rested in the hands of provincial and general councils. All meetings of provincial synods included both bishops and presbyters. 'The *Presbytery* were in every City, a necessary standing Council to their respective *Bishops*... And together with their Bishops therefore they met in a *Diocesan Synod*, upon all great Causes; and without their Advice and Consent, nothing of Importance was, or could be determin'd.'[83] With general councils, presbyters came only as proxies for bishops, but provincial councils that did include presbyters discussed and agreed on all decisions later made by general councils.[84]

Atterbury and Pusey also reached distinctive understandings about where authority within the church resided. Atterbury defended the rights of the lower house of convocation, and Pusey championed the independence of synods from secular authority. In fact, Atterbury concluded that the relative power of the bishops in England had declined, making them less able to fight heresy: 'by the Laws of *England*, [bishops are] confin'd within particular bounds; and beyond those Bounds they are not allow'd to have any Authority to Determine or Punish'.[85] His urgent call for a convocation arose since one could not expect the bishops alone to suppress heresy under those restrictions.

Even though the Church of England was established with the sovereign as supreme governor, the church, Atterbury argued, had not yielded its independence to secular authorities.[86] Yet he feared the declining influence of the clergy. 'Indeed, these Rights of the Clergy do, at present, lie under some Disadvantage' because their power had not 'of late years, been duly Claimed and Exercised'.[87] The clergy must clamour for a convocation to deliberate on matters within their 'Proper Sphere'.[88] All provincial assemblies had these rights 'claim'd and practis'd by them in all Ages of the Church, and in all Christian Countries, and in our own particularly'.[89] He contended that if the metropolitan had the right to call together the clergy in convocation, '[i]t…is likewise accompanied with a *Right* in those of this Province to be so called.'[90]

At the same time, Atterbury remained cautious about overstepping the bounds of propriety with the king. He used flattering language to persuade the king to cooperate: William, he claimed, 'hath discover'd…a Godly Concern for the support of the *Catholick Church* in His Dominions, of which he is the avow'd *Defender*', but he can only succeed when 'the humble Advice of His Clergy assembled in Convocation shall be seasonably and fully laid before Him'.[91] The king therefore had an obligation to call convocation at the same time he summoned a Parliament. 'The Liberties of the Church do, in great measure, run parallel to those of the State; and Both of them must, according to the Nature and Constitution of our English Government, stand or fall together.'[92]

The calling of convocation, however, did not produce the desired results. Constantly prorogued by Archbishop Tenison, the lower house failed to conduct any business. At Atterbury's urging, they posited the right to continue debates on their own, even with the upper house not sitting. The lower house then proceeded to condemn certain writings, notably William Toland's *Christianity Not Mysterious*, presenting their resolution to the outraged Bishops, appalled at the lower clergy's temerity to define doctrine.[93] Atterbury admitted that if the convocation as a whole adjourned, the lower house could not conduct business independently. Even though the upper house had not met, however, the lower could deliberate during synodical days.[94] From Atterbury's prospective, the lower clergy stood as equals to the bishops, certainly a notion the Tractarians, especially Pusey, would have vehemently rejected.

The conflict continued to rage throughout Anne's reign.[95] After the failure to stop occasional conformity and the inability of the lower house of convocation to achieve independence in the face of episcopal opposition, Atterbury again wrote that the church was in danger. 'We are so far degenerated from our good Ancestors, in this respect, that we seem to be another sort of People, and to live in a different Clime. Levity, Lewdness, and Irreligion, are the most prevailing behaviour.'[96] The authority of the church must be brought to bear, and to Atterbury only an independent convocation with a strong lower house could confront these problems.

Atterbury gained a worthy adversary in Benjamin Hoadly, who, because of his services to the Hanoverian kings, ascended the ladder of preferment, becoming successively Bishop of Bangor, Hereford, Salisbury and finally Winchester. Part of that service entailed answering men like Atterbury who advocated a view of the church not pleasing to the Whig ascendancy. Beginning his career as a propagandist during Anne's reign, Hoadly's unabashed loyalty to the Whigs made him a pariah to High Churchmen.[97] His latitudinarian views led him to an understanding of ecclesiology that differed markedly from Atterbury's. As early as 1705, Hoadly, urging his supporters 'to resist and rebel', attacked Atterbury and others who claimed that the church was in danger.[98]

Intense controversy swarmed around Hoadly following his 1717 sermon on 'The Nature of the Kingdom of the Church of Christ'. He depicted the church as solely a spiritual body, with no temporal authority: 'The Church of Christ is the number of men, whether small or great, whether dispersed or united, who truly and sincerely are subject to Jesus Christ alone as their lawgiver and judge.' He warned that 'to set up any other authority in his kingdom… destroys the rule and authority of Jesus Christ as King'.[99] He concluded that Christ's '*Kingdom is not of this World*; that He hath…left behind Him, no visible, humane *Authority*, no *Vicegerents*, who can be said properly to supply his Place; no *Interpreters*, upon whom his Subjects are absolutely to depend; no *Judges* over the Consciences or Religion of his People'.[100] Ministers of the church, like shepherds, guided their sheep to moral respectability. Christ's flock must be 'led and not driven', he insisted.[101] Mundane 'Pomp and dignity' have nothing to do with Christ's kingdom, and the rewards and punishments are strictly spiritual.[102]

Portraying the '*Succession of Prelates from the Apostolical Times*, a Trifle', Hoadly's stance on apostolic succession also antagonized.[103] He claimed that Christ appointed the Apostles to direct and govern only, but the Apostles could not add or subtract from Christ's law.[104] He conceded the crown's unlimited power over the church. In the case of the deprivation of the Non-Juring bishops, Hoadly alleged that William not only revoked their temporal positions but also their spiritual functions.[105] Nevertheless, the church had not gained from an alliance with the State, he wrote sarcastically, 'unless the *Desirable Thing* in *Christ's kingdom* be *Riches* and *Power*'.[106] The alliance with the state has transformed the church into a '*Political Tool*, and an *Engine* of *State*'.[107]

On the issue of occasional conformity, Hoadly opined that while the state does have a right to exclude some citizens from office because of their views, 'I am still of the Opinion, that *Differences* in *Church Matters*, as such, is no ground of such *Restraint*.'[108] Because he did not see a necessary connection between the established church and the state, he rejected depriving Dissenters of 'the *Common Rights* of *Society*', although he maintained that the '*Exclusion* of the *Papists*…was not upon the Account of their *Religion*' but strictly political because they could not be trusted to protect the '*Rights* and *Liberties* of the *Nation*'.[109] Hoadly's call for the repeal of the Test Act infuriated many churchmen,[110] but he contended that '[t]is an Invasion of the Kingdom of Christ to add Sanctions to the Laws of Christ.'[111] Any incursion into the kingdom by human authority to add temporal sanctions or incentives violated Christ's law.[112] He likened it to the persecution under Queen Mary and the Inquisition itself.[113] He claimed that applying the sacrament of holy communion to another purpose than what it was established to do 'is the *Prostitution* of the *Holy Sacrament*'.[114] Overall, Hoadly did not subscribe to the notion that the established church grew as a branch in England of the church catholic, thus undermining its exclusiveness. While this assertion might not have perturbed Atterbury, it certainly would have inflamed Pusey.

On the other hand, William Warburton never questioned the Test Act. In fact, he wrote an entire book defending it, presenting in the process quite a different analysis of the church from that of Atterbury. When he published the work in 1736, some of the controversy had subsided. Discredited as a Jacobite, Atterbury died in exile, although he was later defiantly interred at the West Door of Westminster Abbey.[115] With Whigs dominating the Church, the marginalization of the High Churchmen had increased; suspected of Jacobitism, tainted by their association with Atterbury or the old Non-Jurors, they languished in rural obscurity. The old disagreements, not entirely laid to rest, did however consume less paper pulp. Nevertheless, churchmen remained alarmed about the intensions of the Whig government, especially when Protestant Dissenters launched an attempt to repeal the Test Act in 1736. In this still uncertain atmosphere, Warburton produced his first major work, *The Alliance between Church and State*, appearing just before supporters of the Dissenters introduced the repeal measure in Parliament.[116]

While at least one historian has suggested that few in the church shared Warburton's views,[117] Warburton's defence of the status quo did seem to satisfy many. He certainly did not endure the vituperative attacks that Atterbury and Hoadly suffered. Although a few of his contemporaries disliked his employment of the Lockean social contract theory as his starting point for the alliance,[118] his book went through several editions and many printings, which indicates at least some approbation for his principles.[119] It remained the last word in the controversy until the Tractarians looked afresh at the issue of apostolic succession.[120] Clearly Pusey himself was very familiar with Warburton's writings.[121]

In many respects, Warburton's ecclesiology represents a hybrid between Atterbury's and Hoadly's. On the one hand, he broadly accepted Hoadly's characterization of the church; on the other, his position on establishment more closely resembled Atterbury's, although for pragmatic rather than theological reasons. Warburton attacked the High Church position that asserted the absolute independence of the church 'with all the Prerogatives and Powers', which he regarded as a slightly disguised version of popery.[122] On the other hand, while other authors advocated the church's total subordination to civil control,[123] Warburton pointed to the church's independent creation prior to the secular state. Christ's Kingdom, therefore, is a 'firm and lasting Society...made *such* by divine Appointment'.[124] A religion by law established had existed in all societies, ancient and modern; and in every case where a diversity of religions thrived, some form of a Test Law protected the established church.[125] Thus, Warburton saw no incongruity in an established episcopal church in England and a presbyterian church in Scotland.[126] Some form of sanctioned religion must exist; otherwise man would descend into Hobbesian anarchy. Religion, in constant tension with self-love, had to 'call in a Civil Magistrate as an alley to turn the Balance'.[127] Nor did human laws suffice to control behaviour. Laws cannot compel 'duties of imperfect obligation', such as hospitality, charity, gratitude and love of country.[128] Only the power of religion, 'teaching an overruling Providence the Rewarder of good Men and the Punisher of ill', can enforce them.[129]

Although Warburton advocated the independence of the church as an institution of divine origin, it could only flourish when allied with the state: 'For every sect, or Church, thinking it self alone the true, or a least the most perfect, is naturally pushing to the advancing its own Scheme on the Ruin of all the rest. So that if this succeeds not by *Dint of Argument*...they are apt to have Recourse to *Civil Power*.' The cure was for the government to establish one church, tolerating the others 'but *excluding* them from the *public Administration*, from the admission into *which* these Mischiefs arise'.[130]

The church clearly benefited from this arrangement. Without the mediation of the state, various religious groups are likely 'to fly out into Enthusiasm'. To counteract this and other threats, the church and the state 'must be employed thus to inforce and apply the Influence of Religion... But they can never act conjointly unless in Union and Alliance.'[131] Making the chief magistrate head of the religion, he averred, secured obedience of the people.[132] The church should apply all its influence in the service of the state, and the state shall support and protect the church. One cannot help notice, however, the unevenness of their 'reciprocal Dependency'. While the church did receive state funding, that arrangement encouraged the clergy's best service to the state and, at the same time, 'destroy[s] that mutual Dependency between the Clergy and People, which arises from the former's being maintained by the voluntary contribution of the latter'.[133] The fixed income from the state did not make the clergy autonomous; quite the contrary, 'such Benefits must needs produce the highest Love and Esteem for the Benefactor; which will be return'd out of Motives both of Gratitude and Interest, in the most zealous Labours for the State's Service'.[134] The church likewise gained the aid of civil coercive powers to enforce moral conduct. The church itself could not apply this compulsion, but the state lent its power to the church 'to be employed in the state's service'.[135]

The state profited significantly from the church's concessions: '*The Civil Magistrate becomes thereby Supreme Head of the Church; without whose Approbation and Allowance, she can now decree or determine nothing.*'[136] Since the goal is protection of the church, the protector must have power over the protected: 'The State having *endowed its Clergy*…with coactive Power, these are Privileges that might be perverted to the infinite Damage of the State, had not the Civil Magistrate, in Return, *the Supremacy* of the Church.'[137]

Disputes over ecclesiology therefore figured extensively in the controversies of the early eighteenth century and those swirling around the Tractarians. Pusey, however, could not find much assistance from the earlier controversialists to support his opinions. Warburton's understanding of the nature of the church and its relation to the state clearly did not persuade Pusey. Even more, he rejected Hoadly's approach robustly.[138] On the other hand, Atterbury and Pusey held much in common, although the latter never mentions the former in his writings. While aware of the controversies that disrupted convocation from the reign of William and Mary until the first George, Pusey would certainly not identify with the notorious Atterbury.[139]

Significantly, however, they did share a common concern about the threat they perceived to the church from the Whig politicians. Both reacted to political changes that they believed threatened the church and turned to questions of ecclesiology as a response, defining the church and its relation to the state accordingly. Not coincidentally, they saw this threat coming from new Whig regimes. Moreover, because of Pusey's insistence that the church remain free from outside secular and political forces, he concurred with Atterbury's concern about who held power within the church. Hoadly and Warburton hardly troubled with this issue. Nevertheless, Pusey differed significantly from Atterbury about the locus of this authority. Pusey and the Tractarians faced no firebrand like Hoadly countering their ecclesiology. Although many Victorian churchmen adamantly did object, they did not display the stridency of a Hoadly. Hostility towards Pusey might have been more polite, but it was no less intense than that aimed at Atterbury. Both Pusey and Atterbury wanted to lower the portcullis to defend the citadel of the church. Neither the whiggish Hoadly nor Warburton perceived such a severe threat and consequently advanced quite contrary positions. Nevertheless, the similarities between Atterbury and Pusey might be superficial. Atterbury found his allies among the lower clergy, since the bishops proved unreliable. Pusey discovered that few in England, at least at first, shared his outlook, and so he sought support from the church fathers. On the one hand, Atterbury discredited himself and many who had stood with him by plotting the overthrow of the monarchy, perhaps in an effort to save the church. Expediency rather than principle seemed to direct his steps. On the other hand, Pusey remained within the Church of England despite these attacks and the desertion of so many of his friends to Rome. In the end, Pusey proved the more faithful.

Notes

1 Chadwick, *Spirit of the Oxford Movement*, 3. The relationship between the fear of threats to the church and a high ecclesiology has a long history. For examples of these disputes, see Irenaeus' *Adversus Haereses*; the doctrine espoused by Pope Galasius (d. 496), in Robinson, *Readings in European History*, 72–3; and Boniface VIII's *Unam Sanctum*, in Bettenson and Maunder, *Documents of the Christian Church*, 126. While the proclamations of the Tractarians or the High Church divines of the reign of Queen Anne lacked papal stridency, the sentiment was nevertheless similar. Archbishop William Laud's declarations in his ongoing conflict with the Puritans about the apostolic succession and the authority of the hierarchy represent only a more recent example of this axiom. In each circumstance the defenders of a high ecclesiology supposed the church under attack. For the threats facing the church in the early nineteenth century, see Chadwick, *Victorian Church* (1966–70), 1: *passim*; for the early eighteenth century, see Bennett, *Tory Crisis*, 3–22.
2 Chadwick, *Spirit of the Oxford Movement*, 3.
3 Surprisingly, Bishop Henry Phillpotts also accepted the necessity of emancipation if strict guarantees were in place to protect the Establishment. See Chadwick, *Victorian Church* (1966–70), 1:10.
4 Chadwick, *Victorian Church* (1966–70), 1:10–11.
5 Ibid., 21–3.
6 Ibid., 29.
7 Ibid., 33.
8 Best, *Temporal Pillars*, 297–9.
9 Chadwick, *Victorian Church* (1966–70), 1:113–18.
10 Ibid., 176–7.

11 Liddon, *Life of Pusey*, 1:133.
12 Ibid., 1:198–9.
13 Ibid., 1:273.
14 Pusey to R. W. Jelf, 16 February 1834, quoted in ibid., 1:285.
15 Pusey to Gladstone, 2 February 1836, quoted in ibid., 1:369.
16 Rowell, *Vision Glorious*, 78.
17 Pusey, *Dr Hampden's Theological Statements*, xxix.
18 Chadwick, *Victorian Church* (1966–70), 1:118–21; Pusey to Dr Thurlock, 6 March 1837, quoted in Liddon, *Life of Pusey*, 1:388.
19 For a complete examination of the Jerusalem controversy, see Greaves, 'Jerusalem Bishopric', 328–52.
20 Pusey to Gladstone, 9 April 1846, quoted in Liddon, *Life of Pusey*, 3:71.
21 Ibid., 3:204.
22 Pusey to Mr Justice [J. T.] Coleridge, 9 January 1850, quoted in ibid., 3:211.
23 Pusey to Keble, 13 January 1850, quoted in ibid., 3:216.
24 Pusey, *Sermons during the Season*, vii. 'To belong to the Church, was to be the member of a certain visible body, with little mention of its inward life or union with its Head.'
25 *Tracts for the Times* 2:16.
26 Chadwick, *Spirit of the Oxford Movement*, 15.
27 Pusey, *Fendal v. Wilson*, 22.
28 Pusey, *Eirenicon*, 2:6. In this work, Pusey cited the Immaculate Conception as evidence that the Roman Catholic rather than the English church had drifted from the Apostolic Fathers. Moreover, Roman Catholics went well beyond the early fathers by calling the Roman Catholic Church a co-redemptor (Pusey, *Eirenicon*, passim).
29 Pusey to Bishop-elect Wilberforce, 27 November 1845, quoted in Liddon, *Life of Pusey*, 3:44. He admitted that at first following the teaching of the fathers distressed him: 'I may say, too, I received some things against my will. My bias was to keep the position which those in our Church had usually held. I have mentioned the change in myself to [very] few; because what I had at heart was simply the revival of holiness and true faith among ourselves, and I trusted God in His mercy giving us this "would provide" for the rest.' Some of the things he had resisted included invocation of the saints.
30 Pusey, *Sermons during the Season*, ix.
31 Chadwick, *Spirit of the Oxford Movement*, 39. Chadwick claims that one can 'almost feel the individual's incorporation into the Body'.
32 'Pusey's sermons are shot through with a sense of awe, reverence, and wonder before the grace, mercy, and holiness of God. The adoration of the contemplative before the mystery of the God who, coming down to the lowest part of our need, takes us top himself, and exalts us in Christ to the heavenly places – that is the temper and disposition which he sought to share' (Rowell, *Vision Glorious*, 81). This same sense of wonder permeates Pusey's view of the church.
33 Pusey, *Sermons during the Season*, 2.
34 Pusey to Bishop-elect Wilberforce, 27 November 1845, quoted in Liddon, *Life of Pusey*, 3:43–4.
35 Quoted in Liddon, *Life of Pusey*, 2:140–41.
36 Liddon, *Life of Pusey*, 1:417–20. Liddon posited that Pusey stressed the importance of understanding scripture as well as the fathers in order to quiet Protestant sceptics.
37 Pusey, *Letter to Jelf*, 6. 'Any particular Church owes obedience to the Universal Church, of which it is a part.'
38 Ibid., 2.

39 Pusey to Walter Farquhar Hook, [1838], quoted in Liddon, *Life of Pusey*, 2:48–9.
40 Pusey to Dr Hook, 24 November 1844, quoted in ibid., 2:447. 'I think the sects see further than you do, in that they class "Popery" and what they call "Puseyism" together, i.e. that the Churches and what submits to authority will be on one side in the end, sects and private judgement on the other. The ground seems clearing and people taking their sides for the last conflict, and we shall then see, I hope, that all which hold "the deposit of the Faith"…will be on one side, "the East, West and our own," and those who lean to their own understanding, on the other.'
41 Pusey to Newman, 12 July 1846, quoted in ibid., 2:510.
42 Pusey, *Eirenicon*, 1:65. This book is primarily a discussion of Immaculate Conception and additions to Catholic doctrines by the Roman Catholic Church. In the preface to the second volume, he wrote, 'I mean simply to maintain that its teaching is identical with that of the Fathers… I mean to maintain that the Church of England does hold a Divine authority in the Church, to be exercised in a certain way, deriving the truth from Holy Scripture, following Apostolic tradition, under the guidance of God the Holy Ghost. I fully believe that there is no difference between us in this' (ibid., 2:4–5).
43 Nockles, *Oxford Movement*, 26.
44 Pusey to J. F. Russell, 10 December 1836, quoted in Liddon, *Life of Pusey*, 1:402.
45 Ibid.
46 *Tracts for the Times* 1:21. He referred to councils after the ancient ones as 'mere Latin Councils' (Pusey to Liddon, 13 September 1872, quoted in Liddon, *Pusey*, 4:293).
47 Pusey, *Councils of the Church*, 24.
48 The laity could be witnesses and bishops could seek advice, but the laity exercised no decision-making power. Pusey explained away anything that might appear to demonstrate that the laity had any real power (ibid., 83). For that reason, Pusey later came to dread the establishment of the Lambeth Conferences because of the inclusion of the American bishops (Reed, *Glorious Battle*, 135). Ironically, Pusey reiterated in his sermons that the poor concerned Christ above all (Pusey, *Sermons during the Season*, 29). They are 'the Church's special treasure as the Gospel is their special property, the Church the home of the homeless, the mother of the fatherless'(ibid., 50). Nevertheless, he granted them no power in the church.
49 Pusey raised strenuous objections regarding the proposal to include the laity in the revival of convocation in 1852 (Pusey to Gladstone, 15 January 1852, quoted in Liddon, *Life of Pusey*, 3:344–5).
50 Pusey, *Councils of the Church*, 24–5.
51 Pusey to Keble, [1852], quoted in Liddon, *Life of Pusey*, 3:346. Other Tractarians similarly feared lay participation in a synod. Froude, for instance, criticized Richard Hooker for recommending lay inclusion, which he regarded as whiggish (Pereiro, 'Ethos', 187).
52 Pusey to Bishop William Skinner of Aberdeen, 15 May [1852], quoted in Liddon, *Life of Pusey*, 3:349.
53 Pusey, *Councils of the Church*, 170.
54 Ibid., 89–90. This according to St Cyprian. Nevertheless, even though Pusey placed all authority collectively into the hands of the bishops, he was often less than charitable to them individually. For example he told Newman that he had learned 'to lean on the church instead of bishops' (Pusey to Liddon, 2 July 1870, quoted in Liddon, *Life of Pusey*, 4:231).
55 Pusey, *Royal Supremacy*, 97–8.
56 Pusey, *Fendal v. Wilson*, 20.

57 Liddon, *Life of Pusey*, 4:4–8. Benjamin Jowett's appointment as professor of Greek in the University of Oxford in 1855 and the 1860 publication of *Essays and Reviews* further triggered his anxiety about church authority.
58 'The line of defence of the Church of England in which I was engaged, when the Gorham judgment and its consequent evils burst upon her, consisted in this, that however unsatisfactory many of our relations to the State are, the Church of England had not, by any concession wrung from her, abandoned any trust committed to her by God. Whatever evils there are and have been, the Church has often had to endure them before; and therefore the endurance of them by the Church of England, as the lesser of two evils, is no justification for the hard imputations of being "a State Church", "A creature of the State", which enemies or discontented sons have cast upon her' (Pusey, *Councils of the Church*, 1).
59 Pusey, *Royal Supremacy*, 5.
60 Ibid., 35–6. Pusey then presented a list of seventeen items that the emperor could do in matters regarding the church (ibid., 17–133).
61 Pusey, letter to *The Guardian*, 27 August 1850, quoted in Liddon, *Life of Pusey*, 3:273.
62 Pusey, *Royal Supremacy*, 160–61.
63 Pusey, *Councils of the Church*, 15. One should note the difference between Pusey's assertion and those claims made by Boniface VIII and other medieval popes.
64 Liddon, *Life of Pusey*, 1:281. Pusey's notion of the authority of the church to control its own affairs went beyond other writers. Liddon suggested that earlier tracts focused on the authority of the church, but Pusey's tract on fasting 'differs from its predecessors in the degree of emphasis which it lays on personal and experimental considerations'.
65 Ibid.
66 Nockles, *Oxford Movement*, 67–72.
67 Chadwick, *Spirit of the Oxford Movement*, 4.
68 For instance, Samuel Clarke's supposed Arianism provoked alarms similar to those that drove Newman to study the fourth-century Arians. Church defenders in both periods feared that the government had become infiltrated by those who held the church in low esteem.
69 See Straka, 'Final Phase of Divine Right Theory', 638–58.
70 Tony Claydon argues that William and his advisors, especially Bishop Gilbert Burnett, attempted to overcome these doubts through a policy of courtly reformation. They did not, however, succeed in convincing many of the more traditional churchmen. See Croydon, *William III*, 191–237.
71 Burnet, *History of His Own Times*, 2: 212–15.
72 'I hope none of you will be ever invited, by the specious Arts and Insinuations of Heresy, to depart from it', he continued (Atterbury, 'Of Living Peaceable', in *Sermons and Discourses*, 4:345–6).
73 Ibid., 4:346. '[R]evere her, I beseech you, but in proportion to her Worth; quit not her Communion for any Boasts to more *pure* and *spiritual* worship; not for the Amusements of more *glorious* and *Splendid* one; for the Pretences of these Men who make *reason* Their *God*, without taking in *Revelation* for Their Guide; or for the extravagant Follies and Freaks of *Enthusiasm*.'
74 Atterbury, *Letter to a Convocation-Man*, 2.
75 Ibid., 8. 'It will be said perhaps, that my Lords the *Bishops* have a standing Jurisdiction and Courts of their own, wherein they may proceed and judge of Heresie and censure Persons Guilty of it; that the *Universities* have the like Power within themselves; and

that His *Majesty* by Virtue of His Supremacy, hath Power, according to the Laws of the Lands, to oblige them to do their Duty in this, as well as in other Instances.'
76 Bennett, *Tory Crisis*, 48.
77 Atterbury, *Letter to a Convocation-Man*, 18–19.
78 Ibid., 17.
79 Ibid., 19.
80 Nor did Atterbury explicitly claim that the Church of England stood as part of universal church, along with the Roman Catholic and Orthodox churches.
81 Ibid.
82 Ibid.
83 Atterbury, *Rights, Powers, and Privileges*, 4–5.
84 Ibid., 6. '[T]he *Presbyters* therefore, having Voices in those lesser Synods, their Consent was also in the Definitions of the Greater presum'd and included.'
85 Atterbury, *Letter to a Convocation-Man*, 9.
86 Atterbury, *Rights, Powers, and Privileges*, 98.
87 Ibid., 1.
88 Ibid., 78.
89 Ibid.
90 Ibid., 22.
91 Atterbury, *Letter to a Convocation-Man*, 13. Atterbury also pointed out that calling a convocation was needed to overcome the claim of the 'papists' that 'our Religion is merely Parliamentary, and changeable at the Will of the Prince' (ibid., 15–16).
92 Ibid., 50.
93 Burnet, *History of His Own Times*, 2:283. 'The clergy hoped to recover many lost privileges by the help of his performances: they fanc'd they had the right to be part of the parliament; so they looked for his as their champion, and on most of the bishops, the betrayers of the rights of the Church: this was encouraged by the new ministry; they were displeased with the bishops for adhering to the old ministry; and they hop'd, by the terror of Convocation, to have forced them to apply to themselves for shelter' (ibid., 2:281).
94 Atterbury, *Case of the Schedule Stated*, 2. The archbishop established certain synodical days that either house of the convocation could meet and conduct business if they chose. Normally the lower house would not meet if the upper was not in session. Thus Atterbury's actions, while stickily permissible, did violate tradition and challenged the bishops' authority.
95 'Upon the Queen's accession to the crown, all those angry men, that had raised the flame in the Church, as they treated the memory of the late King with much indecent contempt, so they seemed very confident, that for the future all preferments should be distributed among them, (the Queen having superseded the commission for ecclesiastical preferments,) and they thought they were full of merit, and were so full of hopes' (Burnett, *History of His Own Times*, 2:316).
96 Atterbury, *Axe Laid to the Root*, 8.
97 Hoadly once joined Addison and Steele one 4th of November in drinking to the 'immortal memory of King William III'. Apparently they all got uproariously drunk (John Hoadly to Dr James Watson, 29 March 1772, BL Add. MSS. 32, 329).
98 White Kennett to n.n., 6 December 1705, BL Lans. MS. 1034, f. 4. Ironically, the Tories feared the danger for the church under the administration of the staunchest defender of the Church of England, Queen Anne.

99 Calamy, *Historical Account*, 2:371.
100 Hoadly, *Nature of the Kingdom*, 11–12. Hoadly used almost the exact same language in his rebuttal of Andrew Snape's attacks: the Church, he asserted, was '*a Kingdom not of this World*; that…*the Weapons of a Christian's warfare are not Carnal, but Spiritual*; that a *Spiritual Kingdom*, considered as Such, cannot in the Nature of Things be Supported by *Temporal Methods*; and that Worldly Grandeur, Great Power, and Riches, naturally tend to take off Men's Minds from *True Religion*, and the *True Motives* of it' (Hoadly, *Answer to Snapes*, 42).
101 Hoadly, *Nature of the Kingdom*, 17.
102 Ibid., 18–19. One who would try to overturn these strictures 'evidently destroys the *Rule* and *Authority* of *Jesus Christ*, as *King*, to set up any other *Authority* in *His Kingdom*, to which His Subjects are indispensably and absolutely obliged to Submit their Consciences, or their Conduct, in what is properly called Religion. There are *Some* Professed Christians, who contend openly for such an *Authority*, as indispensably obliges All around them to Unity of Profession; that is, to Profess even what They do not, what They cannot, believe to be true' (ibid., 27–8).
103 Bishop Nicholson to Archbishop Wake, 22 December 1716, BL Add. MSS. 6116, ff. 51–2. Gilbert Burnet, the bishop's son, made the same assertion that it would be especially disadvantageous for the Church of England to have to depend on an unbroken succession from the apostles for his authority to be valid. Therefore, Hoadly stood in good Whig company on this issue (Burnet, *Answer to Mr Law's Letter*, 11–24).
104 Hoadly, *Answer to Dr Snape*, 23. He asserted that 'the Human Engines…of Benedictions, Absolutions, Excommunications *have nothing to do with the Power or anger of God*' (Bishop Nicholson to Archbishop Wake, 22 December 1716, BL Add. MSS. 6116, ff. 51–2).
105 Archbishop Edward Synge to Archbishop Wake, 15 January 1717, BL Add. MSS. 6117, f. 124.
106 Hoadly, *Answer to Dr Snape*, 41.
107 Ibid.
108 Hoadly, *Common Rights of Subjects*, 70. This pamphlet answered one by William Sherlock.
109 Hoadly, *Answer to Dr Snape*, 32.
110 Calamy, *Historical Account*, 2:378.
111 Sherlock, *Answer to a Letter*, 17.
112 Ibid., 25–6; Cockburn, *Short and Impartial Review*, 33.
113 Hoadly, *Common Rights of Subjects*, 301–3.
114 Ibid., 303. Indeed, during the controversy over occasional conformity in 1704, he issued a pamphlet praising the bishops who voted against it, believing that the real danger from the church came from the Roman Catholics and not the Dissenters. In fact, he claimed, Roman Catholics supported the passage of the bill to help alienate Dissenters (Hoadly, *Letter to a Clergy-Man*, 5–6, 11–12). At about the same time he wrote *Persuasion to Lay-Conformity* encouraging dissenters to conform to the Church of England for practical reasons, such as the Christian duty for conformity despite blemishes on the church.
115 Bennett, *Tory Crisis*, 306.
116 Taylor, 'William Warburton', 271.
117 For instance, Taylor, 'William Warburton', 283. Yet as Nockles points out, both Keble and Newman deemed it necessary to criticize Warburton's theory of the church. Clearly they thought he had influence (Nockles, *Oxford Movement*, 70, 202n).

118 'We shall not seek to defend an Establishment and a Test by the Law of this or that State, or on the Principles of this or that Scheme of Religion, but on the great and unerring Maxims of the Law of Nature and Nations' ([Warburton], *Alliance between Church and State*, 6).

119 Even Tobias Smollett made reference to the book in *Humphry Clinker*, although perhaps not in the most flattering light (218). For a complete comparison of Warburton and his contemporaries, see Taylor, 'William Warburton'.

120 Nockles, *Oxford Movement*, 147–9. Nockles argues that from 1760 to 1833, an undercurrent of support for a high ecclesiology was apparent among both High Church and Evangelical writers, yet the discussion did not rise to the level of heated debate experienced in the reign of Anne or among the Tractarians.

121 Pusey heard a series of lectures on Warburton's *Divine Legation* and quoted his other writings on several occasions (Liddon, *Life of Pusey*, 1:62, 380).

122 [Warburton], *Alliance between Church and State*, 48.

123 Ibid., 49–50. He referred to Matthew Tindal's *The Rights of the Christian Church* (London, 1706) and Thomas Gordon and John Trenchard's *The Independent Whig* (London, 1721).

124 Ibid., 99. He did admit that 'tho' from *this* its Nature *alone*, it cannot be demonstrated to be of divine Original: Yet so much may be easily proved, that had it not *this Nature* it could not have *that Original*. For if Religion was designed (as no Religionist can doubt) not only to procure us all Happiness hereafter, but to assist the Promotion of it here, in the best Manner consistent with its Nature; and that this Assistance can be then only effectually imparted when the Religion is *national*, and, that it cannot be made *so* without *Union with the State*, and no reasonable Union can be but *between two real and independent Societies*; then it follows, that if that Religion which pretends to be the last consummate and most prefect Revelation of the Will of God to Man be not a Real Society and independent; its Pretences are false and deceitful.'

125 Ibid., 109. 'The Necessity of a National Religion was, till of late, one of the most uncontroverted Principles in Politics. The Practice of all Nations and the Opinions of all Writers concurred to make it so' (ibid., 33).

126 Ibid., 111. He did not hold the ancient church in the same high regard that Atterbury and Pusey did. He denied as some claimed that the church flourished in the primitive period before Constantine. He argued that the Christian Church was much stronger now with the Established Churches and Test Acts (ibid., 130–31).

127 Ibid., 6–9.

128 Ibid., 10–11.

129 Ibid., 12–13. He argued that not all religions can work effectively in this regard: 'The Papist makes the State a Creature of the Church; the Erastians makes the Church a Creature of the State; The Presbyterian would regulate the Exercise of the State's Power on Church Ideas; The Free-thinker, the Church, by Reason of State; And, to compleat the Farce, the Quaker abolishes the very being of the Church; and the Socinian suppresses the Office of Civil Magistrate.' He pointed out that even in the Church of England, there are significant differences of opinion (ibid., 20).

130 Ibid., 63.

131 Ibid., 53. A church without some outside support would be swallowed up or deviate from the truth, and therefore lose its ability to serve civil society. '*The State was induced to seek this Alliance as the necessary Means of preserving the Being of Religion amongst its Members*' (ibid., 55–7).

132 Ibid., 58. He claimed that veneration would spread over the secular laws as well.
133 Ibid., 59.
134 Ibid., 60–61.
135 Ibid., 67–82.
136 Ibid., 82.
137 Ibid., 83–9. The results are these: '*That no Ecclesiastic of the established Church can exercise his Function without the Magistrate's Approbation and Allowance*', but the conferring of the character of clergy would continue as it had before the alliance since the magistrate cannot make a clergy. 2. '*That no Convocation, Synod, or Church Assembly hath a Right to sit without the Permission and express License of the Magistrate; Nor when they do sit, by virtue of that Permission, to act in a judiciary Manner, without a new and particular License for that Purpose.*' 3. '*That no Member of the Established Church can be excommunicated or expelled the Society without the Consent and Allowance of the Magistrate.*'
138 For instance, Pusey criticized Hoadly in a letter to Keble and supported William Law in his disputes with Hoadly, at one point erroneously linking Hoadly with the Arians. See Pusey to Keble, 14 February 1842, in Liddon, *Life of Pusey*, 2:238, 279.
139 Pusey would have been unlikely to have cited Atterbury as an ally in his ecclesiological disputes, because Atterbury's Jacobite connections had ruined his reputation. That Pusey was unaware of Atterbury's writings and opinions, on the other hand, seems incompatible with his studies of church councils in general and English convocations in particular. He produced *The Councils of the Church from the Council of Jerusalem A.D. 51, to the Council of Constantinople A.D. 381* as part of a 1000-year study of councils in response to the calling of convocation in 1852 (Liddon, *Life of Pusey*, 3:341–54). Moreover, he knowledgeably referred to actions taken by various English convocations. See for instance ibid., 1:417; 3:210; 4:269. Finally he made several references to early eighteenth-century writers, including Hoadly, who would have discussed the issues Atterbury championed and undoubtedly Atterbury himself (for example, ibid., 2:115).

Chapter Six

PUSEY'S EUCHARISTIC DOCTRINE[1]

Carol Engelhardt Herringer

Introduction

The Victorian Church of England was riven by a heated conflict over the meaning and nature of the Eucharist. Traditionally Anglicans could believe either that the consecrated bread and wine were used as, but not changed into, Christ's body and blood – which was known as the virtualist view – or that Christ was present only to the worthy communicant, which was the receptionist view. The rather peaceful coexistence of these two views was challenged beginning in the late 1830s, when the Tractarian doctrine of the Real Presence introduced theological and liturgical strife into the established church.[2] This doctrine held that Christ was 'really' present in, or in conjunction with, the consecrated bread and wine. The doctrine quickly found adherents in the Scottish Episcopal Church as well; and by the 1860s ritualists had introduced liturgical practices associated with it – including bowing to the altar, kneeling during communion and even reserving the sacrament – at the parish level.[3]

This new doctrine was denounced by traditional Anglicans who were horrified by what seemed to them to be crypto–Roman Catholicism. While the preferred form of dispute was through the spoken and written word, some of the more excitable opponents of the doctrine disrupted church services, and clergymen who preached the doctrine were prosecuted in church and civil courts. The controversies were so fierce and so prolonged partly because, while they were about liturgy and doctrine, they were also about deeper issues of whether the Church of England was Catholic or Protestant and whether material objects could have a central role in Christian worship.

Edward Bouverie Pusey was one of the earliest and most prominent of the Victorian Anglicans who articulated the doctrine of the Real Presence. His first contribution to the *Tracts for the Times* was Tract 81 (1836),[4] a catena of authorities on the Eucharist as a sacrifice, a position that is related to the

Real Presence. He preached several major sermons before the University of Oxford on the Real Presence – *The Holy Eucharist a Comfort to the Penitent* (1843); *The Presence of Christ in the Holy Eucharist* (1853); *Will Ye Also Go Away* (1867) and *This is My Body* (1871) – and published a set of scholarly notes supporting *The Presence of Christ in the Holy Eucharist, The Doctrine of the Real Presence, as contained in the Fathers from the Death of S. John the Evangelist to the Fourth General Council* (1853). He also defended the doctrine of the Real Presence in public letters to Richard Bagot, the Bishop of Oxford (1839) and Charles James Blomfield, the Bishop of London (1851). In addition, the Real Presence was a consistent theme in many of his other sermons, including those on confession, and it was integrally connected (as it was for other like-minded Anglicans) to his views on the sacrament of baptism.[5]

Pusey was also at the forefront of the controversy over the Real Presence. He was the first to suffer formal disciplinary action, when in 1843 he was suspended from preaching before the University of Oxford for two years as a result of preaching a sermon entitled *The Holy Eucharist a Comfort to the Penitent*.[6] He also knew the toll the doctrine took on friendships; later in the 1840s his friendship with Walter Farquhar Hook suffered a break over the liturgical practices related to the Eucharist Pusey championed at St Saviour's, Leeds. He was a fervent supporter of other advocates of the Real Presence; for example, he wrote *The Real Presence of the Body and Blood of our Lord Jesus Christ the Doctrine of the English Church, with a Vindication of the Reception by the Wicked and of the Adoration of Our Lord Jesus Christ Truly Present* (1857) in aid of Archdeacon George Anthony Denison when he was brought up on charges of false teaching for his Eucharistic doctrine. (Denison's legal troubles lasted from 1854–57; he was finally acquitted on a technicality.) Pusey's friend Alexander Penrose Forbes, Bishop of Brechin, also supported Denison by publishing his 1857 charge to his clergy. The charge's defense of the doctrine of the Real Presence led to Forbes's being censured and admonished by the Episcopal Synod in 1860. Pusey's efforts in this case were private and ultimately futile and he did not attend Forbes' trial for fear of antagonizing the judges.[7] A decade after Forbes' charge was issued, the clergyman William James Early Bennett, who in 1850 had been forced to resign from St Paul's, Knightsbridge and St Barnabas', Pimlico, for his ritualistic practices, flirted with legal trouble when his *Plea for Toleration in the Church of England* (1867), a public letter to Pusey which dealt with the Real Presence in the Eucharist, led the Church Association to take legal action.[8]

In spite of Pusey's significance to the development of this doctrine that was central to what came to be called Anglo-Catholicism and contributed to battles within the Church of England over doctrine and ritual, no scholarly work has focused on his beliefs regarding the Real Presence. Henry Parry

Liddon's magisterial *Life of Pusey* does not detail the belief (although it does pay attention to the controversies it created) even though the primary focus is Pusey's role in the Oxford Movement and Anglo-Catholicism. While Alf Härdelin's *The Tractarian Understanding of the Eucharist* is a magnificent survey of Tractarian Eucharistic thought, including its place in Anglican theology, it pays more attention to John Henry Newman, Richard Hurrell Froude, John Keble, and Robert Isaac Wilberforce than to Pusey. More recent treatments of Pusey's life and thought, including the collection of essays in *Pusey Rediscovered*, David Forrester's *Young Doctor Pusey: A Study in Development* and Owen F. Cummings' survey of Eucharistic thought in the catholic (broadly defined) tradition, *Eucharistic Doctors: A Theological History*, also pay little or no attention to Pusey's Eucharistic beliefs.

However, we cannot understand Pusey without understanding the doctrine of the Real Presence and the controversies it generated. The Eucharist was central to Pusey's theology and the doctrine of the Real Presence was key to his belief that the Church of England was one branch of the universal Catholic church. Pusey's Eucharistic beliefs shaped how he understood the world, his place in it and the continuing intervention of the divine. Those who seek to understand Pusey's relationship to the church, the material world in which he lived and most significantly to his God (for Pusey's deeply personal relationship with the Trinity was mediated in many ways by the sacrament of the Eucharist) must understand this doctrine. Recapturing Pusey's Eucharistic theology may also change our understanding of the man. Pusey's reputation then as now was that he was an austere, even rigid, man. This reputation has only been enhanced by the contrast with his close friends Keble and Newman. However, this reputation is not entirely fair to Pusey, for he did have passions and affections. Certainly he loved his wife and family.[9] He had spiritual passions as well, and the Trinity was clearly the centre of his life. These spiritual passions are revealed by examining his Eucharistic beliefs.

The Doctrine and Its Discontents

Pusey's doctrine of the Real Presence can be described very simply. It held that Jesus was really but not carnally or corporally present in or in conjunction with the consecrated bread and wine.[10] As Pusey stated in the introduction to his controversial sermon, *The Holy Eucharist a Comfort to the Penitent*, 'I believe the consecrated elements to become, by virtue of His consecrating Words, truly and really, yet spiritually and in an ineffable way, His Body and Blood.'[11] Near the end of his life, he offered a similar explanation: 'God consecrates by us His priests mere elements of the world to be sacramentally, spiritually, supernaturally, His Body and Blood.'[12] Pusey always insisted that Christ's presence was not physical: 'There is no physical union of the Body and Blood of Christ with the bread and wine. Yet where the consecrated bread is, there, sacramentally, is the Body of Christ; where the consecrated wine is, there[,] sacramentally, is the Blood of Christ.'[13] For Pusey, this was the essence of the Real Presence: that Christ was truly present, although not in any way that the senses could apprehend. The doctrine was later also called the Real Objective Presence, to affirm that Christ's presence was not subjective. Pusey explained the addition of the word 'Objective' thus: 'Finding that the words "Real Presence" were often understood of what is in fact a "Real Absence", we added the word "Objective", not as wishing to obtrude on others a term of modern philosophy, but to express that the Life-giving Body, the res sacramenti, is, by virtue of the consecration, present without us, to be received by us.'[14]

In asserting the Real Presence Pusey denied all other Eucharistic beliefs, including transubstantiation, consubstantiation and the belief that the Lord's Supper was a mere memorial.[15] He rejected these 'carnal, sensual thoughts'[16] and attributed them to 'one source, viz. that man would understand the mysteries of God; i.e. he would have the mystery no longer a mystery; he would know "*how*" the things of God are, and set aside, more or less disrespectfully, what he cannot understand'.[17] Not surprisingly, he was more condemnatory towards Zurich and Geneva than towards Rome. While he thought that transubstantiation was 'carnal' and 'presumptuous'[18] (and possibly responsible for 'the miserable state of Roman Catholic countries in general'[19]), he condemned Zwingli and Calvin for having explained away Christ's presence and thereby destroying the sacrament.[20] In Pusey's view the doctrine of the Real Presence followed a *via media* between the 'errors' of Roman Catholicism and those of what Pusey called 'ultra-Protestantism'.[21] It differed from transubstantiation in that there was no change to the consecrated elements, and it differed from Protestant views in that Christ was present to the worthy and unworthy alike, during as well as after the church service.

The apparent simplicity of the doctrine notwithstanding, it was difficult to explain how Christ could be 'really' present in a spiritual way. Pusey was forced to go to some lengths to explain that what was real was not necessarily what was apparent to the senses, or natural, as he did in his 1853 sermon.

> The Presence…has been termed Sacramental, supernatural, mystical, ineffable, as opposed *not* to what is real, but to what is natural… We know not the manner of His Presence, save that it is not according to the natural Presence of our Lord's Human Flesh, which is at the Right Hand of God; and therefore it is called Sacramental. But it is a Presence without us, not within us only; a Presence by virtue of our Lord's words, although to us it becomes a saving Presence, received to our salvation,

through our faith. It is not a Presence simply in the soul of the receiver, as 'Christ dwells in our hearts by faith'; or as, in acts of Spiritual, apart from Sacramental, Communion, we, by our longings, invite Him into our souls... For He is truly present, for us truly to receive Him to the salvation of our souls, if they be prepared by repentance, faith, love, through the cleansing of His Spirit, for His Coming.[22]

In its certainty that Christ was 'truly present' and 'not…simply in the soul of the receiver', this formulation was clearly a rejection of the traditional Anglican theories of the Eucharist described above, for it definitively linked Christ's presence to the consecrated bread and wine. Both traditional theories clearly demarcated the material objects of bread and wine from Christ's body, a demarcation which the doctrine of the Real Presence erased. As will be seen, the doctrine's challenge to traditional Anglican beliefs helped to inspire widespread anger against Pusey for preaching the doctrine.

To explain how the bread and wine could become Christ's body and blood, Pusey and other supporters of the Real Presence posited that Christ had a spiritual body, which was the spiritual manifestation of his resurrected and ascended body, which was in heaven.[23] However, they did not attempt to explain how the presence was achieved other than stating the necessity of the priest's repetition of the words of institution.[24] Beyond that, Pusey said that how Christ was present was beyond human knowledge: 'He Who is God and Man, is with us as God only, except that, in some way known to Himself, He, while abiding in heaven in His natural mode of being, causes His Body sacramentally to be with us.'[25] In fact, he actively cautioned against trying to understand how Christ was present, warning that 'It *is* a temptation, to require too precise theories, to desire to be able to state clearly that which is beyond all understanding.'[26] Pusey consistently refused even to speculate on how the presence was obtained; he was satisfied believing that it was there. And because it was there, the quotidian objects of bread and wine were changed. The clearest explanation Pusey could give was to say that

> The Body and Blood of Christ are not present there, after the manner of a body. Yet it would not be true to say, 'This is *mere* bread'; for this would be to deny the Real Presence; and so the fathers deny, that it is any longer '*mere* bread'. But it is true to say, 'This is the Body of Christ'. For this does not deny that it is bread as to its earthly substance; but speaks of it, as to its heavenly.[27]

In a British culture that was both anti–Roman Catholic and unaccustomed to thinking that inanimate objects could have an unseen reality, the proposition that the consecrated bread and wine were really but not tangibly also some other things was difficult for many Anglicans to grasp. Many simply rejected the doctrine, believing that, as an anonymous clergyman stated, 'the "real presence" of Christ is not *in the elements* either before or after consecration, but that what the priest delivers to the communicants is bread and wine *only* in their simple and natural substances, neither changed into, nor compounded with any thing else'.[28] Some of Pusey's opponents who left a written record of their objections to the doctrine were parish clergymen, rather than Oxbridge scholars or members of the Anglican hierarchy, which suggests a strong level of grass-roots opposition to the doctrine.

While Pusey's determined opponent the anti-Tractarian and anti-ritualist John Harrison, Vicar of Fenwick, called the Real Presence 'an unnatural mode of presence of human invention',[29] many of Pusey's Anglican opponents assumed that the Real Presence was actually consubstantiation[30] or transubstantiation.[31] Unwilling or unable to accept the concept of a spiritual body,[32] they often accused the Tractarians of believing that Jesus' body was present in the consecrated bread,[33] the consequence of which must be that Christ was being eaten.[34] Thus they could dismiss the Real Presence as either a pagan doctrine, in which a material object was worshipped,[35] or as a ridiculous one, as Harrison did when he questioned 'how can Christ's real body and blood be present in the consecrated elements, so present in them in all parts of the world, and so present in each infinitesimal part of the elements that a communicant, whether saint or sinner, receives in the smallest portion of bread a whole Christ, body, soul, and divinity, and the same in each drop of wine'.[36]

These reactions are significant because they help show why Pusey became the focus of popular animosity during his lifetime. Even those who were uninterested in Eucharistic theology could absorb the message that Pusey and his ilk were promoting a Roman Catholic doctrine, which in popular culture meant a doctrine that was foreign, pagan, and hostile towards British liberty.[37] More subtly, these reactions also reveal a discomfort with the doctrine's positing a new way of thinking about the relationship between the material and the spiritual, which suggested that material objects could be the means of transmission of a spiritual reality.

Pusey's Defense of the Real Presence

Pusey was too conservative to advocate a doctrine he thought was new. He, like other supporters of the Real Presence, consistently asserted that the doctrine was a traditional one, that it had been instituted by Jesus at the Last Supper, held by the early church and adopted by the Church of England from its earliest origins. As with many Victorian Anglicans, his version of history skipped over the Middle Ages in order to avoid the corruption attributed to the medieval church and transubstantiation.[38]

Supporters of the Real Presence relied on a literal interpretation of Jesus's words of institution at the Last Supper – 'This is My Body'; 'This is My Blood'[39] – as the strongest evidence for the doctrine.[40] Pusey wrote *The Real Presence of the Body and Blood of Our Lord Jesus Christ* 'to vindicate the literal interpretation of our Blessed Lord's words, "This is My Body"',[41] after having warned a few years earlier that 'Reverence for the word of God requires, that we should not tamper with its apparent meaning, on any preconceived notions of our own.'[42] In support of this literal interpretation, he cited the use of the same phrases in the synoptic Gospels,[43] phrases that were emphasized and confirmed by Paul.[44] While Pusey and other supporters of the Real Presence did acknowledge that elsewhere Jesus had spoken metaphorically – as when he compared himself to the vine, the door, the resurrection and the good shepherd[45] – they said it was clear when he meant his words to be taken metaphorically and when they were to be taken literally. For example, Pusey said that the repetition of Jesus' words of institution in the Gospels of Matthew, Mark and Luke meant that they were to be taken literally, but he warned that taking Scriptural passages like 'the Word was made Flesh' literally could lead to heresy.[46] Pusey believed that Jesus had prepared his followers to take his words of institution literally by his statements likening his flesh to bread which must be eaten to secure eternal life.[47] The sheer repetition of this concept, he said, was evidence that 'our Lord, with unwearied patience, bringeth this one truth before us in so many forms', and so one would realize that 'He means to inculcate, that life in Him is His chief gift in His Sacrament, and to make a reverent longing for it an incentive to our faith.'[48] One senses here Pusey's own weariness in constantly defending a belief he thought should be self-evident.

The bulk of the academic evidence for the belief came in Pusey's university sermons, rather than his parochial ones. In keeping with the Tractarian desire to trace a Catholic Church of England back to the patristic period, Pusey defended his Eucharistic beliefs as being those of the church fathers, including Tertullian, Origen, St Cyprian, St Firmilian, Eusebius, St Irenaeus, St John Chrysostom, Theodoret, Facundus, Ephrem of Antioch, St Athanasius, Justin Martyr, St Cyril, St Basil, St Gregory of Nazianzum, St Macarius, Eusebius, Eusthathius and St Augustine.[49] The multiplicity of these authorities, Pusey asserted, revealed that the Real Presence was supported by 'the uniform teaching of the Fathers of every Church and of every variety of mind, in every sort of writing, Epistles, Homilies, Treatises, &c.'[50] This fact was, he said, known even to the ignorant: 'This doctrine of the Real Presence all who know ever so little of the ancient Fathers and Councils, know to have been taught from the first.'[51]

Undaunted by the reality that there was no patristic consensus about the nature of the Eucharist,[52] Pusey generously offered quotations from the fathers to support his contention that they shared his belief in the Real Presence. St Cyprian, St Augustine, St Jerome, St Ambrose, St Athanasius, Eusebius and Theodoret all spoke, he said, of 'our being inebriated by the Blood of our Lord';[53] while St Cyril believed that faithful communicants 'hav[e] received into ourselves, bodily and spiritually, Him who is by Nature and truly the Son'.[54] When the fathers did not exactly support the Real Presence he made excuses; for example, he said that they understood that the consecrated bread and wine had both an inner and an outer reality, and so they could speak of 'bread' and 'wine' when they meant 'Body' and 'Blood'.[55] The paucity of relevant quotations forced Pusey to use the fathers in support of related topics, as when Origen and St Cyril were brought in to support using the word 'propitiation' in reference to the Eucharist.[56] Such usage gave the doctrine of the Real Presence the appearance of having more patristic support than Pusey was able to muster. Another tactic for inflating the amount of patristic support was to string quotations together with little or no analysis.[57] Pusey could also exploit the fact that patristic works on the Eucharist were written in a poetic rather than a theologically precise style by noting that the fathers' use of figurative speech was simply their style, and then concluding that it did not argue against their acceptance of the Real Presence.[58] Thus he could calmly conclude that 'This doctrine [was] so uniformly attested [to] by Christian antiquity'.[59]

Pusey's most difficult and important task was to defend his Eucharistic beliefs as being traditionally Anglican. He was convinced that they were, and he repeatedly expressed surprise that they should be controversial. As he said in his 1842 *Letter* to William Howley, Archbishop of Canterbury, the Tractarians 'have revived nothing in common but the acknowledged practices of our Church'.[60] He always insisted, somewhat disingenuously, that in his public works he was 'maintaining what I believed, and do now equally believe, to be a doctrinal statement of the Church of England'.[61] It was for this reason, he said, that he had 'not set about proving my agreement with the other formularies of our Church, because I did not imagine the possibility of any disagreement. I did not defend, what I did not imagine to be open to attack'.[62] Repeated assertions by his opponents that his premise was wrong did not change his mind that, as he assured Bishop Blomfield, 'I believe simply the teaching of our Church, in the Catechism, the Articles, and the Eucharistic Service.'[63]

Pusey often invoked the historic phrase used by the Church of England (and adopted from the Roman Catholic liturgy) 'under the form of bread and wine', which he connected to Jesus' words of institution: 'since our Lord says, "This is My Body", "This is My Blood", the Church of England believes that "under the form of Bread and Wine", so consecrated, we "receive the

Body and Blood of our Saviour Christ"'.[64] He traced this phrase back to the establishment of the Church of England, arguing that 'the phrase "under the form of bread and wine" came into our Theology in the time of Henry VIII, being ultimately derived from the Confession of Augsburg',[65] which he claimed upheld the theory of the Real Presence.[66] Its inclusion in the *Book of Homilies*, both in 1547 and when the homilies were reprinted in 1560 after the accession of Elizabeth I, he cited as proof that the Church of England had, even during the Tudors' religious changes, believed in the Real Presence.[67] He also argued that the care the rubrics took with the consecrated bread and wine, including covering the remains with a linen cloth reminiscent of Jesus' shroud, 'shews that the Church of England believes an abiding objective Presence of the Body and Blood of Christ in the elements, apart from the act of reception'.[68]

The Articles were potentially a bigger obstacle, although Pusey reassured himself that Articles 25, 27 and 28 'have this in common; that they begin by rejecting the Zwinglian heresy, whether as to the theory of Sacraments generally, or as to the two great Sacraments specially'.[69] The specifics of Articles 28 and 29, which are the two that deal most directly with the Eucharist, were more daunting to those who supported the Real Presence, but Pusey valiantly rose to the challenge.

Article 28, 'Of the Lord's Supper', repudiated transubstantiation but also opposed the belief that Christ was 'really' present in stating that faith was necessary to receive Christ in the Eucharist: 'insomuch that to such as rightly, worthily and with faith, receive the same, the Bread which we break is a partaking of the Body of Christ; and likewise the Cup of Blessing is a partaking of the Blood of Christ'. This Article further affirmed the role of the communicant's faith and seemed to deny any local or 'real' presence when it stated that 'The Body of Christ is given, taken and eaten, in the Supper, only after an heavenly and spiritual manner. And the mean whereby the Body of Christ is received and eaten in the Supper, is Faith.'[70]

However, relying on a loose interpretation of words, Pusey read the Article as supporting the Real Presence. This is clear in his *Letter to the Bishop of London*, in which he offers his interpretation of Article 28 in the bracketed phrases.

> I believe that 'the Body of Christ is given, taken, and eaten', [given by the Priest and taken by the people] 'only after a spiritual and heavenly manner' [i.e, not in any carnal, or physical, or earthly manner, but spiritually, sacramentally, truly, and ineffably]. And I believe that 'the means whereby the Body of Christ is received and eaten in the Supper is Faith'. For assuredly Faith only perceives, faith only receives His Presence, or Himself.[71]

Pusey began by reiterating the words of the Article before moving on to reinterpret the words so as to change the Article's meaning. In effect, he rewrote the Article. He first emphasized the physical transfer of the bread from priest to communicant, in order to reassure the bishop that he was merely confirming and amplifying the words of the Article. Having lulled his reader into believing that he was merely meditating on the words of the Article, he then reinterpreted the second phrase – 'only after a spiritual and heavenly manner' – by juxtaposing 'spiritual and heavenly' with 'carnal, or physical, or earthly'. Having opposed 'spiritual and heavenly' to 'carnal, or physical, or earthly', he could then align 'spiritual' with 'sacramentally, truly, and ineffably' so that the Article affirmed that Christ was 'truly, and ineffably' present.

Having proven (to his own satisfaction, at least), that the Article confirmed a spiritual presence that aligned with the 'real' presence of the Tractarian doctrine and opposed a carnal presence, Pusey could conclude that the reference to faith in the next sentence was to the faith of the individual recipient that allowed him to perceive Christ. This assertion, of course, was a rejection of the traditional Anglican belief that the reception of Christ was spiritual only. Essentially, Pusey found a way around Article 28's stipulation that faith was necessary to receive Christ by opining that faith was necessary to *know* that one was receiving Christ, so that unworthy receivers would receive but not know that they were receiving the spiritual body and blood of Christ.

The cumulative effect of these reinterpretations was to make the Article reaffirm the Tractarian doctrine of the Real Presence. Elsewhere he referred to recently discovered documents by Bishop Edmund Guest (also Gheast), Bishop of Rochester, to bolster this interpretation; Pusey argued that 'the framer of the Article himself…intended by these words, "after a spiritual and heavenly manner", "only to exclude the grossness and sensibleness in the receiving of Christ's Body"'.[72]

Article 29, 'Of the wicked, which eat not the Body of Christ in the Lord's Supper', likewise is at odds with the view integral to the Real Presence that all, worthy and unworthy alike, received Christ in the Eucharist. However, Pusey redefined 'partaker' so that it meant one who was in unity with Christ, leaving unworthy communicants to receive Christ but none of the benefits.[73] He argued that 'It [Article 29] does not say, that the wicked "cannot be partakers *of the Body and Blood of Christ*". It says "are in no wise *partakers of Christ*". Plainly, the wicked and such as be void of a lively faith, so long as they remain such, are not, and cannot be, "partakers of Christ"'.[74] Thus he could argue that they received Christ, but to their damnation:

> the body of the Article denies, that 'the wicked, though they do carnally and visibly press with their teeth the Sacrament of the Body and Blood

of Christ', are 'partakers of Christ'; the heading denies, in the Scriptural sense of the words, that [']they so eat the Body of Christ, as to dwell in Christ'. He who does not *so* eat the Flesh of Christ and drink His Blood, that he should dwell in Christ and Christ in him, does not eat or drink them at all, *for any purpose or effect for which Christ gave them*. And so God, in Holy Scripture, frequently speaks of that which is not done according to His will, as if it had not been done at all.[75]

Here again Pusey rewrote the Article, and thus revised Anglican tradition. His redefinition of the word 'partaker' allowed him to ignore the rather clear language of the Article and convince himself that the Article confirmed a central proposition of the Real Presence, which was that Christ was present regardless of the communicant's faith.

Pusey's reinterpretation of these two Articles so that they supported his Eucharistic beliefs was breathtaking in its creativity, especially for one who had argued that Jesus' words of institution should be taken literally.[76] It also raises the troubling question of whether he acted cynically or sincerely. Given the centrality of the Real Presence to his life, it seems logical that he was sincere, for he would not want to base his faith on a lie. Yet the question remains whether he was at all troubled by the lengths he needed to go to convince himself that while 'in the Liturgy, Catechism, Articles and Homilies, there are attestations to the Real objective Presence, there is not one word to contradict it'.[77] It is impossible to answer this question, which lingers like a shadow across Pusey's reputation as a churchman and a theologian.

Pusey also invoked Anglican divines in support of the doctrine of the Real Presence. In the preface to the published version of *The Holy Eucharist a Comfort to the Penitent* he asserted, 'My own views were cast (so to speak) in the mould of the minds of Bishop Andrews and Archbishop Bramhall, which I regarded as the type of the teaching of our Church. From them originally, and with them, I learnt to receive in their literal sense, our Blessed Lord's solemn words, "This is My Body"'.[78] However, he offered surprisingly few direct quotations from the divines, few of whom were as obliging as Lancelot Andrewes, Bishop of Winchester, who urged that '*Christ Himself, the Substance of the Sacrament*, in and with the Sacrament; out of and without the Sacrament, wheresoever He is, is to be adored.'[79] More often he relied on divines who agreed with him on issues related to the Real Presence. Because a frequent charge against the Real Presence was that it implied multiple sacrifices by Christ, he cited Anglicans from the sixteenth and seventeenth centuries, including John Overall, Bishop of Norwich; Andrewes; John Bramhall, Archbishop of Armagh; and Matthew Scrivener as agreeing with him that there was only one sacrifice.[80] This was, in fact, a non-controversial position; no Anglican believed that Christ had made the sacrifice more than once. This proliferation of quotations gave the appearance that the doctrine of the Real Presence was advocated by some of the most famous Anglican divines.

Pusey's assertion that this was a traditional doctrine was greeted with outrage by many Anglicans. John Milner, Chaplain in Ordinary to the Duke of Edinburgh, spoke for many when he declared that 'that *not one single authority quoted supports his view* [of the Eucharist]'.[81] Many rejected Pusey's claim to understand Jesus' words of institution at the Last Supper, asserting that the Gospel's 'Facts, facts which can be understood in every age',[82] were on their side. Harrison, who in several works strenuously rejected the Tractarian Eucharistic doctrine articulated by Pusey, argued that the word 'is' should not be taken literally, as Christ had not yet died when he said the words of institution.[83] If the words were taken literally, then 'is' would refer to that specific piece of bread in Jesus' hand[84] and that specific cup or its contents,[85] or it would mean that Jesus' suffering and death on the cross were to be constantly re-enacted,[86] which would have the grave consequence of 'entirely overthrow[ing] the evidence for miracles, and by necessary consequence the Christian religion'.[87] Claude Bosanquet, Vicar of Christ Church, Folkestone, insisted that the word 'is' should be interpreted as 'signifies'[88] because the apostles would have been 'troubled' if they thought Jesus meant them to take the words of institution literally.[89] Fundamentally, though, they could not imagine how a body could be anything but a material body. As Harrison said, 'Our blessed Lord had but one body, and when He uttered the simple words, "This is my body", even if we suppose He meant His real body, and not a memorial of it, He could not mean any indefinite number of bodies; but how the bread could be a body at all, much less an indefinite number of bodies, we are utterly at a loss to conceive.'[90]

Pusey's reliance on the fathers fared equally poorly. In one of the few non-Anglican intrusions into the debate, the Congregationalist minister Henry J. Bevis dismissed references to the fathers on the grounds that they often disagreed with each other and the pagan past of some of them meant that they were in error;[91] while Harrison accused Pusey of misinterpreting the fathers, who at times were unreliable in their interpretation of Scripture[92] and other times contradicted Pusey's assertions:[93] 'He affixes his own meaning to the sacramental language of the Fathers, and assumes that they teach his doctrine.'[94]

Finally, Pusey's opponents – one of whom tagged Pusey as 'the champion of (as I think) the opposers of our Church's doctrine'[95] – agreed that, as Harrison said, 'Dr Pusey's doctrines on the Holy Eucharist can be proved to be contrary to the doctrine of the Church of England.'[96] As an anonymous clergyman stated, the Articles were 'entirely opposed to any notion of

Christ's being present in or with the elements, and evidently agrees with the doctrine of the real intercommunion of the believer with his Lord, in his own institution, not externally but internally, not by receiving Him in or through or with or by the elements, but *by faith* after a heavenly and spiritual manner'.[97] Pusey's opponents noted that Articles 28[98] and 29,[99] as well as the communion exhortation,[100] declared that the faith of the recipient was necessary to receive Christ. Milner discounted Pusey's use of Bishop Geste's letter, saying that 'the Presence he [Geste] meant to assert in the letter was an exclusively spiritual Presence; and…he intended to exclude any localised Presence, whether of Christ's natural or of His glorified Body'.[101] Thus, he concluded smugly, 'Bishop Geste, explained by himself, will turn out to be a most unruly witness in the hands of the Ritualists.'[102] Finally, against Pusey's invocation, however vague, of the divines, one young anonymous clergyman cited Whitby, Lightfoot, Hammond, Turton, Grotius 'and the host of able divines who have entirely overthrown the literal and Romish interpretations'[103] of the Eucharist. William Goode, rector of St Margaret Lothbury, London, and the author of several pamphlets against Pusey's doctrine of the Real Presence, pointed out that it was inaccurate to quote any divines who used the term 'Real Presence', because they did not use it in the same sense that it was used currently,[104] while Harrison said that, contrary to Pusey's interpretation, Andrewes did not take 'this is my body' literally.[105]

Pusey's Motivations

Pusey consistently defended the doctrine as being both Scriptural and traditional and rejected any charge that it derived from any erroneous interpretation on his part.[106] However, a close reading of his sermons and other writings suggests that he had more personal, and perhaps not wholly conscious, reasons for believing in the Real Presence. One motivation was connected to his priestly vocation: because the doctrine emphasized a sacramental view of the world, it allowed him to define the Church of England as a catholic church. On a more intimate personal level, the doctrine addressed his powerful sense of sin, by providing him with both a motive for disciplining the body and a source of joy to balance the despair caused by his sinfulness. This multiplicity of motivations helps to explain why he advocated the doctrine so firmly and for so long.

Privately and publicly, Pusey often used the doctrine to posit a solely catholic identity for the Church of England. If the doctrine of the Real Presence could be traced from the New Testament and the early church to the foundation of the Church of England, then the established church was catholic and not Protestant. This was of course a key argument of Tractarians, who were intent on proving a catholic identity for the established church. Using tradition as well as Scripture to argue for the Real Presence was also a way to argue for the catholic identity of the Church of England, for Protestants professed a reliance on Scripture alone, whereas Catholics also invoked tradition.

Catholicism emphasizes mystery as well as tradition, and the doctrine also allowed Pusey to defend the sense of mystery in religion. He frequently referred to the Eucharist with terms such as 'this holy mystery' and 'the all-holy Mysteries'.[107] As has been shown, he often denied human ability to understand how Christ was present in the Eucharist. Adamantly refusing to explain how Christ was present in the Eucharist was not only good sense, as Anglican tradition had no explanation, but also allowed him to insist on the mysterious power of God and the limits of human reason. Thus he insisted that 'communion with God is evidently supernatural, produced by an influence of God above the order of nature'.[108] In a world that was turning from religious to scientific explanations for events, and where Higher Criticism was gaining influence in Biblical scholarship, a reliance on divine mystery could allow priests like Pusey – who were the ones who facilitated the transformation of the bread and wine – to assert the continued validity of religion. Supporters of the doctrine of the Real Presence never articulated this as a motivation; it was likely an unconscious motivation, and in any event to acknowledge secular influences would undermine the doctrine. However, their frequent reminders that the means of Christ's presence was a mystery suggest a desire to assert their own significance as priests and Biblical scholars who, if they could not explain the mystery, could at least position themselves as best able to recognize it.[109]

This emphasis on the mystery and tradition of the Eucharist was not, however, merely a way for Pusey to increase his power and that of his fellow priests. Like other Tractarians he valued the sacraments over preaching, for he believed the sacraments were the most direct means of communicating God's grace; that they were 'unlike every thing [sic] else even in the intense fullness of the Christian life'[110] because they 'are part of the glories of the Incarnation of the Son of God... They are gifts of "God manifest in the flesh".'[111] He was even willing to believe that there were sacraments beyond the two officially recognized in the Church of England, although not with the same status as baptism and the Eucharist.[112] Thus it is not surprising that he, like other Tractarians, advocated holding more frequent – weekly and even daily – communion services.[113] As Pusey described it, receiving communion was almost a physical means of connection with Christ, and therefore more satisfying than other forms of worship, such as prayer.[114] His communion sermons frequently spoke of the union between the worshipper and the divine: 'The Holy Eucharist is plainly the closest union of man with God.'[115] He reminded communicants that '*in* faithful Christians God the Father, God the

Son, and God the Holy Ghost dwell; they are said to be thus *inhabited* by the Three Persons of the Blessed Trinity'.[116] Therefore, one should approach the communion table 'as if thou wert coming to thy Saviour's side'.[117]

The close relationship between the worshipper and the divine engendered by communion was, Pusey assured many congregations, a source of great joy.[118] In a sermon preached at Christ Church Cathedral, Pusey described Christ as a stalwart and close companion who could provide strength for the fight and joy for the future. He urged the Oxford undergraduates to remember that Christ was their constant companion.

> Christ redeems us not, my younger brethren, to part with us. He cometh not to us, to part from us; He cometh to abide with us, if we will have Him. He will come to us in holiness, righteousness, sanctification, redemption, if we will long for Him, – if in faith and charity we will receive Him. He will cleanse your dross, slake your feverishness, chase away foul thoughts, re-create your decay, drive off Satan, gather you up into Himself. He will strengthen you against temptation, lift you up above those miserable, maddening, seducing pleasures of sense, and give you a foretaste of heavenly sweetness, of blissful calm, of spiritual joy, of transporting love, of unearthly delight, in His own ever-blessed, ever-blessing, Presence. Martyrs of old went to their last conflict 'fortified', S. Cyprian says, 'with the protection of the Body and Blood of Christ'. By His Body and Blood will Christ prepare *you* for *your* conflict. Satan stands in awe of you.[119]

Christ here is the faithful lover who will fortify the communicant in the struggle against evil and bring him certain joy. As Pusey describes it, Christ's presence is almost palpable; he is there to support the communicant and to inspire him with the heavenly bliss that awaits. Here Pusey must have been drawing on his own experience of Christ in his prayer life.

The many losses Pusey suffered made this joy all the more necessary to him. His younger brother Henry had died in 1826; more devastatingly, his wife, Maria, died in 1839, and an infant daughter had predeceased her. Liddon notes that Maria's death was a turning point for Pusey: 'This sad crisis in his life could not but influence also his preaching. From this time forward the nothingness of this world, the disciplinary value as well as the atoning power of the Cross, the awfulness and reality of the Day of Judgment, assume a new prominence in his sermons.'[120] Other deaths followed: his favourite child, Lucy, died in 1844, and in the 1850s he lost three people close to him – first his sister-in-law, Lady Emily, in 1854 (whose death was especially hard on Pusey); her husband, Philip Pusey, died the following year; and in 1858 his adored mother, Lady Pusey, died. And of course he lost his great friend and fellow leader of the Oxford Movement when Newman converted to Roman Catholicism in 1845. Although they maintained a correspondence, the two friends were never as intimate as they had been previously. All these losses make it unsurprising that Pusey sought a loving, comforting presence that he could not lose.

The centrality of the Eucharist also helped Pusey mitigate his own sense of sinfulness. Like many Victorian Christians, he saw sin as an ever-present danger; he once warned a congregation that 'there are many paths to hell; one only, and that a narrow one, to Heaven'.[121] For those who had sinned, he advocated auricular confession (which was a very controversial practice in the Victorian Church of England).[122] He also hoped that 'more frequent communion should involve a change of life, more collectedness in God, more retirement, at times from society, deeper consciousness of His Presence, more sacredness in our ordinary actions whom He so vouchsafeth to hallow, greater love for His Passion which we celebrate, and carrying it about, in strictness of self-rule and self-discipline, and self-denying love'.[123]

Even in a culture that was focused on human sinfulness, especially in comparison to attitudes in the preceding and following centuries, Pusey was fixated to an unhealthy extent on his own sins, to the point of seeing tragedies and setbacks as punishments for specific sins. He attributed the deaths of his wife and daughter to his own sinfulness,[124] and he had the church of St Saviour's, Leeds, built as penance for the sins he believed caused his wife's death. When he returned to the pulpit for the first time after his 1843 suspension, he called the suspension a time in which God had chosen for him to be cleansed for his '"secret faults," which He knoweth'.[125] With such a stern view of himself – one which drew disapproval from Keble and Newman[126] – Pusey would, not surprisingly, seek for hope of forgiveness and salvation in the Eucharist.

To this point, there is nothing very surprising about Pusey's motivations for defending the Real Presence, a doctrine which brought him closer to God and allowed him to redefine the Church of England solely as a Catholic institution. However, the Eucharist also figured in his compulsions about the body, a compulsion that was notable even among Victorian Christians. Pusey was especially concerned with bodily sins, and his private life shows a desire to tame bodily desires. He wore a hair shirt and would have practiced self-flagellation if his health had permitted;[127] he restricted the highest order of the Society of the Holy Cross (SSC) to celibates; he fasted and ordered his wife and children to fast, even when they were ill.[128] He also, in the 1830s, required his wife to sell her jewellery; she donated the proceeds to charity.

The doctrine of the Real Presence gave Pusey another reason to justify his desire for physical chastisement. Because participating in the Eucharist was a bodily act – the communicant ate and drank, and knelt during the consecration and upon receiving – Pusey wanted to ensure that the body would be undefiled by actual sin.[129] He warned an Oxford congregation that, because Christ came to the communicant's body, foul language could not emit from the body.

> He comes to dwell in you. Ye will not then utter, with lips which belong to Christ, words of profaneness, or of refined or coarse indecency, which ye would be shocked to utter in your parent's presence... Ye are not your own; ye are joined to Christ; ye will not profane what is not yours, but Christ's.[130]

In retrospect, we who live in a culture that condones public coarseness may smile at Pusey's optimism, given the realities of undergraduate life. However, Pusey's advocacy of clean language was just one aspect of his quest for bodily purity. This is clear in his warning to undergraduates against masturbating before receiving the Eucharist.

> As you would reverence the Holy Sepulchre, so and yet more reverence yourselves, your own bodies, which, our Church says, have been 'made clean by His Body, and washed with His most Precious Blood'. Reverence, beforehand, your souls and bodies. If ye believe Christ and His Word, ye know that, when ye do come to the Holy Eucharist, ye come to the Communion of the Body and Blood of Christ. Were He Himself visibly present, and ye to come into His Presence, ye would not, just before ye came into His Presence, defile your imaginations, or, whether men know of it or no (ye whom it concerns, know what I mean), first fever your own frames, and then, in a way which Christ forbids and hates, remove that feverishness.[131]

In this and two other sermons – another on the Eucharist and one on confession – Pusey's discussion of masturbation, which he called 'sin' and 'a violation of nature' that would bring forth a scourging from God,[132] was typically Victorian. He warned that the terrifying consequences of this secret sin passed from one boy to another, and included 'lunacy or idiotcy' and even 'early death'.[133] Whereas medical practitioners of the period were concerned with the physical consequences of the practice,[134] Pusey was more concerned with the spiritual consequences, especially separation from Christ. It is the conjunction of this concern with what Pusey saw as sexual deviancy with the Eucharist – a solemn, public sacramental ritual – that is shocking to the modern reader. It suggests that he saw the body, or at least the male body, as especially prone to sin and in need of regulation and even public rebuke. Here the concept of Jesus' spiritual body is also relevant: given Pusey's obsession with the body, it seems likely that he was reassured by the belief that he encountered a Saviour whose earthly presence was no longer physical.

Perhaps that intense concern for bodily purity was the natural result of the strain under which Pusey, as one of the leading spokesmen for the Real Presence, laboured. The doctrine of the Real Presence remained controversial throughout the Victorian period, and Pusey suffered greatly for his adherence to it. Besides being suspended from preaching before the university from 1843–45, he was regularly pilloried in the press for his beliefs. However, the controversies did not cause Pusey to back down; on the contrary, he remained engaged in defending the Real Presence his whole life. This commitment to a controversial doctrine suggests that there was one other reason why Pusey – who believed that suffering was a sign that one was chosen by God[135] – adhered to it. If the world he rejected, the world of Protestants and parliamentary members, rejected the doctrine and made him suffer for it, he must be right; he must be doing God's work.

Notes

1 Some of the research used in this essay was conducted thanks to funding from the National Endowment for the Humanities, St Deiniol's Library (now Gladstone's Library) and Wright State University. I am grateful to these institutions for their support.
2 Pusey credited Henry Philpotts, the Bishop of Exeter, with first using the term 'Real Presence' to describe the belief in 1839. See Pusey, *Letter to the Archbishop of Canterbury*, 56.
3 All of the Six Points, which were defined at the annual meeting of the English Church Union in 1865, concerned the Eucharist. The Six Points defended the use of Eucharistic vestments, the eastward position of the celebrant at the Eucharist, candles on the altar, mixing water and wine in the chalice, the use of wafer bread and the use of incense.
4 The formal title of this work was *Catena Patrum: No. 4: Testimony of Writers in the Later English Church to the Doctrine of the Eucharistic Sacrifice, with an Historical Account of the Changes Made in the Liturgy as to the Expression of That Doctrine*. This was the first original Tract published on the Eucharist.
5 For example, Pusey articulated the complementary relationship between the two sacraments thus: 'Baptism gives; the Holy Eucharist preserves and enlarges life. Baptism engrafts into the true Vine; the Holy Eucharist derives the richness and fullness of His life into the branches thus engrafted. Baptism burns in Christ's tomb, and through it He quickens with His life; the Holy Eucharist is given not to the dead, but to the living' (Pusey, *Holy Eucharist a Comfort*, 6). For further discussion of the relation of Pusey's Eucharistic beliefs to his sacramental beliefs generally, see Härdelin, *Tractarian Understanding*, chapter 2, esp. 99–103.
6 While the suspension elicited protests from Tractarians, it was insufficient for other Anglicans. H. C. Woodgate, for example, wrote a letter to the Bishop of London asking that the sermon 'be formally brought before the Proper Ecclesiastical Doctrine' (Woodgate, letter to the Bishop of London, n.d. [1843?], Liddon Bound Volumes 37).

7 An account of the controversy and the trial itself is found in Strong, *Alexander Forbes*, chapter 4. For an account of William Ewart Gladstone's failed attempts to avoid the trial, see Strong, 'High Churchmen and Anglo-Catholics'.
8 Bennett escaped legal sanctions when he substituted 'real and actual' for 'visible' to describe Christ's presence in the consecrated elements.
9 For more on Pusey's family life, see the essays by K. E. Macnab and Ian McCormack in this collection. Fr Barry Orford of Pusey House is working on an edition of the recollections of Maud Milner. She was a friend of Pusey's daughter Mary Brine, and Pusey was her confessor. Her notes reveal Pusey as a kindly, considerate and good-humoured man, as well as a devout one.
10 As the doctrine evolved over several decades, was never formally accepted by the Church of England and was caricatured by its opponents, there were minor variations in how it was articulated.
11 Pusey, *Holy Eucharist a Comfort*, 3. Near the end of his life, he offered a similar explanation: 'God consecrates by us His priests mere elements of the world to be sacramentally, spiritually, supernaturally, His Body and Blood' ([Pusey], *Spiritual Letters*, 218).
12 [Pusey], *Spiritual Letters*, 218.
13 Pusey, *Real Presence*, xvii. He had earlier assured the Bishop of London that 'I have never taught any thing physical, corporeal, carnal, but spiritual, sacramental, Divine, ineffable' (Pusey, *Letter to the Bishop of London*, 69).
14 Pusey, *This is My Body*, 40.
15 Pusey, *Real Presence*, 2–3; [Pusey], 'Holy Communion: Exceeding Danger', 91; Pusey, *Presence of Christ*, 14–15. For an extended discussion of transubstantiation and consubstantiation, see notes A and B in Pusey, *Doctrine of the Real Presence*, 1–53.
16 [Pusey], 'Holy Communion: Exceeding Danger', 91.
17 Ibid.
18 Pusey, *Letter to the Bishop of Oxford*, 134.
19 Ibid., 136.
20 Ibid., 132.
21 Pusey used the term 'ultra-Protestant' frequently in his *Letter to the Bishop of Oxford*. See 22, 39, 55–9, 61, 89, 111, 125, 143, 173, 182, 202, 203.
22 Pusey, *Presence of Christ*, 21–2.
23 For descriptions of Jesus' spiritual body, see Hook, *The Eucharist*, 11; Beeman, *Ritualism*, 139–40; Bennett, *Examination*, 35.
24 Pusey, *This is My Body*, 40.
25 Pusey, *Real Presence*, 114.
26 Pusey, *Presence of Christ*, 12.
27 Pusey, *Real Presence*, xxi.
28 A Clergyman, *Answer to Dr Pusey's Sermon*, 3; see also 16.
29 Harrison, *Answer to Dr Pusey's Challenge*, 32.
30 A Clergyman, *Answer to Dr Pusey's Sermon*, 22–3; Lee, *Some Remarks*, 14–15.
31 Bosanquet, *The Lord's Supper*, 7; Garbett, *Review of Dr Pusey's Sermon*, vii–viii, xv–xxii, l–li;1; Meller, *Dr Pusey and the Fathers*, 9–10; Milner, *Remarks on the New Doctrine*, 9–12; Edison, *Doctrine of Dr Pusey's Sermon*, 34; Harrison, *Answer to Dr Pusey's Challenge*, 19–20; Lee, *Some Remarks*, 14–15.
32 Garbett, *Review of Dr Pusey's Sermon*, vi; Harrison, *Answer to Dr Pusey's Challenge*, 34.
33 Edison, *Doctrine of Dr Pusey's Sermon*, ix, 10, 16; Garbett, *Review of Dr Pusey's Sermon*, xxxiii; Milner, *Remarks on the New Doctrine*, 13, 26.

34 Meller, *Dr Pusey and the Fathers*, 14.
35 Garbett, for example, apprehended a 'sensuous and semi-pantheistic philos of the Tractarian school' (Garbett, *Review of Dr Pusey's Sermon*, xxxii).
36 Harrison, *Answer to Dr Pusey's Challenge*, 3.
37 The literature on the Victorian popular understanding of Roman Catholicism as a pagan, foreign religion of oppression is extensive; see my *Victorians and the Virgin Mary: Gender and Religion in England 1830–85* (Manchester: Manchester University Press, 2008), esp. chapter 3; Walter Arnstein, *Protestant versus Catholic in Mid-Victorian England: Mr Newdegate and the Nuns* (Columbia and London: University of Missouri Press, 1982); Dominic Janes, *Victorian Reformation: The Fight over Idolatry in the Church of England, 1840– 1860* (Oxford: Oxford University Press, 2009), chapter 4; Maria LaMonaca, *Masked Atheism: Catholicism and the Secular Victorian Home* (Columbus, OH: Ohio State University Press, 2008); D. G. Paz, *Popular Anti-Catholicism in Mid-Victorian England* (Stanford, CA: Stanford University Press, 1992); John Singleton, 'The Virgin Mary and Religious Conflict in Victorian Britain' (*Journal of Ecclesiastical History* 43 [1992]: 16–34).
38 This discomfort did not, however, stop Victorian Anglicans from embracing Gothic church architecture as the truest expression of religion. This apparent contradiction is explained by the fact that English champions of the Gothic defined the style as a genuinely English architectural style.
39 Mt 26:26–28; Mk 14: 22–23; Lk 22:17–19.
40 See, for example, Pusey, *Presence of Christ*, 16–17, 21, 23, 26–9, 32–5; Pusey, *This is My Body*, 15–24. Note E of Pusey's *Doctrine of the Real Presence* was also devoted to defending a literal interpretation of Jesus' words. See also Pusey, 'Holy Communion: Exceeding Danger', 92; Pusey, *Real Presence*, 88.
41 Pusey, *Real Presence*, xi.
42 Pusey, *Presence of Christ*, 29.
43 Ibid., 27.
44 Pusey, *Presence of Christ*, 27, 32; Pusey, *Real Presence*, 294, 307–8.
45 Pusey, *This is My Body*, 20; Pusey, *Will Ye Also Go Away?*, 13; Cheyne, *Six Sermons*, 23–4.
46 Pusey, *Presence of Christ*, 27, 18.
47 Pusey reminded the congregation of Jesus' use of metaphorical images, including that he was the bread of life and that his flesh and blood must be consumed to have eternal life. See Pusey, *Holy Eucharist a Comfort*, 8. Other sermons repeated at least some of these images; Jn 6:53–6 was the topic of his sermon 'Holy Communion: Privileges'.
48 Pusey, *Holy Eucharist a Comfort*, 8.
49 See Pusey, *Real Presence*, 279–93; Pusey, *Presence of Christ*, 37–66. Härdelin notes that the 'appeal to Antiquity' was typical of the Tractarians as well as of Anglicans more generally. See Härdelin, *Tractarian Understanding*, 42–5.
50 Pusey, *Presence of Christ*, 47.
51 Pusey, *This is My Body*, 26.
52 For an overview of the ideas of some of the most important fathers, see Kilmartin, *The Eucharist in the West*, chapter 1.
53 Pusey, *Letter to the Bishop of London*, 194.
54 Pusey, *Holy Eucharist a Comfort*, 14.
55 Pusey, *Doctrine of the Real Presence*, 75–90, 121–31.
56 Pusey, *Letter to the Bishop of London*, 32.
57 See, for example, Pusey, *Presence of Christ*, 48–66.
58 Pusey, *Doctrine of the Real Presence*, note I, 94–118.

59 Pusey, *Real Presence*, 293.
60 Pusey, *Letter to the Archbishop of Canterbury*, 88.
61 Pusey, *Real Presence*, 3. He repeatedly insisted that the views in his 1843 sermon were those of the Church of England; see his protest to the vice chancellor and the preface to *Holy Eucharist a Comfort*, 3.
62 Pusey, *Real Presence*, 3. Pusey frequently made similar assertions about the orthodoxy of his beliefs: for example, he assured the Bishop of London, 'I fully believe, and have anew adopted, every statement of the Church of England on the doctrine of the Holy Eucharist' (Pusey, *Letter to the Bishop of London*, 240). In his *Letter to the Bishop of Oxford*, he declared that his beliefs were those he had 'learnt…from the same Mother, the Church of England', or things on which the church had not pronounced (10). See also Pusey, *Real Presence*, 4.
63 Pusey, *Letter to the Bishop of London*, 55.
64 Pusey, *Presence of Christ*, 22.
65 Pusey, *Real Presence*, 23.
66 Ibid., 23–84.
67 Pusey, *Presence of Christ*, 5, 22–84, 159–60; Pusey, *Real Presence*, 158–9.
68 Pusey, *Real Presence*, 231–2.
69 Ibid., 195.
70 This Article also rejected the practice of reservation of the Eucharist, promoted by ritualists because of the belief that Christ was present in, or in conjunction with, the Eucharistic bread and wine: 'The Sacrament of the Lord's Supper was not by Christ's ordinance reserved, carried about, lifted up, or worshipped.'
71 Pusey, *Letter to the Bishop of London*, 55.
72 Pusey, *Real Presence*, 203–4.
73 Bennett, *Examination*, 65–6; Pusey, *Real Presence*, 252, 255–6.
74 Pusey, *Real Presence*, 252. He made this argument at length; see 244–58.
75 Ibid., 255–6.
76 In fairness to Pusey, those on both sides of the debate over the Eucharist were willing to defend both plain language and interpretation of language, depending on which suited their purposes.
77 Pusey, *Real Presence*, 237. His friend G. C. Berkeley agreed with Pusey. In a letter dated 2 July 1843, he asked rhetorically of the 1843 sermon, 'where is it contrary to our Formularies?' (Pusey House, PUS 19/2). The assertion that there was no contradiction to the Real Presence was, of course, correct, but only because it had not been thought of during the sixteenth-century reformations.
78 Pusey, *Holy Eucharist a Comfort*, 3.
79 Quoted in Pusey, *Real Presence*, 316. See also Pusey, *This is My Body*, 41; Pusey, *Will Ye Also Go Away?*, 27.
80 Pusey, *Letter to the Bishop of London*, 44–7.
81 Milner, *Remarks on the New Doctrine*, 5. See also Bosanquet, *The Lord's Supper*, 9.
82 Bevis, *Popery of Puseyism*, 6.
83 Harrison, *Answer to Dr Pusey's Challenge*, 26–7.
84 Goode, *Nature of Christ's Presence*, vii–viii.
85 Harrison, *Answer to Dr Pusey's Challenge*, 33.
86 Ibid., 25.
87 A Clergyman, *Answer to Dr Pusey's Sermon*, 26.
88 Bosanquet, *The Lord's Supper*, 16–17. See also A Clergyman, *Answer to Dr Pusey's Sermon*, 27; he argued that 'is' should be translated as 'represents'.

89 Bosanquet, *The Lord's Supper*, 19.
90 Harrison, *Answer to Dr Pusey's Challenge*, 32.
91 Bevis, *Popery of Puseyism*, 6–8.
92 Harrison, *Answer to Dr Pusey's Challenge*, 16–17, 23–4.
93 Ibid., 6, 9–12. See also Meller, *Dr Pusey and the Fathers*, 19–20, 30–31.
94 Harrison, *Answer to Dr Pusey's Challenge*, 13; see also 18. When Pusey did not respond to Harrison's charges, Harrison challenged him again in his *Letter to Pusey*.
95 A Clergyman, *Answer to Dr Pusey's Sermon*, 1.
96 Harrison, *Answer to Dr Pusey's Challenge*, 6. See also Edison, *Doctrine of Dr Pusey's Sermon*, 26.
97 A Clergyman, *Answer to Dr Pusey's Sermon*, 13.
98 Goode, *Nature of Christ's Presence*, 30; Edison, *Doctrine of Dr Pusey's Sermon*, 36–7, 57.
99 A Clergyman, *Answer to Dr Pusey's Sermon*, 3; Edison, *Doctrine of Dr Pusey's Sermon*, 8; see also 15.
100 A Clergyman, *Answer to Dr Pusey's Sermon*, 4.
101 Milner, *Remarks on the New Doctrine*, 22–3.
102 Ibid.
103 A Clergyman, *Answer to Dr Pusey's Sermon*, 27.
104 Goode, *Nature of Christ's Presence*, 1:vi.
105 Harrison, *Answer to Dr Pusey's Challenge*, 23–4.
106 See, for example, Pusey, *Holy Eucharist a Comfort*, 3, 8, 12, 15–19; Pusey, *Letter to the Bishop of London*, 28–31, 59–60, 69–70, 150; Pusey, *Letter to the Bishop of Oxford*, 126–9, 130–32; Pusey, *Presence of Christ*, 14, 16–17, 22; Pusey, *Real Presence*, xv, xvii, 161, 244–58, 307–8; Pusey, *This is My Body*, 26, 37–9; Pusey, *Will Ye Also Go Away*, 13–14.
107 Pusey, 'Holy Communion: Exceeding Danger', 99, 100.
108 Pusey, *This is My Body*, 11.
109 Clerical supporters of the doctrine of the Real Presence frequently alluded to the 'mystery' of Christ's presence. See, for example, Carter, *Spiritual Instruction*, 2; Cheyne, *Six Sermons*, 4; Grueber, *The Presence, the Sacrifice*, 25; Keble, *On Eucharistical Adoration*, 40, 132; Neale, *Sermons on the Blessed Sacrament*, 39, 46. Pusey also used the term 'mystery' to refer to Christ's presence; see Pusey, *Holy Eucharist a Comfort*, 10, 12; Pusey, *Letter to the Bishop of London*, 61–2; Pusey, *Letter to the Bishop of Oxford*, 129; Pusey, *Will Ye Also Go Away?*, 3–4, 11–12, 19–20.
110 Pusey, 'Holy Communion: Privileges', 106.
111 Ibid., 107.
112 Pusey, *Letter to the Bishop of Oxford*, 5–16.
113 Pusey, *Holy Eucharist a Comfort*, 12; Neale, *Sermons on the Blessed Sacrament*, 5; Wilberforce, *Doctrine of the Holy Eucharist*, 305–11; Carter, *Blessings of the Sacrament*, 10–12, 26–9. Weekly communion is stressed in the sermons in Dodsworth, *Discourses*.
114 Pusey, 'Holy Communion: Privileges', 106–7, 110–13.
115 Pusey, *Presence of Christ*, 9.
116 Pusey, 'Holy Communion: Privileges', 94.
117 Pusey, 'Holy Communion: Exceeding Danger', 103.
118 For more on the sense of joy in Pusey's preaching, see Ian McCormack's essay in this volume.
119 Pusey, *Presence of Christ*, 68–9.
120 See Liddon, *Life of Pusey*, 2:109.
121 Pusey, 'Holy Communion: Exceeding Danger', 97.
122 The first 25 pages of Pusey's *Letter to the Bishop of London* were dedicated to defending confession as spiritually useful and approved by Anglican tradition.

123 Pusey, *Holy Eucharist a Comfort*, 22.
124 See Liddon, *Life of Pusey*, 2:109, 3:94–5.
125 Pusey, 'Entire Absolution', 257.
126 See Liddon, *Life of Pusey*, 2:109.
127 Reed, *Glorious Battle*, 20.
128 Forrester, *Young Doctor Pusey*, 66–8, 70–71.
129 See Pusey, *Real Presence*, chapter 3.
130 Pusey, *Presence of Christ*, 71.
131 Pusey, *Presence of Christ*, 69–70.
132 Pusey, *Will Ye Also Go Away?*, 21.
133 Pusey, *Will Ye Also Go Away?*, 22.
134 The medical doctor William Acton remains the most famous of those who warned of the supposedly dire consequences of masturbation, as well as of frequent intercourse, for men, in *The Functions and Disorders of the Reproductive Organs, in Childhood, Youth, Adult Age, and Advanced Life, Considered in the Physiological, Social, and Moral Relations* (1857).
135 Pusey, *Letter to the Bishop of Oxford*, 3–4.

Chapter Seven

PUSEY, ALEXANDER FORBES AND THE FIRST VATICAN COUNCIL

Mark Chapman

Ecumenism in the 1860s[1]

The 1860s were marked by a sense of crisis among many Anglicans who had sought a degree of rapprochement with the Roman Catholic Church. There was a fear that if the ultramontane faction gained control of the Vatican, future hope for reunion would disappear. Many Anglo-Catholics therefore sought to do as much as they could to support the more moderate and ecumenically open faction. What success there had been in discussions with Roman Catholics was founded on a common front against the all-pervasive rationalism of the nineteenth century.[2] Edward Bouverie Pusey, the undisputed leader of the Anglo-Catholic movement, played an important role in ecumenical activity in the mid-1860s, producing his first *Eirenicon* in 1865,[3] and two further volumes in the years leading immediately up to the First Vatican Council, both of which took the form of letters to John Henry Newman.[4] By the 1860s Pusey had grown too old and too busy to travel regularly, which meant that he had to rely on younger friends to promote his interests on the Continent: he did not work in isolation, but he encouraged others in their ecumenical endeavours and foreign trips. This chapter addresses one central figure in this collegial approach to ecumenism: Alexander Penrose Forbes (1817–1875),[5] Bishop of Brechin, a younger colleague and protégé who remained one of Pusey's most devoted followers. Forbes, who, as a Scottish bishop had rather more time at his disposal than an Oxford professor, in some ways functioned as Pusey's eyes and ears in ecumenical encounters in the late 1860s. He also reveals some of the fundamental differences in the understanding of Catholicism between Anglo-Catholics and Roman Catholics, which were simply heightened after the First Vatican Council (1869–70).

Forbes adopted a similar 'eirenical' method to Pusey in his major work, *An Explanation of the Thirty-Nine Articles*.[6] In a manner reminiscent of Newman in the controversial Tract 90 of 1841, which had been republished by Pusey in 1866 as part of his earlier efforts to promote the Anglican cause, Forbes tried to show how the English Reformation formularies could be understood in 'the Catholic sense'.[7] To do so he used a theological method which was shared with many Anglo-Catholics, which was based on what he called the 'organic identity' of the Church of England before and after the Reformation.[8] Like Pusey, Forbes adopted a 'catholicism of the word' which made explicit use of those written dogmatic formulations which had been accepted *de fide* by the undivided church.[9]

Forbes, as the first Tractarian bishop, had come under the spell of Pusey and other Anglo-Catholic leaders including Charles Marriott (1811–1858) and Newman while he was a student at Brasenose College, Oxford from 1840 to 1844. He later served as curate under Thomas Chamberlain at St Thomas's, Oxford, one of the first ritualist parishes in the Church of England. After a short period at Pusey's church, St Saviour's in Leeds,[10] he was elected Bishop of Brechin in the Scottish Episcopal Church under the influence of Samuel Wilberforce, the newly appointed Bishop of Oxford, and William Ewart Gladstone.[11] He was consecrated in October 1847 while just over the canonical age of thirty. Although Forbes was interested in reunion with other Catholic Christians through the whole of his episcopate, he was particularly active in reunion discussions in the years leading up to the First Vatican Council.[12]

Most importantly, Forbes greatly welcomed the idea of an ecumenical council as a way of encouraging reunion among all catholic Christians against the common foe of rationalism. In his charge to the Diocese of Brechin in 1863, for instance, he spoke at length about the importance of church unity, primarily as a way of countering the scepticism of the nineteenth century. For Forbes, the unity of the church was a sign of its sanctity. Whenever the 'holiness of the Church has waxed cold', he felt, 'the power of Unity has weakened also'.[13] Indeed, according to Forbes, any sin on the part of a Christian injured the church's sanctity and thereby impaired its unity. Unity was crucial in the fight against infidelity, which had become particularly prevalent in Germany, 'the great focus of modern thought'.[14] Against the vague pietism to which so many seemed to resort as a solution to the problems of unbelief, Forbes called for something more concrete, feeling that this did not 'touch the root of the matter'.[15] Instead Forbes held that the heart of the solution rested in rediscovering the authority of the church.[16] Such authority was to be found in the divine truth, which was 'exhibited and perpetuated' in the visible form of the mystical Body of Christ, which, 'till the end of the world' became the 'ultimate authority in religion – the living exposition of the faith'.[17] This had an obvious implication: 'anything which impairs the authority of the Church must affect the Ground of faith'.[18] Consequently, the unity of the church became an imperative.

Forbes outlines three possible types of unity: first, 'latitudinarianism or syncretism', which supposes that Christianity has no 'definite message'.[19] Second, there were those who clamoured for an 'essence' of Christianity, even though it was unlikely that there would ever be agreement on how this might be constituted.[20] A third option was what he called the 'unity of the Church of Rome' with its remarkable blend of different languages and peoples.[21] The problems with this type of unity, however, were, first, that this excluded 'the grand old Church of East, so venerable in her traditions, so rigid in her maintenance of the deposit'.[22] Secondly, it was deficient in its exclusion of what Forbes called 'the great Anglo-Saxon race' which had become dominant in the 'civilisation of the world'. Finally, the exclusion of the Protestant bodies and the 'comparative failure of Christian mission' were hardly likely to overcome 'the increasing infidelity among the thinking classes over Europe'. Consequently, according to Forbes, Christian unity required something far more comprehensive – nothing short of a new ecumenical council.[23] His book, *An Explanation of the Thirty-Nine Articles* marked his efforts to clear the ground for precisely what sort of faith was required in order to participate in an ecumenical council.

The similarity between the methods of Pusey and Forbes is far from accidental: although seventeen years his junior, Forbes was also one of Pusey's closest confidants. Pusey had initially suggested to Forbes that he should write the *Explanation*,[24] and throughout 1867 he offered his assistance to Forbes in the writing of the book.[25] It was consequently hardly surprising that Forbes should have dedicated the work to Pusey in a lengthy and highly adulatory epistle.[26] Christian truth, for Forbes, was to be found principally in the dogmatic formularies of the undivided catholic church rather than in the belligerent apologetics of the Reformation. Like many Anglo-Catholics of his time, Forbes was a firm believer in what Diarmaid MacCulloch has called the 'myth of the English Reformation'.[27] This myth was one of continuity based on the idea that the Church of England had survived more or less intact through the sixteenth century. When divested of its polemics, the Reformation was of minimal importance, and simply helped remove the worst excesses of the popular catholic system. For Forbes, the Church of England was a national institution far older than the English state.[28] He advocated a dogmatic system based on the certainty of both the apostolic church and the witness of the fathers. In typical Tractarian fashion, therefore, he claimed that it was through the church that God communicated an inspired set of truths, which were preserved intact by the divinely instituted hierarchy. Truth was entrusted once and for all to bishops as successors of the apostles.[29] The loss of dogmatic certainty, Forbes held, would lead to moral anarchy since '[d]ogma is to morals as cause to effect, will to motion. Christian morality is dogma in action, or practical faith.'[30] Forbes thus shared the Anglo-Catholic fixation on absolute and unshakeable certainty secured by the apostolic succession of bishops. This at once guaranteed the Christian faith and upheld the moral fabric of society.

Although Forbes's book was structured as an exposition of the Thirty-Nine Articles of Religion and made prodigious use of the Pusey's own method of extremely lengthy citation from the fathers, it also covered a range of current topics not explicitly mentioned in the Articles. These included the infallibility of the church, which was of obvious importance given the impending Vatican Council. Forbes held that dogmatic inerrancy could be upheld only by the teachings of the undivided church, which meant that after the schism between East and West there could be no definition of new dogmas without a general council.[31] As he noted in a letter to his friend, the German church historian Ignaz von Döllinger, he could not accept the idea of doctrinal development, which simply pointed to 'an aggravation of the consequences of the fatal divorce between Historic Truth and Dogma, to my mind one of the most dangerous conditions of these times'.[32] Consequently, the only possible definitive solution to both division and unbelief was to be found in a new truly ecumenical council which would be composed of all the bishops from the scattered branches of catholic Christendom, East and West. Only in this way could the 'rent vesture' of Christ be repaired.[33] While this was obviously more rhetorical than practical, Forbes felt a degree of hope that he might be able to swing opinion in Rome away from ultramontane intransigence in the common front against liberalism.

Forbes and the First Vatican Council

After the international situation had become moderately more settled following the Austro–Prussian War of 1866, on 29 June 1867 Pius IX announced a council of all the bishops of the Roman Catholic Church which was set to be a climax of his pontificate.[34] This spurred Forbes into action. Together with Pusey, he believed that certain influential figures in the Roman Catholic Church might secure a hearing for the Anglican bishops at the council or at least a discussion of a list of propositions which summarized the Anglican position. This would serve a twofold purpose: first, it would provide a basis for the future reunion of divided Christendom, and, secondly, it might also help to moderate Roman opinion and prevent the declaration of infallibility. Some Roman Catholics were equally anxious that convening a council would lead to a definition of papal infallibility. It was possible that the prospect of reunion with Anglicans might help to influence opinion in Rome and prevent a dogmatic declaration as inopportune. Thus, while he rejoiced in the forthcoming council, Newman wrote to Pusey:

> I don't like that half and half way in which it sets people by the ears – I am not denying the Pope's Infallibility – but questions arise, as to what are the conditions of his exercising the gift – no such difficulties (*to* me) arise as to a General Council. Now is the time, if a *large and strong* body of united Anglicans could address the council, being willing to be reconciled.[35]

To test the waters, Forbes went to Rome via France in February 1868, where he met with Archbishop Georges Darboy of Paris, armed with a letter of introduction from Pusey.[36] Darboy wrote to Pusey with his impressions of Forbes and was suitably optimistic about the effect dogmatic propositions might have in Rome.[37] However, during his visit to Rome, Forbes became dispirited about the possibility of success in having any propositions heard, partly because, as a Scottish bishop, he felt that he was quite unrepresentative of English opinion.[38] Pusey wrote to Newman that Forbes had come back from Rome 'disappointed'. He 'purposely did not consult any of the Cardinals etc., being so discouraged as for any hope, under the present Pope'.[39] Newman replied that 'any one in England would have confidently said beforehand how he would be received at Rome. The central authority cannot *profess* to relax.'[40] Newman consequently thought that it was vital that any propositions would need to have the support of a significant number of churchmen to stand any chance of being heard in the Vatican.

Matters had become increasingly pressing after the promulgation of the Bull of Indiction convening the council on 29 June 1868 which was to begin on the feast of the Immaculate Conception (8 December) the following year.[41] In the autumn of 1868, Pusey attempted to draw up a list of propositions which might provide a negotiating position in Rome. He had included the contentious issues of the invocation of the saints, purgatory, and the seven sacraments.[42] He submitted them to Newman for a preliminary judgement, who thought it crucial to gather together a large number of signatories, including 'three or four Bishops of the Church of England, 50 Professors (Fellows of Colleges would count as such), 200 clergy'. They would need to be able to say that they, together with a significant number of congregations, 'say 150, were desirous of coming into communion with the Holy See, that they were willing on the question of the Anglican Orders to submit to the decision of the Council'. What was crucial, according to Newman, was that the Vatican would need to be persuaded that there were significant numbers of people behind the idea of reunion, rather than simply a few individuals. A problem, however, was that Pusey's friendship with the French bishops would prove suspicious to the Vatican authorities, who would be likely to ask: 'Why does not Dr. Pusey apply through the Bishops of England?' He consequently went on to suggest that Pusey might organize some German episcopal support through the Archbishop of Mainz, Wilhelm, Baron von Ketteler (1811–1877), as well as through Döllinger, who might also be able to draw on the support of Professor F. H. Reusch of Bonn.[43] What was crucial, however, was that Pusey would have to supply a list of names who might be persuaded to convert, which, as Newman admitted, was highly unlikely.[44]

Pusey wrote back to Newman, however, noting that Forbes's 'report of the state of the ecclesiastical mind in Italy made me give up the idea of sending propositions to Rome'. Despite the good will of the Bishop of Orleans, who had offered to take the propositions to Rome personally and obtain a secret opinion about them, Pusey gave up the plan altogether. Besides, Pusey wrote, as long as Cardinal Henry Edward Manning was at the helm of the English Catholic Church any 'organic reunion' would be impossible.[45]

Shortly afterwards Pius IX made a predictable snub to Anglicans. In what Pusey afterwards described as 'an absorbing and anxious move',[46] the *Weekly Register* announced that while the Pope had issued invitations to the forthcoming council to the bishops of the Orthodox churches, even though they were not in communion with the Holy See; the Anglican bishops had not been invited. They were simply included among the '*acatholici*' who had been addressed by the Pope in his letter *Omnibus Protestantibus* of 13 September.[47] Furthermore, the actions of the Italian Government had grown so extreme that the political situation in Rome was becoming increasingly tense.[48] Many moderates were being pushed into the ultramontane camp.

Forbes and Victor de Buck

Despite the setback brought about by *Omnibus Protestantibus* which had the practical effect of nullifying the validity of Anglican orders, it nevertheless seemed to Pusey and to Forbes that there was a moral imperative on the part of the Church of England to do all it possibly could to ensure that the door remained open for the future possibility of corporate reunion. Pressing the ecumenical cause required finding sympathetic Roman Catholics to work against the formal declaration of papal infallibility. To this end, Forbes began a lengthy correspondence with the Belgian Jesuit priest and Bollandist, Victor de Buck (1817–1876).[49] De Buck had earlier published a sympathetic article on Anglicanism in 1854,[50] and was a friend of Félix Antoine Philibert Dupanloup,[51] who had encouraged him to 'get

Anglicans to the Council'.[52] Forbes, who also produced lives of the saints,[53] wrote to de Buck on 24 January 1869 with a copy of his *Explanation*. He commented on the 'recent letters of Pius IX' which questioned Anglican orders while admitting those of the Eastern churches. This, he claimed, would do little for the perception of the Roman Catholic Church among Anglicans.[54] After a favourable response from de Buck, Forbes replied with a eulogy to Anglicans: 'You cannot know the beautiful lives of many who profess her tenets.' Perhaps overstating his case, he spoke of the 'strong virile piety of her men' and the 'unspeakable purity of her women' as well as of the high quality of her clergy.[55]

In a long letter of 8 March 1869 de Buck wrote to Forbes: 'Vous êtes beaucoup plus catholique que nous ne le pensez.' He claimed that the forthcoming council offered one of the best opportunities since the Reformation for reunion, and that either Forbes or Pusey should represent the Anglicans. If they felt unable to attend then at the very least there should be a presentation of Anglican doctrine, which de Buck would convey to Rome. He concluded by asking: 'What are the superstitions which we ought to combat? What are the balancing and complementary truths which ought to be more and more placed in the light?'[56] After Forbes had replied commenting on a number of the accusations traditionally made by Roman Catholics that the wealth of the Church of England served to prevent many from converting to Rome,[57] de Buck wrote back to Forbes, noting that 'Manning and many others were beneficed in the Anglican Church for many years.' If they were in bad faith and were rogues and scoundrels, he asked rhetorically, 'how with such bad moral characters have they been promoted to Orders and the Episcopate?'[58]

Forbes showed de Buck's long letter to Pusey, who was suspicious about de Buck's motives. According to Pusey, de Buck 'tacitly calculates on the effect which the sight of so many Bishops assembled from different parts of the world would have upon some two or three and that they would give way'.[59] Pusey returned to the idea of propositions, summarizing the issues arising from possible attendance at the Vatican Council and what would be implied in signing the Creed of Pius IV. Again he counselled the production of a set of doctrinal propositions. 'My own idea, ever since my visit to France', Pusey wrote to Liddon on 24 March 1869, 'has been to formulize propositions and see whether any real authorities would accept them.' However, he did no more about formulating them since he was aware of Forbes's reluctance on the matter. He also sensed a possible Protestant backlash.[60]

Forbes wrote to de Buck on 10 April 1869 once again saying that he did 'not represent anyone'. He made his point with great clarity:

> Even if I came on my alone [i.e., own], as an individual Bishop to testify to the tradition of my own Church, I should expose myself to reclamations

and protests on the part of the protestant-minded laity of the Church to whom Popery as they understand it is extremely hateful and associated with Mary's burnings and wretched Ireland. I would represent none but the Unionist school of thought in the Church, which you know has no definite organization as such, though some Societies such as the English Church Union exhibit some phases of it.[61]

A few days later de Buck wrote to Pusey in optimistic mood claiming that one of the reasons for summoning a council was to bring about a reconciliation between Rome and the High Church party. He felt that Forbes should attend the council since if he thought himself a catholic bishop then he should consider himself invited.[62] Forbes showed de Buck's letters to Pusey, who replied that it would be worth assembling a list of those whom they could be said to be representing. He also pressed for the production of propositions or declarations, which might help the forthcoming council 'lay the foundations of union, by way of explanation: or they might declare that to any considerate body, who should wish to reunite itself, they would grant such and such things'.[63]

In May de Buck wrote to Forbes to inform him that he was going to Rome and asking whether he could be of any help in promoting the Anglican cause.[64] Forbes showed the letter to Pusey, who advised extreme caution: 'I think that the only answer to the enclosed is "kindest thanks"'.[65] Forbes wrote to de Buck that he was 'very unsanguine of any happy result'. He went on: 'The English High Church Party have been so trained to believe in Tradition, and to appeal to the Early Church, that they look upon this doctrine [infallibility] with the utmost dislike.'[66] Forbes and Pusey spent some time drawing up a number of dogmatic propositions, which would contain both positive and negative statements: 'The negative will contain the formulary of that which we Anglicans do not believe of the popular modes of expressing certain doctrines. The positive will say what we hold on the subject as Catholic Christians in communion with the Church of England.'[67] For Anglicans schooled in the fathers, the idea of development and what they regarded as its logical outcome in infallibility threatened the doctrinal consensus of the undivided church.

Pressing the Anglican Case

Meanwhile, de Buck visited Rome from the end of May, returning to Belgium in early July 1869. After cutting off the signature, he showed Forbes's letter of 6 June to a number of senior officials as a sign of Anglican seriousness about reunion.[68] Liddon describes this visit using an unsourced and confidential account that was prepared afterwards. De Buck had communicated with one of the leading voices among the so-called *Intransigenti*, Luigi Maria Cardinal

Bilio (1826–1884), Secretary of the Supreme Sacred Congregation of the Holy Office. De Buck reported on his conversations with Forbes and Pusey, whom he described respectively as 'Episcopus Z. et Oxonienses'. He 'added that the "doctores Oxonienses" were now busily engaged in preparing a statement of faith which was to be brought to Rome by the Bishop of Orleans'. He made three suggestions to Bilio: first, 'a small committee should be appointed at Rome of men full of learning and discretion, with Cardinal Bilio at its head', which would have to be capable of 'distinguishing dogma from unauthorized opinions'. All converts, he suggested, except perhaps William Lockhart and Newman, should be excluded. Secondly, he asked that all 'exasperating newspaper gossip and comment should be stopped on both sides, a truce which the Archbishops of Westminster and Dublin and the Bishop "Z." and Dr. Pusey might well arrange'. Finally, in order to avoid the accusation that the council was not truly ecumenical, the Anglican bishops should be invited, as '*episcopi dubii*, or at least as *episcopi a multis habiti*'.[69]

When he returned to Belgium, De Buck wrote immediately to Forbes, commenting on the deep interest there had been among Roman officials for the Anglican cause. '[I] have constantly impressed upon them that they ought to treat you and the writings that come from Oxford as S. Hilary treated the semi-Arians in his book De Synodis, that I consider you as near to the Kingdom of God, as the Semi-Arians [sic] a little before their union with the Catholic Church & c. All this has been well received. I did not encounter in the men I spoke to any prejudice against you.'[70] Discussing his own role as an official Jesuit theologian at Rome he claimed that 'we have the most entire liberty to say everything'. He concluded by suggesting that he thought it 'desirable that your exposition of doctrine should be ready for the commencement of the Council or at least that the part ready should be presented'.[71] He suggested that each proposition should be divided into three (instead of two as Pusey had intended): 'on each point they should define (1) *quid sit credendum*, (2) *quid credi non debeat*, (3) *quid credi non possit*; and the propositions should be ready for the first meeting of the Council'.[72]

In July Forbes visited the Continent, spending three weeks at Hohenlohe in Bavaria, where he managed to gain some inside information about what was likely to happen at the forthcoming council.[73] Forbes's German friends led him to believe that the *Syllabus of Errors*, the Assumption, as well as papal infallibility, would be declared dogmas. He lamented to de Buck: 'We Anglicans are men of tradition and we cannot accept as dogma what is so new and doubtful as the proposed points.'[74]

De Buck replied to Forbes, thinking that he had become disillusioned by some of the correspondence in the Jesuit monthly, *Civiltà Cattolica*.[75] Forbes responded to de Buck that his information had come from diplomatic sources. While he hoped that the 'fanatical party' would not meet with success, he nevertheless noted, 'one cannot deny that they need to be watched'. He went on to differentiate between 'northern' and 'southern' forms of catholicism especially in their approaches to history: 'You must recollect that if these matters are brought to the vote, the great preponderance of Bishops of the Romanesque, in opposition to the Teutonic and Slav races, will tend to make resistance difficult. The unhistorical training in the Italian and Spanish seminaries affords little hope of resistance on their parts.' He also dreaded 'any theory of human politics, as also any theory of human philosophy being erected into dogma'. Attacking the idea of doctrinal development he commented: 'On the old principles of the faith being implicitly given from the beginning, it could not be so erected, but now Christianity is too much regarded as a philosophic idea capable of development and evolution, not as a depositum once for all given in its integrity.' He would not be able to sign the Creed of Pope Pius IV, since it was a symbol of individual submission rather than corporate reunion. Besides, he went on, it contained dogmatic difficulties 'alike to Romans and Anglicans'. There were 'many points on which it would be impossible to assert the unanimous consent of the Fathers', which included transubstantiation, papal powers, and the withdrawal of the chalice. 'I demur also to the term, unless explained, of the Roman Church being the mother and mistress of all churches. Surely Jerusalem was the Mother church [sic] and there can be no mistress.' Forbes also took issue with the idea that the council was ecumenical, finding it offensive that Anglicans had been 'mixed up with Socinians and all Protestants', positioned even lower than 'the withering heretical communities in the East'. Nevertheless, despite these reservations, he concluded that the council was likely to do 'great good' and that he would proceed with his task of drawing up a list of propositions (the *Regula Fidei*), although 'with less hope of any good result'.[76]

Newman too was interested in Anglican representation at the council, since he had come to think that 'the moderate party will have hard work enough in hindering some extreme measures being carried'.[77] In September 1869 he wrote to Pusey: 'I suppose it has not entered into your mind to go to Rome yourself.' If he went he would be able to 'know just what the Bishops of different countries thought. I think you would find them all of one mind as regards the position of the Church of England.' 'I am quite sure', Newman continued, 'that every one would be rejoiced to see you and that you would receive kindnesses on all hands'. If Pusey was not able to attend, Newman asked whether anybody else might go instead of him: 'I don't think they would go out of their way except they were sure that by doing so they brought important people into the Church. They would want a *quid pro quo*.' Although Newman realized that Forbes's position as a bishop meant that it would be impossible for him to attend, he nevertheless concluded: 'I do really think one or two learned Anglicans would tend to soften the antagonism which exists in so many quarters.'[78] Pusey, however, remained convinced that it would not be productive to attend. He replied to Newman noting that although he would find 'great individual kindness', he would be better off finishing his final *Eirenicon*. He concluded with a less-than-optimistic appraisal of de Buck's request for dogmatic propositions: 'I suppose some of us will send propositions to the care of Dupanloup, which De Buck is very urgent to have done: but I suppose it will have no result, except, please God, for hereafter.'[79]

Later in the autumn de Buck was required by the Supreme Congregation to stop his correspondence with 'heterodox Anglicans'.[80] Despite this, however, he continued to receive letters from his Anglican contacts. Forbes wrote to him as the bishops were assembling in Rome. Even though he held out little hope for reunion, Forbes nevertheless promised to proceed with dogmatic propositions.[81] Although he had been warned off by the General of the Jesuits and his old Spanish seminary tutor, De Buck replied to Forbes shortly after the council had begun, trying to persuade him to attend and reassuring him that he would be treated well.[82] In January 1870 he wrote once again to Forbes hoping that he would reconsider his position, and also hoping that Manning would not be appointed to any commission on Anglican affairs. He gave details of his visit to Cardinal Antonio Saverio de Luca, reporting that he had instructed him what to say at the Council on Anglicanism.[83]

Forbes replied to de Buck in February 1870 clarifying his position for the sake of Cardinal de Luca, who, Forbes suggested, might be shown the letter.[84] He even expressed a degree of optimism, noting that he had begun 'to conceive hope that something may be done in a matter so fraught with important results to the interests of Christianity'. With the cardinal in mind he concisely outlined the position of the Anglo-Catholics. This letter, which forms what amounts to a declaration of faith and a position statement of what is necessary for reunion, remains unpublished. Before moving to the specific propositions, Forbes begins with a reiteration of the importance for High Churchmen of 'the corporate unity of Christendom as one great remedy of the advancing and all-devouring Rationalism of the nineteenth century'. The five propositions express first, a catholic understanding of all documents to be signed in the sense that they are to be 'illustrated by the references to the consent of the Early Fathers which these documents recognize'. Second, Forbes continued, the Reformation schism was to be deplored, although there were nevertheless 'many incidental advantages that flowed from it – e.g. the freedom of the use of the Holy Scriptures and the destruction of many of the superstitions which defiled the Church and which called for reform long before the too long delayed Council of Trent'. Third, Forbes recognized that 'not only is salvation to be had in Anglicanism, but that they have valid Sacraments, and that grace flows to them through those Sacraments'. Forbes reaffirmed his belief that Anglican orders were valid, and that the 'English Church has had a special duty in the matter of Evidential Theology'. Indeed, he continued, 'the English Church, far short as she has come of her ideal, has yet continued by God's grace to operate for good'. This was proved by the 'mighty religious revival of the last forty years' with its rebuilt churches and 'higher standard of faith and practice both among Clergy and laity'. At the same time, however, Forbes denounced the 'excess of the cultus of our dear Lady' and 'such exaggerated expressions...that the Pope is an incarnation of God'. This, Forbes held, was the 'real bar to what Dr. Pusey has happily termed healthful reunion'. Finally, he acknowledged that 'the condition of Anglicanism in reference to the great Church of the West is unsatisfactory, and that the prospects of the Church of England, politically, are not encouraging.' On the one hand, there was the prospect of disestablishment and re-alignment where the Calvinists would merge with the Dissenters. On the other hand, the Catholic party, 'without injury to its convictions', might rest 'under the Chair of St Peter'. This, it seems, was Forbes's ultimate hope: 'We may not live to see it', he concluded, 'but surely to lay the foundation of such a work as this must be well pleasing to our Gracious Saviour, Whose prayer for unity sounds forth from the Upper Chamber of Jerusalem through all time to the ends of the earth. "Ut hi omnes unum sint, sicut tu Pater etc. Fiat voluntas Tua, Domine Iesu, Fili Mariae. Amen."'[85] After he wrote this letter, Forbes appears to have received no more letters from de Buck before the conclusion of the council – the injunction from the Holy Office was presumably eventually heeded.[86] There is no sign that the letter was ever shown to the cardinal. Besides, Luca was shortly afterwards removed on account of his sympathy with Bishop Joseph Georg Strossmeyer, an opponent of papal infallibility during the council.[87]

Conclusion

These doctrinal propositions succinctly summarize the Anglican position as understood by Forbes: however much the Anglo-Catholics had achieved in bringing the Church of England to the Roman Catholic position, there was a very long way to go. While there might be some hope of an eventual realignment of all Christians as more Protestant-minded Anglicans united with the Free Churches, there was inevitably a huge gulf between catholic-minded Anglicans and those who clamoured for a declaration of infallibility. This meant that by the summer of 1870 the worst fears of the reunionists were realized. Although some bishops absented themselves, the council voted during a great storm on 18 July 1870 almost unanimously in favour of the declaration of infallibility. Later, even those had been opposed agreed to the declaration.[88]

Enthusiasts for reunion were forced to think again about whether there could ever be any hope for future reconciliation between the churches.

Forbes was deeply disappointed by the outcome of the council. In his September 1871 charge to his diocese he reacted strongly to the definition of infallibility as a denial of history.[89] While he felt that nobody could deny the significance of the council and everybody, whatever one's individual view, had to have an interest in what went on in the Roman Catholic Church, he nevertheless asked about the council: 'Is it a healing balm?'[90] After briefly tracing the history of the development of papal authority,[91] he arrived at a rhetorical climax when he reached the nineteenth century: 'The appeal to history is now heresy. The consent of the people is nothing.' He went on: '[B]y a strange irony, the instruments of civilisation, the telegraph and the iron way, carry the commands of the Apostle of reaction and obscurantism into the most distant villages and hamlets. The *quod semper, quod ubique, quod ab omnibus* is discredited for ever. There is one living oracle of God, from whose lips all men are to receive the truth.'[92] Since there could be no limits to the authority of the pope, according to Forbes, it was impossible to know how this might develop or what might be added to the content of the faith.

Having pointed to the problems with the declaration of infallibility, Forbes then turned his attention to what he called the 'English branch of the Catholic Church' and whether it was a 'present manifestation of the faith once delivered to the saints'.[93] While he saw the Reformation as a purification of some of the grosser superstitions of the past, he likened the religious changes to a 'carious tooth'. 'The removal causes the pain to cease, but the natural arch of the mouth is destroyed, and the gradual destruction of all the rest proceeds from that very removal.' This meant that the Reformation was 'neither so good nor so bad as people say'.[94] After listing some of its grosser excesses, he nevertheless concluded that 'there was something that justified the English Reformation, and that justification is found in the late proceedings of the Vatican Council'. The Reformers, as was vindicated by the actions of Pius IX, 'felt an intolerable abuse which must be got rid of at any price'.[95]

Forbes went on to claim that since the Anglicans were not summoned to the council, they could not be bound by its teachings. Indeed, with the absence of the Eastern churches along with the Anglicans, there was no sense in which it could be regarded as ecumenical. Besides, he continued, clearly demonstrating his understanding of the development of doctrine, councils were themselves limited in what they could do:

> A Council cannot create new objects of faith. It may proclaim what is an article of faith, but only in accordance with the Holy Scripture and tradition; and Christianity is a revelation, not a philosophy. It is impossible for a doctrine with such antecedents as the Papal Infallibility to have the

elements of antiquity, universality, and consent, which the common law of Christendom has ever demonstrated as the guarantee of the truth of doctrine. It is again and again contradicted by the fact of History.[96]

Nevertheless, Forbes claimed, the council would still have a profound influence on the future of human thought. Even though it was summoned out of a 'sincere desire to promote the interests of Christianity', and 'as a panacea for the infidelity and materialism of the age', it could never succeed: 'I cannot think that the type of Christian life produced by the school of Infallibility will have the masculine strength to cope with the errors of the times, putting aside the truth or falsehood of the doctrine. On the contrary, I believe that it will tend to widen the gap that exists already between the intellect and the piety of Europe; that it will drive the educated classes into infidelity, and sap the foundations of the social order by erecting into dogma an impossible theory of life.'[97] In distinction, the Church of England did not require such a sacrifice of the intellect. Instead it maintained nothing more than the simple creed of apostolic times and the 'bonds of sacramental union with the Church of the Fathers'.[98] This required a serious study of history and had nothing to fear from science. Examples of such a method could be found in the German catholic school of men such as Möhler and Döllinger, as well as in textual criticism: 'We rest upon a sure foundation', he concluded, 'certain things have by legitimate authority been defined to be true; we accept that authority, and therefore any scientific or biblical difficulties adjust themselves to this.'[99]

In the end, then, Forbes's 'catholicism of the word', with its foundation in the written documents of history, which he had learnt from Pusey and which he shared with other Anglo-Catholics, had been ruled out as heresy by the new authority of a papacy able, as he saw it, to ignore history and define 'new objects of faith'. Whether any hopes for reunion could be salvaged after the council was an open question which was very rapidly addressed by a number of Anglo-Catholics: if Roman Catholicism had shut itself off from the rest of Christendom in its absolutist sanctuary, then perhaps national forms of Catholicism – including those of the East – were the most obvious alternative. After all, they at least retained a sense of the centrality of history. For most Roman Catholics, however, what Forbes called a 'dogmatic identity'[100] was an insufficient criterion for defining the Catholic church: Catholicism was not a fixed set of doctrines given to the early church, but was a far more complex phenomenon able to develop over time under the influence of authoritative – and now infallible – interpreters of the faith. Thus, against the secularism of the modern world, which was threatening to remove the temporal power of the papacy completely, a decisive and infallible authority seemed necessary.

A devotional, populist, yet absolutist rhetoric was thus formulated against the backdrop of the increasing political insecurity of the Vatican.

Notes

1. The current literature on the Anglo-Catholicism and ecumenism is surprisingly modest. See Brandreth, *Œcumenical Ideals*, and Stuart, 'Roman Catholic Reactions'. On Pusey, see Greenfield, 'Such a Friend'; Strange, 'Reflections on a Controversy'; and Geck, 'Edward Bouverie Pusey', esp. 120–23. See also Pawley, *Rome and Canterbury*, chapters 10, 11.
2. On this, see Christopher Dawson's seminal interpretation in *Spirit of the Oxford Movement*, xi–xii, 140–44. The connections between Puseyism and conservative movements have been discussed by Franklin in *Nineteenth-Century Churches*, esp. chapter 5. See also Aston, *Christianity and Revolutionary Europe*, esp. chapter 8.
3. *The Church of England a Portion of Christ's One Holy Catholic Church, and a Means of Restoring Visible Unity: An Eirenicon, in a Letter to the Author of 'The Christian Year'*, hereafter referred to as the *Eirenicon*.
4. *First Letter to the Very Rev. J. H. Newman in Explanation Chiefly in Regard to the Reverential Love due to the Ever-blessed Theotokos, and the Doctrine of her Immaculate Conception; with an Analysis of Cardinal de Turrecremata's Work on the Immaculate Conception*, hereafter referred to as the *First Letter to Newman*; *Healthful Reunion as Conceived Possible before the Vatican Council: The Second Letter to the Very Rev. J. H. Newman, D.D.*, hereafter referred to as the *Second Letter to Newman*. The latter work was initially published as *Is Healthful Reunion Impossible? A Second Letter to the Very Rev. J. H. Newman, D.D.* (London: Rivingtons, 1870). I have discussed Pusey's contribution to ecumenism in detail in 'A Catholicism of the Word and a Catholicism of Devotion: Pusey, Newman and the first *Eirenicon*' and 'Pusey, Newman, and the End of a "Healthful Reunion": The Second and Third Volumes of Pusey's *Eirenicon*'.
5. On Forbes see Strong, *Alexander Forbes*; Perry, *Alexander Penrose Forbes*; Mackey, *Bishop Forbes*; Allchin, *Alexander Penrose Forbes*; *Forbes of Brechin*. See also Pawley, *Rome and Canterbury*, esp. chapter 11; Brandreth, *Œcumenical Ideals*, chapter 5.
6. Forbes, *An Explanation of the Thirty-Nine Articles: Volume One: Arts I–XXI with an Epistle Dedicatory to the Rev. E. B. Pusey D.D.; Volume Two: Arts XXII–end*. The two volumes were numbered consecutively. On the importance of this book, see my essay, 'An Ecumenical Front against Liberalism'. This section summarizes that essay.
7. Forbes, *Explanation of the Thirty-Nine Articles*, 1:xxx.
8. Ibid.
9. Chapman, 'Catholicism of the Word', 167–90.
10. Mackey, *Bishop Forbes*, chapters 5–7.
11. On Gladstone's friendship with Forbes, see 'Prefatory Note' addressed to Gladstone in Mackey, *Bishop Forbes*, vii–viii.
12. Strong, *Alexander Forbes*, chapter 6.
13. Forbes, *Notes of Unity*, 9.
14. Forbes, *Notes of Unity*, 12. On this, see Chadwick, *Victorian Church* (1987), 2:75–111.
15. Forbes, *Notes of Unity*, 13.
16. Ibid., 14.
17. Ibid., 16.
18. Ibid.

19 Ibid.
20 Ibid., 17.
21 Ibid., 18.
22 Ibid.
23 Ibid., 19–20.
24 Forbes, *Explanation of the Thirty-Nine Articles*, 1:iii.
25 Liddon, *Life of Pusey*, 4:145.
26 Forbes, *Explanation of the Thirty-Nine Articles*, 1:iii–iv.
27 MacCulloch, 'Myth of the English Reformation', 1–19.
28 Forbes, *Explanation of the Thirty-Nine Articles*, 1:xxv.
29 Ibid., 1:289, 1:423.
30 Ibid., 1:132–3.
31 Ibid., 1:iii.
32 Forbes to Döllinger, no date, probably 1867, in Forbes Papers, Pusey House, Oxford. Forbes was well acquainted with Döllinger's writings and visited him in 1865 (Forbes to Gladstone, 8 May 1865, in Mackey, *Bishop Forbes*, 175). He cites his *Gentile and Jew* in *Notes of Unity*, 4. On Döllinger and the council, see Buschkühl, *Great Britain and the Holy See*, 133–45.
33 Forbes, *Explanation of the Thirty-Nine Articles*, 2:812–14.
34 Pius had earlier assembled large gatherings of bishops in Rome, as, for instance, for the canonization of the Japanese martyrs in 1862 which attracted 255. More than 500 bishops and 20,000 priests attended the celebration of the supposed 1800th anniversary of the martyrdom of SS. Peter and Paul on 29 June 1867 at which he convened the council. See Chadwick, *History of the Popes*, 181–214; Butler, *Vatican Council*, 1:84; Hales, *Pio Nono*, 277; Albiergo, 'Das erste Vatikanische Konzil', 386–412, 388.
35 Newman to Pusey, 10 July 1867, in Newman, *Letters and Diaries*, 23:265.
36 Liddon, *Life of Pusey*, 4:153.
37 Darboy to Pusey, 21 March 1868, in Liddon, *Life of Pusey*, 4:154.
38 Strong, *Alexander Forbes*, 210.
39 Pusey to Newman, 11 May 1867, in Newman, *Letters and Diaries*, 24:78.
40 Newman to Pusey, 24 May 1868, in ibid., 78–80.
41 Butler, *Vatican Council*, 1:88.
42 Pusey to Newman, 31 August 1868, in Newman, *Letters and Diaries*, 24:136.
43 Franz Heinrich Reusch (1823–1900) was professor of theology in Bonn; when he was excommunicated in 1872, he became one of the leading Old Catholic theologians.
44 Newman to Pusey, 4 September 1868, in Newman, *Letters and Diaries*, 24:136–8; Liddon, *Life of Pusey*, 4:154–6.
45 Pusey to Newman, [September] 1868, in Liddon, *Life of Pusey*, 4:154.
46 Pusey to Newman, 6 October 1868, in Liddon, *Life of Pusey*, 4:161.
47 See Liddon, *Life of Pusey*, 4:159; Noether, 'Vatican Council I', 227–8. The document is reprinted in Eugenio Cecconi, *Storia del Concilio Ecumenico Vaticano* 1: part ii, documents, 82–5; and Butler, *Vatican Council* 1:93–6.
48 Chadwick, *History of the Popes*, chapter 6.
49 Strong, *Alexander Forbes*, 212–23. Richard Simpson of *The Rambler* had sent a copy of Pusey's first *Eirenicon* to de Buck, who reviewed it positively in *Études Religieues, Historiques et Littéraires* in March 1866. See Jurich, 'Ecumenical Relations', 271ff.; Pawley, *Rome and Canterbury*, 219.
50 Jurich, 'Ecumenical Relations', 245. See also Pawley, *Rome and Canterbury*, 219–21.
51 Strong, *Alexander Forbes*, 212. De Buck also corresponded with Richard Simpson, a Catholic convert of liberal sympathies, and Richard Littledale, a ritualist priest.

52 Liddon, *Life of Pusey*, 4:174.
53 Strong, *Alexander Forbes*, 212.
54 Forbes to de Buck, 24 January 1869, Liddon Bound Volumes 6.
55 Forbes to de Buck, 24 February 1869, cited in Strong, *Alexander Forbes*, 213–14.
56 De Buck to Forbes, 8 March 1869, translation in Liddon Bound Volumes 6.
57 Forbes to de Buck, 13 March 1869, in Jurich, 'Ecumenical Relations', 493–4.
58 De Buck to Forbes, 16 March 1869, Liddon Bound Volumes 6.
59 Pusey to Forbes, no date [March 1869], Liddon Bound Volumes 5.
60 Pusey to Liddon, 24 March 1869, in Liddon, *Life of Pusey*, 4:175.
61 Forbes to de Buck, 10 April 1869, in Liddon Bound Volumes 6. Forbes here refers to the *Union Review* produced by the enthusiasts of the Association for the Promotion of the Unity of Christendom. On this, see Chapman, 'Fantasy of Reunion', 49–74.
62 De Buck to Pusey, 14 April 1869, Liddon Bound Volumes 6.
63 Pusey to Forbes 3 May 1869, Liddon Bound Volumes 5.
64 De Buck to Forbes, 15 May 1869, Liddon Bound Volumes 6.
65 Pusey to Forbes, 19 May 1869, Liddon Bound Volumes 6. This section is a postscript to the letter of 5 May, which was presumably not sent to de Buck until afterwards.
66 Forbes to de Buck, 20 May 1869, Liddon Bound Volumes 6.
67 Forbes to de Buck, 6 June 1869, Liddon Bound Volumes 6. See also Liddon, *Life of Pusey*, 4:177–8.
68 De Buck to Forbes, 7 July 1869, Liddon Bound Volumes 6.
69 Liddon, *Life of Pusey*, 4:178–9. Liddon refers to Cecconi, *Storia del Concilio Ecumenico Vaticano* 1: part ii, 301 n. 2.
70 De Buck to Forbes, 7 July 1869, Liddon Bound Volumes 6.
71 Ibid.
72 Liddon, *Life of Pusey*, 4:179.
73 Strong, *Alexander Forbes*, 219. It is feasible that the informant was Prince Hohenlohe, the Bavarian Prime Minister who was anxious about the possible effects of infallibility on church–state relations. See Hohenlohe-Schillingsfürst, *Denkwürdigkeiten*, 1:351–430. English translation by Chrystal, *Memoirs of Prince Chlodwig*, 326–406. See also Butler, *Vatican Council*, 1:97–8.
74 Forbes to de Buck, 10 July 1869, Liddon Bound Volumes 6; Strong, *Alexander Forbes*, 220.
75 The edition of 6 February 1869 first openly raised the issue of infallibility (345–52). See Hales *Pio Nono*, 284. Much correspondence followed. See Buschkühl, *Great Britain and the Holy See*, 131. De Buck to Forbes, 16 July 1869, Liddon Bound Volumes 6.
76 Forbes to de Buck, 24 July 1869, Liddon Bound Volumes 6.
77 Newman to Pusey, 12 September 1869, in Newman, *Letters and Diaries*, 24:331–2.
78 Newman to Pusey, 16 September 1869, in Newman, *Letters and Diaries*, 24:333; Liddon, *Life of Pusey*, 4:182.
79 Pusey to Newman, 17 September 1869 in Liddon, *Life of Pusey*, 4:182–3; in Newman, *Letters and Diaries* 24:333.
80 The decree was passed on 17 November 1869. See Liddon, *Life of Pusey*, 4:186.
81 Forbes to de Buck, 2 December 1869, Liddon Bound Volumes 6.
82 De Buck to Forbes, 13 December 1869, Liddon Bound Volumes 6. See also Liddon, *Life of Pusey*, 4:186.
83 De Buck to Forbes, 27 January 1870, Liddon Bound Volumes 6.
84 Forbes to de Buck, 20 February 1870, Liddon Bound Volumes 6. Liddon dates this letter to the end of December 1869 (*Life of Pusey*, 4:187–8).
85 Ibid.

86 Liddon, *Life of Pusey*, 4:186. They resumed correspondence later, largely on the subject of hagiography (Strong, *Alexander Forbes*, 223, citing Jurich, 664).
87 Liddon, *Life of Pusey*, 4:187. See *The Guardian* (26 January 1870), 82.
88 Hales, *Pio Nono*, 310; on the debates, see Butler, *Vatican Council*, 2:119–67; Chadwick, *History of the Popes*, 213–14. There were 533 placets to 2 non placets.
89 Forbes, *The Church of England*. See Strong, *Alexander Forbes*, 224–5.
90 Forbes, *The Church of England*, 5–6.
91 Ibid., 8–16.
92 Ibid., 15.
93 Ibid., 16.
94 Ibid., 23–4.
95 Ibid., 27.
96 Ibid., 28.
97 Ibid., 28.
98 Ibid., 29.
99 Ibid., 30.
100 Forbes, *Explanation of the Thirty-Nine Articles*, 1:xxv.

Chapter Eight

PUSEY AND THE SCOTTISH EPISCOPAL CHURCH: TRACTARIAN DIVERSITY AND DIVERGENCE

Rowan Strong

Edward Bouverie Pusey became directly involved with the Scottish Episcopal Church in the 1850s and 1860s as a consequence of two major issues. The first occurred as a result of the accusation of heresy and the subsequent trial of Bishop Alexander Penrose Forbes of Brechin from 1857 to 1860, over his teaching about the 'Real Objective Presence' of Christ in the Eucharist. The second was the prospective relinquishing of their indigenous Communion Office by the Scottish church in the early 1860s. Both these issues were causes for Pusey and the Tractarians in England because they were seen to be threats to their doctrinal position. In examining these two Scottish Episcopalian developments not only can Pusey's attitude to the Scottish Episcopal Church be teased out, but also the existence of diversity, and even divergence, among the Tractarian leadership can be noted. This divergence is important because there has been a tendency in the historiography of Anglo-Catholicism to play down Tractarian differences in favour of presenting the Oxford Movement in a more unified way.

As with so much interpretation of the Oxford Movement, it was Dean Richard Church who did so much to cement this impression of Tractarian uniformity in his classic account. Church, with his nostalgic personal remembrance of many of the actors in the Movement, created in his book a sunlit scenario of 1830s Oxford University. The need for acting in concert was identified early on,[1] and as long as this was upheld the Movement went forward, until John Henry Newman's separation and secession broke it apart within Oxford. This presentation of strong Tractarian unity was facilitated by Church's limpid account of the Movement as a circle of intimate friends under

Newman's leadership, in which John Keble and Pusey, though important, are essentially outsiders.

> But indeed, by this time, out of the little company of friends which a common danger and a common loyalty to the Church had brought together, one, Mr Newman, had drawn ahead, and was now in front. Unsought for...the position of leader in a great crisis came to him, because it must come... [I]t was the force of genius, and a lofty character, and the statesman's eye, taking in and judging accurately the whole of a complicated scene, which conferred the gifts, and imposed inevitably and without dispute the obligations and responsibilities of leadership. Dr Pusey of course was a friend of great account, but was as yet in the background, a venerated and rather awful figure, from his position of mixing in the easy intercourse of common-room life, but to be consulted in emergencies. Round Mr Newman gathered...members of his intimate circle, bound to him not merely by enthusiastic admiration and confidence, but by a tenderness of affection, and a mixture of the gratitude and reliance of discipleship with the warm love of friendship, of which one has to go back far for examples, and which has had nothing like it in our days at Oxford.[2]

The presentation of a gloriously united Movement has not just predominated among Anglo-Catholic writers and historians, but it has also been adopted by major scholars. Owen Chadwick, in his suggestively entitled 1960 book, *The Mind of the Oxford Movement*, was too good a scholar to overlook the differences and even the contradictions of the Oxford Movement associates.[3] Yet his construction of a Movement mind (or 'Spirit' as he put in the title of the re-issued book in 1990) impelled him to a presentation of Tractarian unity. This overarching metaphor meant Chadwick subordinated the admitted differences under the metaphor of a 'movement of minds' in which the thought of Keble, Pusey and Newman had identifiable united characteristics that went on to form a recognizable Oxford Movement theology.[4] Even more recently, with regard to the subject of this essay, Peter Nockles affirmed there was a common Tractarian Oxonian 'affection' for the Scottish Episcopal Church, based on the Scottish Church's history of anti-Erastianism, and its High Church theological tradition as a witness to the Catholic truth of the early church; while its consecration of the first bishop in the newly independent United States of America seemed to vindicate the Movement's fundamental stance on episcopacy as the *esse* of catholicity.[5] This pan-Tractarian affection for the Scottish Episcopal Church will be questioned in this essay.

This essay does not want to dispute that there was such a thing as an identifiable Oxford Movement, or that there were indeed coherent theological and ecclesiastical positions taken by the Tractarian leadership. What it does argue is that coherence has been rather overdrawn in historical accounts and examinations of the Movement, in comparison to the diversity and divergences that existed between the Tractarian leadership. This essay will seek to illustrate this variegated nature of the Movement by the leadership's contrasting attitudes to the Scottish Episcopal Church. In addition, the connection between Pusey and Scottish Episcopalianism has not been substantially explored in the existing scholarship. It was a subject completely disregarded in the last collection of scholarly essays on Pusey, published in 1983 as part of the bouquet of publications around the Oxford Movement's 150th anniversary.[6]

Of course, by the 1850s, when Pusey became connected with Scottish Episcopalian developments, Newman had already departed from both the Movement and the Church of England. Indeed, until Newman began corresponding from 1840 with Episcopalian priests considering conversion to Roman Catholicism he appears to have had no connection with Scottish Episcopalianism.[7] Even in that correspondence with a Scottish priest expressing doubts about the catholicity of his present ecclesiastical position Newman makes no overt mention of the Scottish church, confining his Anglican references to the English church and English divines.[8] Richard Hurrell Froude also, while evidently aware of the Scottish church, appears little concerned about it. There is only one mention of it in his letters published posthumously, where he comments in an 1833 letter that 'it would be a great thing to have a true church in Germany; in Scotland it seems to be thriving'; a reference that can only be to the Episcopal Church given Froude's marker of ordination in the apostolic, that is, episcopal, succession as the mark of such a true church.[9]

This cursory attention at best to Scottish Episcopalianism by Newman and Froude is in marked contrast to the understanding and position of Keble. Keble valued the Scottish Episcopal Church before the advent of the Oxford Movement, largely because he had been raised by his father to be an Orthodox High Churchman, thus becoming heir to a tradition that had long battled on behalf of the legally persecuted and impoverished Scottish church.[10] It is highly possible, though I cannot prove it, that Keble was made aware of the catholicity and trials of the Episcopal Church by Dr Martin Routh, longtime president of Magdalen College, and leading High Churchman, for whom the Episcopal Church was a major cause of his life.[11] Keble first made Routh's acquaintance when his father took him up to Oxford in an unsuccessful attempt to gain entrance to the university at the early age of 14. Later, as an undergraduate and subsequently in his life, Keble had a relationship with Routh that his biographer describes as a life-long 'respectful acquaintance'.[12] It seems very unlikely that Routh would not have shared with Keble his support for the Scottish church and shaped Keble's High Church position accordingly. As a Tractarian Keble frequently expressed his warm theological approbation of the northern church and, as is well known, Keble stated his (possibly rhetorical) intention to join the Episcopal Church should the Church of England in his estimation apostasize.[13] Keble was also prepared to make his support for the High Church tradition of the Episcopal Church more tangible. For a man devoted to his parish of Hursley, in 1844 he nevertheless made the journey to form part of the High Church and Tractarian coterie that celebrated the opening of the Marchioness of Lothian's Tractarian church at Jedburgh.[14] Keble also accepted a canonry of the cathedral built on the little island of Great Cumbrae, the somewhat bizarre Tractarian project of George Boyle, the sixth Earl of Glasgow.[15] He would twice make the trip north to be present at the trial of Forbes for heresy in 1860 over the bishop's teaching of the real physical presence of Christ in the Eucharist.[16]

Compared with the well-established sympathy of Keble for the Episcopal Church, and the scanty knowledge and concern of Newman and Froude, Pusey came to a concern for the northern church much later than Keble, but more substantively than the other two Tractarian leaders. In part, this was because he was not raised in the warm Orthodox tradition as Keble was. Pusey was brought up in an English aristocratic Tory home that was of the high and dry establishment type, with a focus on good works and a horror of experiential fervour, his overbearing father leaving the room if conversation began to broach religion in such a way.[17] Pusey's subsequent ecclesiastical career, until he became friends with Keble, was more influenced by the liberal scholarship of Noetic Oxford than by High Church sighing for the preservation of the purity of apostolic episcopacy in England and Scotland.[18]

Pusey became substantively concerned with Episcopalianism in Scotland through his friendship with his younger disciple Forbes, subsequently Bishop of Brechin. Forbes was from a leading upper-middle-class Episcopalian family; his grandfather and father were influential in the counsels of the tiny church. Alexander had come up to Oxford in 1840 at the rather older age of 23 after having to relinquish a career in the civil service of the East India Company because of ill-health. At the university Forbes was drawn into Tractarian circles around Newman but became particularly influenced by Pusey, perhaps because he was an older man and less susceptible to the ready discipleship that Newman attracted from undergraduates usually years younger than Forbes. By 1840 Pusey himself had begun to demonstrate greater sympathies for Tractarianism as he began to resile from his previous liberalism. He had commenced his connection with the Oxford Movement with his 1833 tract on fasting, and by the 1840s had become identified in the popular press as the Tractarian leader, especially after Newman's 1845 conversion. After Forbes took his degree at Oxford Pusey appointed him to the Tractarian foundation of St Saviour's, Leeds, of which he was the founder and patron; and it was from St Saviour's that the Scotsman was elected in 1847 Bishop of Brechin by nine of the ten priests who were all the clergy of the diocese.[19]

Forbes became the principal proponent of the Oxford Movement in Scotland and, within the Movement, had a British-wide profile as the first Tractarian to be elevated to the episcopal bench, even if that bench was merely the rather homely one shared by the seven bishops of the miniscule Scottish Episcopal Church.[20] Given the Tractarian glorification of the episcopate as virtually the only *esse* of the Catholic Church, having one of their own among the successors to the apostles seemed a foretaste of better things to come.

Scotland therefore impinged itself more personally onto Pusey's consciousness with the elevation of his younger friend in 1847. But this awareness became involvement when, in 1857, Forbes delivered his first official charge to the clergy of his diocese on the real, corporal presence of Christ in the Eucharist. One of Forbes's clergy, William Henderson (the unsuccessful candidate for the position of Bishop of Brechin in 1847) presented him to the Episcopal Synod of the other six bishops for heresy for this teaching in that charge. Forbes subsequently turned to the theological skills of his mentor, as well as to Keble, for help in constructing his defence. The machinations that ensued between 1857 and Forbes's eventual trial and tame conviction in 1860 have been described in detail elsewhere.[21] What the Eucharistic Controversy of the 1850s does, however, is provide us with an insight into Pusey's views of the Scottish Episcopal Church through his correspondence with Forbes during these years.

Forbes's charge on the Eucharist forms one of a number of public statements of support for a physical presence of Christ in the Eucharist among Tractarians and High Churchmen that made the Eucharist Controversy a *cause célèbre* in British church circles in the mid-nineteenth century. There was the prosecution of George Anthony Denison, the orthodox Archdeacon of Taunton, for three sermons on this subject in Wells cathedral in 1854 that was upheld 1856, and then reversed on a technicality in 1857. Pusey himself had earlier entered the lists in 1843 with his sermon before the University of Oxford, 'The Holy Eucharist a Comfort to the Penitent', in which he had upheld the Eucharist as both a 'Real Objective Presence' of Christ and a commemorative sacrifice. For this sermon Pusey had been judged guilty of heterodoxy by the university and officially suspended from preaching before it for two years.[22] He again preached a sermon on 'The Real Presence' in 1852, but this time without official censure (though he expected it), and published on this topic in 1853 and again in 1857. A Tractarian Eucharistic theology was, therefore, a major concern for Pusey and was also expressed in his campaign to build Eucharistic-centred churches across Britain, of which St Saviour's, Leeds, was his own personally funded example.[23] Pusey's attitude, therefore, towards the Scottish Episcopal Church at this time has to be read in the context of his prolonged support for an Anglican Eucharistic theology that was more explicitly in the Catholic tradition of a genuine physical presence of Christ in the sacramental bread and wine. Clearly, Pusey would not have been disposed to be sympathetic towards a church which was putting his disciple and friend on trial for teaching what he himself had upheld publicly for years; for which he had previously endured official and public ecclesiastical censure; and which was one of the motivations for his long-standing campaign for the remodelling of Anglican churches and parochial practice.

A constant theme of Pusey's throughout the Eucharistic Controversy in the Scottish Episcopal Church was the hubris of its few bishops acting as though they could determine doctrine on a matter that had not been explicitly defined by the Anglican Church. Pusey first touched on this complaint in a letter probably written in 1859: 'It is ridiculous for 4 or 5 Bishops to be putting on the airs of a General Council, and abrogating the right of laying down as to matters of faith what never has been laid down, and condemning what has not been condemned.'[24] Pusey was also anxious lest such a definition by the Scottish bishops should lead to a persecution of those who upheld a Eucharistic presence along the lines of himself and Forbes.[25] Though the Scottish church was comparatively tiny, Pusey was evidently concerned about its influence beyond Scotland, at a time when other British bishops in England and Ireland were largely antithetical towards Tractarians. Pusey therefore viewed Scottish Episcoplianism within a pan-Anglican, or at least a British Anglican, context. This was in marked distinction to the disregard of Froude and Newman, and also to that of the Church of England generally (the Orthodox excepted) during the previous century.

In October the same year, writing to Keble, and now expecting Forbes's condemnation by the other bishops, Pusey complained of a 'half-believing laity' among Episcopalians influencing the bishops against the toleration of Forbes's teaching. Pusey dreaded that, with an antagonistic laity, there would be an irrevocable condemnation by the bishops; and because it came from the episcopate it might be widely understood as an official ecclesiastical definition of doctrine against Tractarian Eucharistic teaching.[26] But two days later he wrote to his fellow Tractarian leader to blame the bishops instead of the laity. Again he bemoaned the reprehensible possibility of a small group of bishops overturning orthodox doctrine. That Pusey saw the issue in these fundamental terms is evident from his comment that if Forbes relinquished his see in the event of such a condemnation it would be equivalent to an orthodox bishop (presumably in the fourth century) doing so upon being deposed by an Arian – something Pusey maintained no orthodox bishop would have done. An angry Pusey had little time or respect for the Scottish bishops repudiating, as he saw it, the truth of the early church upheld by its greatest theologians.

> It is, of course, an unheard of thing that some six Bishops should have the power of deposing a seventh without any appeal. The appeal ought to be with the whole Communion. But this is obviously impossible to get. Those Scotch Bishops seem to me like monkeys, dressed up like men, giving themselves great airs and talking big. They profess their own unacquaintance with the Canons, talk of 'feeling their way', and yet are going to condemn the whole Primitive Church, and would depose, if they could, S. Greg[ory]. Naz[ianzus]., S. Ambrose and S. Augustine.[27]

This was a considerable alteration of his views on the episcopate from his liberal days, when he repudiated the idea that bishops exercised any divinely guided authority over doctrine; that position, he had asserted, would be to make a human polity the *esse* of the church.[28] But Pusey in the 1850s had now come to accept what he previously rejected, and he was still concerned that such a condemnation would result in a Tractarian persecution spreading from Scotland to England, so Forbes should think of himself as 'fighting the battle for the Faith in England' also.[29] It was this possibility of the detrimental effects for Tractarian belief spreading from Scotland to England that was a principal motivation for Pusey's involvement in the affairs of the Episcopal Church at this time, alongside concern for a friend and defending the faith as they saw it. As far as Pusey was concerned, adopting the predominant Branch Theory of the church most clearly enunciated by William Palmer's *Treatise of the Church of Christ* (1838), the Scottish church, as a branch of the Church Catholic, could only teach what the early church taught.[30]

By the beginning of 1860 Pusey was hard at work drafting possible portions of Forbes's theological defence, in the face of the increasing likelihood of a public trial, notwithstanding the various attempts to head a trial off by both the bishops and Forbes's friends. Forbes was depressed at what he thought was the general unacceptance of his teaching among the laity of his diocese, and was expressing his belief that the Scottish church was 'unsound'. Pusey now thought it best he should resign before the bishops 'proceed to extremities', presumably meaning that the bishops would convict Forbes of heresy and depose him.[31] Pusey was also writing to Keble in ways that suggest he saw a distinction in this matter between the wider Scottish church and their largely English bishops. 'I think too that the Scotch Bishops dislike what they call English influence, which is what most of them (being Englishmen) are using against the poor Scotch Church.'[32] By July the sentence partly condemning Forbes had been delivered, leaving Forbes dejected and dispirited and, as Pusey put it, 'disappointed as to the small amount of faith in what we believe on the Holy Eucharist in the Scotch Church'.[33] Pusey believed that Forbes was suffering the depressing effects of a disillusionment that his Tractarian belief was shared by many Anglicans, something Pusey asserted he and Keble did not share. Pusey had always known, he claimed to Keble in another letter about Forbes's brokenness on the matter, how little faith there was in a 'Real Objective Presence, though I suppose that there is much faith in a real reception'.[34]

In the succeeding decade Pusey again became involved with the Scottish Episcopal Church, once again because of his friendship with Forbes. In the 1860s the bishop was now striving to defeat the relinquishing by his church of its traditional Eucharistic rite, the Scottish Communion Office. There were important demographic changes behind this shift within Scottish Episcopalianism. Scotland had been experiencing for half a century the effects of substantial English and Irish migration into the lowlands of Scotland, drawn by the growth of Scottish industries in that region.[35] These in-comers were often members of the Church of England or the Church of Ireland, with no familiarity with native Scottish Episcopalianism or the Scottish Communion Office. They identified their religion with the worship of the Book of Common Prayer and the liturgy of Holy Communion in that prayerbook. They were impatient with any difference from a familiar Anglicized culture and as many of these immigrants were Low Church (the Irish particularly) they disliked the High Church Episcopalian attachment to the Communion Office.[36] In addition, the effects of Anglicization – the cultural dominance of England – were beginning to be experienced among the Scottish urban middle class, as well as the Scottish aristocracy where Episcopalianism was strong. Englishmen also predominated among the small group of Scottish bishops; and even the other native Scot among them, William Wilson of Glasgow, disliked the Communion Office for its lack of conformity with the Book of Common Prayer.[37]

The increasing Anglicization of this Scottish church over the Communion Office also developed a specific English ecclesiastical dimension for the majority of the bishops and those, who like them, supported conformity with the Church of England. Clergy ordained by one of the Scottish bishops were still legally disbarred from holding a benefice in the Church of England. It was the vestige of the penal laws that had been imposed against Scottish Episcopalians for their Jacobitism during the eighteenth century. In 1860, in response to a remit from the Diocese of Moray and Ross, the bishops initiated an approach to the English bishops to have the clerical disabilities repealed in Parliament. But as a consequence of this Scottish request, the *quid pro quo* of English episcopal support for repeal of the clerical disabilities looked like being the rescinding of the Scottish canon that gave the Scottish Communion Office primary authority in the Scottish church over the Eucharistic liturgy of the Book of Common Prayer.[38] Consequently, the early 1860s saw a tussle within the church. On the one side were Episcopalians attached to the native Episcopalian tradition centred on the Communion Office. This rite went directly back to mid-eighteenth century. It was an adaptation by Bishop Thomas Rattray of the Holy Communion liturgy in the abortive 1637 Book of Common Prayer devised for Scotland with the support of Charles I. On the other side was an increasingly influential section of the church which wanted conformity with the Church of England, and the demotion and even the discarding of the Scottish Communion Office. Forbes was particularly attached to the Office because he valued the presence of an *epiclesis* in that liturgy, the mixing of water and wine in the chalice and the prayer of oblation as part of the Eucharistic Prayer, all of which were absent in the 1662 prayerbook. He believed these ceremonies were a liturgical expression of a belief in the physical presence of Christ in the Eucharistic elements.[39] The outcome, in 1863, was a compromise in which the English rite was to be used in all new congregations, unless the incumbent and a majority of the congregation desired the Scottish Office; but the English rite was now to be the one used in all diocesan and national gatherings. This led directly to the parliamentary act in 1864 that removed the Scottish Episcopalian clerical disabilities in the Church of England.[40]

Pusey referred to the troubles over the Scottish Communion Office in a letter to Keble in March 1862, where he wonders if it is not 'too late to stop this fatal Procrustean plan of the English and Scotch bishops?'[41] The next month he was referring to the plan of the majority of the Scottish bishops as a 'suicidal surrender'. He knew that the threat to the Scottish Office derived from the evangelical Archbishop of Canterbury, John Bird Sumner, because he opined that 'Even half a measure would not meet the wishes of Abp. S., who speaks of nothing but an unconditional "authoritatively setting aside" and even then "a great obstacle" only will be removed.'[42] This knowledge in all likelihood came from Forbes who, like all the other Scottish bishops, had been apprized the previous month that it was a condition set by Sumner for the English bishops supporting in Parliament the repeal of the disabilities. This was the first time the clerical disabilities had been linked to the rescinding of the Scottish liturgy, but from then on the two were locked together in an English-designed marriage. It would now not be possible for the Scottish bishops to have one without the other. It was a condition set by Sumner that had to be taken seriously because of the influence that evangelicals had in politics, through Lord Shaftesbury's influence in ecclesiastical matters with the prime minister, Lord Palmerston.[43]

Knowing that this bargain was in the offing, Pusey went on to express to Keble his distaste for it. 'It is the shadow in the water for which the dog parted with the substance. The surrender in any degree would be disgraceful to the Scotch Church, alienating their friends, sacrificing belief, gaining loss.'[44]

However, in a letter to Forbes in May 1862 Pusey expressed a more moderate interpretation about the whole matter. To Forbes he presented it as 'an ecclesiastical, not a doctrinal move'. It derived, he argued, from a sense among the Scottish bishops that their position in Scotland was an isolated one which could be strengthened if they were 'ecclesiastically more closely united' with the Church of England. In this seeking a greater unity with their larger sister church the Scottish bishops would not, Pusey maintained, be doing anything displeasing to Christ, which was the only thing that mattered. It would only be to give up the Scottish Office 'in order to make the Scotch Church more evidently one with the English'. He did agree that every effort needed to be made to keep the Office, but this was more a matter of prudence, in not harming the piety of many Episcopalians who saw it as 'the expression of their devotion'. Pusey, ever sanguine, compared the possible loss of the Scottish Office to the Gorham Judgement – the upholding by a civil court in 1850 as allowable a Calvinist clergyman's objections to baptismal regeneration. Pusey blithely argued that the case had caused faith to grow and spread rather than the reverse. Presumably Pusey here meant that an attack on the Catholic teaching of baptismal regeneration in that case had caused that doctrine to be defended more publicly and ardently than beforehand. Consequently, an attack on the Scottish Office would similarly see it ably and publicly defended. He urged Forbes not to see division over the Scottish Office as a separation on matters of fundamental faith. As with the Gorham Judgement, Pusey claimed it was not divisions over baptismal regeneration within the Church of England that had harmed the faith of the church, but the decision by some to separate from the Church of England. 'The secessions, not divisions, have hurt faith.'[45] The implication was that divisions over the Office did not mean that the Catholic faith was imperilled in Forbes's church.

But this construction of the issue by Pusey, as being less serious than Forbes believed it to be, as a matter of ecclesiastical order not of faith, is at odds with what he wrote to Keble earlier that year. In that correspondence Pusey had portrayed the Scottish church in relinquishing the Office as 'sacrificing belief' and losing something substantial; it would be a 'suicidal surrender'. The explanation for the milder argument to Forbes becomes clearer in a letter Pusey wrote to Keble in January the following year. There he described Forbes as being 'nervous and desponding' about the whole matter, something that Pusey, as a friend and confidante, had been only too well aware of in his friend throughout the Eucharistic Controversy, and which he now saw also in this storm over the Scottish liturgy. Pusey told Keble that, because of Forbes's morbid disposition about the whole Scottish church at this time putting in peril his position within it, 'I dare not *write* about these matters.' The emphasis reveals that it was only writing to Forbes that Pusey dreaded. But his encouragement to Forbes to visit him in Oxford through these periods of intense personal anxiety indicates that Pusey preferred personal interaction as a more subtle and satisfying way to engage in these controversial trials with his depressed friend. This pastoral concern to be most effective in counselling and consoling Forbes comes out explicitly later in the letter. 'I shape my advice to what I think he [Forbes] would bear. He is sensitive about these matters, far beyond myself; and I have to soothe, as far as I may, his sensitiveness.'[46]

This evidence raises an objection to the very stark picture of Pusey offered by Paul Avis in the first edition of his seminal work on ecumenical theology, *Anglicanism and the Christian Church* (1989). In an analysis of Pusey's theology that pulls no punches, Avis portrays Pusey as a former theological liberal whose decline into 'guilt-mongering' was prompted by the deaths of his father, Bishop Lloyd – another father figure – his daughter and his wife. These tragedies produced a Pusey who, as a liberal, was alive and vibrant; but who, as a Tractarian, was reactionary and insensitive under the prodding of his excessive penitential responses to his demanding God.[47] While I consider Avis's picture of the theological changes in Pusey to be more or less accurate, I believe his picture of the humanity of Pusey is too broadly and severely drawn. A person such as Avis painted Pusey to be would not have been able to hold the friendship of warm, human individuals such as Keble, or sensitive ones like Forbes. His responsive pastoral handling of the depression and anguish of Forbes during the challenges of the 1850s and 1860s; his ability to moderate and tailor his views to take account of his friend's condition and the repeated visits of Forbes to Pusey in search of succour, I believe demonstrate that Pusey, though undoubtedly overly severe and at times brutal in his asceticism, was also capable of human warmth and compassion.

Pusey put his more muted construction of the controversy to Forbes again in an undated letter in 1862. It would be best to accept the English rite as an unaltered whole, rather than accept alteration to the Scottish Office as a couple of the bishops wanted. Pusey thought it had probably been a mistake for the Scottish church to legislate for a different rite in the first place as it was 'so small a body'. It would be 'stronger, if identical with England, if in doing so it did not displease God'. Adopting the English liturgy was, in other words, 'a matter of policy' not of faith.[48]

So what was Pusey's true position with regard to the Scottish Episcopal Church and its Scottish Communion Office? Was it a struggle over a purely ecclesiastical arrangement that did not affect the catholic faith; or was it, as Forbes believed, a threat to one of that church's most important local expressions of catholicity with regard to the Eucharistic presence of Christ?

Pusey steadfastly all his life maintained that the Book of Common Prayer was a satisfactory witness to Catholic truth, as had been initially set out in Tractarian theology by Newman in Tract 3 of the *Tracts for the Times*. The communal worship of the prayerbook, however, did need to be supplemented by books for personal catholic devotion, something Pusey devoted himself to in repeated adaptations of Roman Catholic works of spiritualty for Anglican use.[49] Pusey reiterates this position in the correspondence on the Scottish Communion Office when he posits to Forbes that if the bishops adopted the English liturgy it would be one in which 'the power of the Act of Consecration is more brought out' than it was in the Scottish rite.[50] Presumably Pusey was adopting the common Roman Catholic view that the words Jesus said over the bread and wine in the institution narrative are the consecrating moments in the Eucharistic Prayer. These words were more highlighted in the English rite, where the Eucharistic Prayer ends immediately after their recitation by the priest, than in the Scottish rite where the prayer goes on after the institution narrative into the prayer of oblation.

From this exploration of Pusey's connection with the affairs of the Scottish Episcopal Church over a period of nearly ten years in the late 1850s and 1860s, what can be said about his views of that Scottish church? In the first place, it meant that Pusey, like Keble but unlike Newman and Froude, was personally associated with manifestations of Anglicanism beyond England. In this respect, Pusey's Scottish participation connects with his direct concern for the imperial spread of Anglicanism which Ruth Teale has outlined as substantive.[51] This attention to the development of colonial Anglican Churches was principally in furtherance of the Tractarian agenda of the fundamental importance of the episcopate, something their followers would honour more in theory than in practice. Consequently, Pusey's Anglicanism developed a pan-British and even a global dimension that stands in contrast to the two other early Tractarian leaders. Froude, because of his early death, probably had little time to do so, being largely caught up in characteristic acerbic and radical concern for his own English church. Newman appeared largely unconcerned for Anglicanism beyond England. Despite having contributed to coining 'Anglicanism' as an ecclesial concept, Newman seemed often during the 1830s and 1840s to be paying more attention to his own mental construction of the church of the early Christian centuries than he did for his own contemporary church outside England. It was Pusey who did most among the original Tractarian leaders to make their movement one that had a genuine concern with Anglicanism beyond the boundaries of England.

That awareness of Scottish Episcopalianism, though genuine, was of course partial and distorted. It did not include much awareness of the native tradition of Scottish Episcopalianism that was expressed in attachment to the Scottish Communion Office. It certainly did not have any sympathy with the Evangelicalism of many Anglicans in Scotland who kept themselves separated from the Episcopal Church. It could hardly be otherwise, given that Pusey largely, but not completely, received his understanding of Scottish matters from a single source, Forbes, who was also a Tractarian; and both men were locked in a battle over a Christ's physical presence in the Eucharist, a Tractarian belief they held dear. However, that battle also meant that Pusey was also unsympathetic to what he saw as an Anglicizing agenda foisted upon an undeniably Scottish church by its largely English bishops. Yet Pusey, at the same time, was upholding his own Anglocentric bias, being rather dubious about the wisdom of such a small church having a Eucharistic rite that was distinctive and different from the Church of England in the first place.[52]

This brief exploration into some aspects of the evolution of an Anglo-Scots dimension to the Movement Pusey found himself giving his name to in popular awareness points to a need for a wider historiographical exploration of the first decades of the Oxford Movement. I have argued elsewhere for a historical investigation that is broader than the present excessive focus on John Henry Newman;[53] and a movement that impacted Scotland from at least the 1840s needs to be assessed in terms of its comparative development in all the lands and cultures of the British Isles. Enough has been said here to indicate the connections between leading Anglicans involved in the Movement to suggest that such a British approach to the study of the Oxford Movement would lead to a more complex assessment of its development. Notwithstanding the increasing dominance of an expanding Anglicized culture in nineteenth-century Britain, the Oxford Movement found its way very quickly after its inauguration into a diversity of Anglican cultures in the British and Irish islands, including Anglo-Irish and Gaelic Scots, not to mention peasant northeastern farming- and fisher-folk and an aristocracy that was in the vanguard of the promotion of Anglicized culture.[54] A greater awareness and attention by historians to this cultural diversity of the various groups affected by the Movement, not to mention the different British nations the Movement expanded into, would see the history of the Oxford Movement escape the Anglocentricity that has often in the historiography restricted its importance to the University of Oxford and the Church of England. Indeed, it is too little attended to in English scholarship on the Movement how remarkably quickly it expanded and grew beyond the confines of Britain and began to influence Episcopalians and Anglicans in North America and the furthest reaches of the British Empire.[55] There it was a background influence in the development of an Anglicanism that claimed more independence from the state on the divine basis of the church and the episcopate found, for example, in the counsels of Bishop Broughton of Sydney and George Augustus Selwyn of New Zealand.[56] The Oxford Movement must be more understood as both an imperial and a trans-Atlantic movement within years of its English inauguration.

Pusey's awareness of a British Anglicanism, partial and Anglocentric as it was, finds a small acknowledgement in his major work on Anglican ecclesiology. This was his first *Eirenicon*, published in 1865 in pursuit of the Tractarian dream of a reunion between the Church of England and the Roman Catholic Church. There Pusey affirmed, against the criticisms of Henry Edward Manning, that the doctrine of the real physical presence of Christ in the Eucharist upheld by Forbes had 'been vindicated in the Church of Scotland'.[57] It is a tiny grain in the Tractarian sandcastle Pusey was building in his book. He proposed that the Church of England, as a perpetuator of apostolic truth and a bulwark of catholicism, had a spiritual, rather than an ecclesial, union with that larger catholic church. Whatever the value of Pusey's major argument in the book, the mention of the Scottish Episcopal Church is a small indication that by this time Pusey's consciousness of his church was wider than that of the Church of England. Though that pan-Anglican awareness was limited to Pusey's theological writing, and did not include personal visits to either Scotland or the colonies, it was an important contribution in making the Oxford Movement, in which Pusey found himself a reluctant leader, a global phenomenon.

Notes

1 Church, *Oxford Movement*, 93.
2 Ibid., 114–15.
3 Chadwick, *Mind of the Oxford Movement*, 30.
4 Ibid., 231.
5 Nockles, 'Our Brethren of the North', 656–8.
6 Butler, *Pusey Rediscovered*.
7 Strong, 'In Search of Certainty', 511–29.
8 Newman, *Letters and Diaries* 8: 337–8, 345–6, 348, 355–8, 365, 368–70, 390, 402–4, 406–7.
9 *Remains of Richard Hurrell Froude*, 302.
10 Nockles, *Oxford Movement*, 66, 88–9, 153; Strong, *Episcopalianism in Nineteenth-Century Scotland*, 31–2.
11 Middleton, *Dr Routh*, 65–75.
12 Battiscombe, *John Keble*, 11.
13 Nockles, 'Our Brethren of the North', 673.
14 Strong, 'Coronets and Altars', 398.
15 Perry, *Oxford Movement in Scotland*, 61.
16 Strong, *Alexander Forbes*, 146, 151.
17 Lough, *Dr Pusey*, 1.

18 Frappell, 'Science', 165.
19 Strong, *Alexander Forbes*, 1–46, 52.
20 In 1800 Scottish Episcopalians were estimated only to number around 15,000 adults; by 1851 there were 43,000 adherents. There was a larger 'Anglican' population in Scotland in the mid-nineteenth century, but they were divided between High Church congregations in communion with the Scottish bishops and a minority of separate Evangelical congregations. The collapse of Episcopalian numbers had occurred in the late eighteenth and early nineteenth centuries from their position in the late seventeenth century when they had constituted about one-third of Scots when they were ejected from the Church of Scotland in 1689. This was a result of penal legislation because of their non-juring Jacobitism, coupled with an impoverishment, that left that the church unable to resource resistance to Evangelical evangelization in their Highland and northeast strongholds. See Strong, *Alexander Forbes*, 12–13, 229.
21 Strong, *Alexander Forbes*, chapter 4.
22 Liddon, *Life of Pusey*, 2:306–9, 3:422–6.
23 Franklin, 'Tradition', 150–51.
24 Pusey to Forbes, 6 July [? 1859], Brechin Diocesan Archives, Dundee University, 1. 1. 153.
25 Pusey to Forbes, undated, Brechin Diocesan Archives, Dundee University, 1. 1. 154.
26 Pusey to Keble, 11 October [1859], Pusey House, PK (Pusey to Keble correspondence) v.
27 Pusey to Keble, 13 October 1859, Pusey House, PK v.
28 Avis, *Anglicanism*, 208–9.
29 Ibid.
30 Pusey to Keble, 1859, Pusey House, PK v.
31 Pusey to Keble, 4 January 1860, Pusey House, PK v.
32 Pusey to Keble, n.d., Pusey House, PK v.
33 Pusey to Keble, 1 July 1860, Pusey House, PK v.
34 Pusey to Keble, 4 December 1860, Pusey House, PK v.
35 Morris, 'Urbanisation and Scotland', 73–102; Morgan and Trainor, 'The Dominant Classes', 103–37; Nenadic, 'The Rise of the Urban Middle Classes', 109–26.
36 Meldrum, *Conscience and Compromise*.
37 Strong, *Alexander Forbes*, 130.
38 Strong, *Alexander Forbes*, 163, 165.
39 Strong, *Episcopalianism in Nineteenth-Century Scotland*, 10; Strong, *Alexander Forbes*, 171.
40 Strong, *Alexander Forbes*, 181–6.
41 Pusey to Keble, possibly 27 March 1862, Pusey House, PK vi.
42 Ibid.
43 Strong, *Alexander Forbes*, 164–5.
44 Pusey to Keble, possibly 27 March 1862, Pusey House, PK vi.
45 Pusey to Forbes, 2 May [1862], Brechin Diocesan Archives, Dundee University Library, Br MS 1. 3. 613.
46 Pusey to Keble, 1 January 1863, Pusey House, PK vi.
47 Avis, *Anglicanism and the Christian Church*, 205–6, 212.
48 Pusey to Forbes, n.d. [1862], Brechin Diocesan Archives, Dundee University Library, Br MS 1. 3. 682.
49 Denison, 'Dr Pusey as Confessor', 225–7.
50 Pusey to Forbes, n.d., Brechin Diocesan archives, Dundee University library, 1. 3. 682.
51 Teale, 'Dr Pusey and the Church Overseas', 185–209.

52 Pusey to Forbes, n.d. [1862?], Brechin Diocesan Archives, Dundee University Library, Br MS 1. 3. 682.
53 Strong, 'The Oxford Movement and the British Empire'.
54 Strong, *Episcoplianism in Nineteenth-Century Scotland*, chapters 2, 3, 6.
55 Among the essays published in 1933 on the centenary of the Oxford Movement, Edward Hardy Jr alerted English scholarship to the influence of Tractarianism in the Episcopal Church in the United States by the end of the 1830s: Edward Rochie Hardy Jr, 'The Catholic Revival in the American Church', in N. P. Williams, *Northern Catholicism: Centenary studies in the Oxford and Parallel Movements* (London: SPCK 1933), 87–8. But this trans-Atlantic dimension has been missing in most historiography since that time. Ironically, even a major overview of the Movement by a North American scholar is silent on the Atlantic dimension of Tractarianism: O'Connell, *Oxford Conspirators*.
56 Strong, *Anglicanism and the British Empire*, chapter 5.
57 Pusey, *Eirenicon*, 30.

BIBLIOGRAPHY

Archival sources

Acland, Henry W. Papers. Pusey House, Oxford.
British Library, London.
Forbes, Alexander Penrose and George Frederick Boyle. Correspondence, 1844–1875. Brechin Diocesan Library Manuscripts. Archives, University of Dundee, Dundee.
Forbes, Alexander Penrose. Papers. Pusey House, Oxford.
Liddon Bound Volumes. Pusey House, Oxford.
Liddon, Henry Parry. Manuscript of *Life of Edward Bouverie Pusey*. Pusey House, Oxford.
Milner, Miss [Maud]. 'Reminiscences of Dr Pusey'. Pusey House, Oxford.
Pusey, Edward Bouverie and John Keble. Correspondence. Pusey House, Oxford.
Society of the Most Holy Trinity. Statutes, 1861. Ascot Priory Archive, Ascot.

Printed sources

Albiergo, Guiseppe. 'Das erste Vatikanische Konzil (1869–1870)'. In *Geschichte der Konzilien vom Nicaenum bis zum Vaticanum II*, edited by Guiseppe Albiergo, 386–412. Düsseldorf: Patmos, 1993.
Allchin, A. M. *Alexander Penrose Forbes: The Search for Unity*. Dundee: University of Dundee,1975.
Allchin, A. M. *Participation in God: A Forgotten Strand in Anglican Tradition*. London: Darton, Longman and Todd, 1988.
Allchin, A. M. 'Pusey: The Servant of God'. In *Pusey Rediscovered*, edited by Perry Butler, 366–90. London: SPCK, 1983.
Allchin, A. M. *The Silent Rebellion: Anglican Religious Communities 1845–1900*. London: SCM Press, 1958.
Anson, Peter F. *The Call of the Cloister: Religious Communities and Kindred Bodies in the Anglican Communion*. London: SPCK, 1964.
Anson, Peter F. *Fashions in Church Furnishings*. London: Faith Press, 1960.
Aston, Nigel. *Christianity and Revolutionary Europe, c.1750–1830*. Cambridge: Cambridge University Press, 2002.
Atterbury, Francis. *The Axe Laid to the Root of Christianity: or, A Specimen of the Profaneness and Blasphemy that Abounds in Some Late Writings*. London: John Morphew, 1706.
Atterbury, Francis. *The Case of the Schedule Stated, Wherein an Account is Given of the Rise and Design of that Instrument; And of the Influence It Hath on the Adjournments of the Lower House of Convocation; And all the Authorities, Urg'd in Behalf of the Archbishop's Sole Power to Prorogue the Whole Convocation, are Occasionally Examined*. London: T. Bennet, 1702.

Atterbury, Francis. *A Letter to a Convocation-Man Concerning the Rights, Powers, and Priviledges of that Body.* London: E. Whitlock, 1698.

Atterbury, Francis. *The Rights, Powers, and Privileges of an English Convocation; Stated and Vindicated, in Answer to a Late Book of Dr Wake's, Entitled, The Authority of Christian Princes over Their Ecclesiastical Synods Asserted &c. and to Several Other Pieces.* London: Thomas Bennet, 1700.

Atterbury, Francis. *Sermons and Discourses on Several Subjects and Occasions.* Edited by Thomas Moore. 2nd ed. London: T. Woodward, 1737.

Avis, Paul. *Anglicanism and the Christian Church: Theological Resources in Historical Perspective.* Edinburgh: T&T Clark, 1989.

Battiscombe, Georgina. *John Keble: A Study in Limitations.* London: Constable, 1963.

Beeman, Thomas O. *Ritualism: Doctrine not Dress: Notes of Lectures on Ritualism, the Development of Tractarianism: Published by Request, with Additions, Including Remarks on the Charge of the Bishop of Salisbury.* Cranbrook: Geo. Waters & Son, 1868.

Bennett, G. V. *The Tory Crisis in Church and State, 1688–1730: The Career of Francis Atterbury, Bishop of Rochester.* Oxford: Clarendon Press, 1975.

Bennett, W. J. E. *An Examination of Archdeacon Denison's Propositions of Faith on the Doctrine of the Holy Eucharist, with a Prefatory Letter to the Lord Bishop of Bath and Wells.* Froome-Selwood: published by and for the author; London: Whittaker; London: J. Cleaver, n.d. [1857].

Bennett, William J. E. *A Plea for Toleration in the Church of England, in a Letter to the Rev. E. B. Pusey, D. D., Regius Professor of Hebrew, and Canon of Ch. Ch. Oxford.* London: J. T. Hayes; Froome-Selwood: W. C. & J. Penny, 1867.

Best, G. F. A. *Temporal Pillars: Queen Anne's Bounty, the Ecclesiastical Commissioners, and the Church of England.* Cambridge: Cambridge University Press, 1964.

Bettenson, Henry and Chris Maunder. *Documents of the Christian Church.* 3rd ed. Oxford: Oxford University Press, 1999.

Bevis, Henry J. *The Popery of Puseyism: Two Sermons.* London: James Paul, n.d. [1845].

Bosanquet, Claude. *The Lord's Supper: A Sacrament, not a Sacrifice.* London: S. W. Partridge, n.d. [1879].

Boulter, B. C. *The Anglican Reformers.* London: Philip Allen, 1933.

Brandreth, H. R. T. *The Œcumenical Ideals of the Oxford Movement.* London: SPCK, 1947.

Brendon, Piers. 'Newman, Keble, and Froude's Remains'. *English Historical Review* 87, no. 345 (1972): 697–716.

Brilioth, Yngve. *The Anglican Revival: Studies in the Oxford Movement.* London: Longmans, Green & Co., 1925.

Brown, David. 'Pusey as Consistent and Wise: Some Comparisons with Newman'. *Anglican and Episcopal History* 71 (2002): 328–49.

Burke, Edmund. *Reflections on the Revolution in France: and on the Proceedings in Certain Societies in London Relative to that Event: in a Letter Intended to Have Been Sent to a Gentleman in Paris.* London: Dodsley, 1790.

Burnet, Gilbert. *An Answer to Mr Law's Letter to the Lord Bishop of Bangor, in a Letter to Mr Law.* London: Timothy Childe, 1717.

Burnet, Gilbert. *Bishop Burnet's History of His Own Times.* 2 vols. London: Thomas Ward, 1727, 1734.

Burton, Edward. *Testimonies of the Ante-Nicene Fathers to the Divinity of Christ.* Oxford: Clarendon, 1826.

Buschkühl, Mathias. *Great Britain and the Holy See.* Dublin: Irish Academic Press, 1982.

Butler, Cuthbert. *The Vatican Council: The Story Told From the Inside in Bishop Ullathorne's Letters.* 2 vols. London: Longmans, 1930.

Butler, Joseph. *The Analogy of Religion, Natural and Revealed, to the Constitution and Course of Nature: A New and Improved Edition*. London: Thomas Tegg, 1829.
Butler, Perry, ed. *Pusey Rediscovered*. London: SPCK, 1983.
Calamy, Edward. *An Historical Account of my Own Life with Some Reflections on the Times I Have Lived In*. 2 vols. London: Henry Colburn and Richard Bentley, 1829.
Carter, Thomas Thellusson. *The Blessings of the Sacrament of the Lord's Supper Practically Explained, and the Duty of Frequently Communicating Enforced*. London: J. G. & F. Rivington, 1835.
Carter, T[homas] T[hellusson]. *Spiritual Instruction on the Holy Eucharist*. 2nd ed. London: Joseph Masters, New York: Pott and Amery, 1871.
Cecconi, Eugenio. *Storia del Concilio Ecumenico Vaticano, Parte Prima: Antecedenti del Concilio*. 2 vols. Rome: Tipografica Vaticana, 1872.
Chadwick, Owen. *A History of the Popes*. Oxford: Clarendon Press, 1998.
Chadwick, Owen. 'The Mind of the Oxford Movement'. In *The Spirit of the Oxford Movement: Tractarian Essays*, 1–53. Cambridge: Cambridge University Press, 1990.
Chadwick, Owen. *The Mind of the Oxford Movement*. Cambridge: Cambridge University Press, 1960.
Chadwick, Owen. *The Spirit of the Oxford Movement: Tractarian Essays*. Cambridge: Cambridge University Press, 1990.
Chadwick, Owen. *The Victorian Church*. Oxford University Press, 1966.
Chadwick, Owen. *The Victorian Church*. 2 vols. 2nd ed. London: Adam and Charles Black, 1966–70.
Chadwick, Owen. *The Victorian Church*. 2 vols. London: SCM Press, 1987.
Chalmers, Thomas. *The Evidence and Authority of the Christian Revelation*. Edinburgh: Blackwood, 1814.
Chapman, Mark David. 'Bischofsamt und Politik: Zur Begründung des Bischofsamtes in der Anglikanischen Kirche'. *Zeitschrift für Theologie und Kirche* 97 (2000): 434–62.
Chapman, Mark D. 'A Catholicism of the Word and a Catholicism of Devotion: Pusey, Newman and the First *Eirenicon*'. *Zeitschrift für neuere Theologiegeschichte/Journal for the History of Modern Theology* 14 (2007): 167–90.
Chapman, Mark D. 'An Ecumenical Front against Liberalism: Bishop Alexander Penrose Forbes of Brechin and *An Explanation of the Thirty-nine Articles*'. *Zeitschrift für neuere Theologiegeschichte/Journal for the History of Modern Theology* 17 (2010): 147–61.
Chapman, Mark D. 'The Fantasy of Reunion: The Rise and Fall of the Association for the Promotion of the Unity of Christendom'. *Journal of Ecclesiastical History* 58 (2007): 49–74.
Chapman, Mark D. 'Pusey, Newman, and the End of a "Healthful Reunion": The Second and Third Volumes of Pusey's *Eirenicon*'. *Zeitschrift für neuere Theologiegeschichte/Journal for the History of Modern Theology* 15 (2008): 208–31.
Cheyne, P. *Six Sermons on the Doctrine of the Most Holy Eucharist*. Aberdeen: A. Brown and Co., 1858.
Church, R. W. *The Oxford Movement: Twelve Years, 1833–1845*. London: Macmillan, 1891.
A Clergyman of His Lordship's Diocese. *An Answer to Dr Pusey's Sermon: The Doctrine of the Church of England, and of Holy Scripture on the Eucharist Shewn to be Entirely Opposed to Dr Pusey; In a Series of Letters to the Right Rev. Charles Thomas, Lord Bishop of Ripon*. London: Seeley, Burnside, and Seeley, 1853.
Cockburn, John. *A Short and Impartial Review of the Lord Bishop of Bangor's Sermon at S. James's Chapel, March 31, 1717: Now after the Several Defences of his Lordship*. London: John Morphew, 1718.

Congar, Yves. *I Believe in the Holy Spirit*. Translated by David Smith. 3 vols. New York: Crossroad Publishing, 1983.

Conybeare, John Josiah. *The Bampton Lectures for the Year 1824: Being an Attempt to Trace the History and to Ascertain the Limits of the Secondary and Spiritual Interpretation of Scripture.* Oxford: The University Press for the Author, 1824.

Croydon, Tony. *William III and the Godly Revolution.* Cambridge: Cambridge University Press, 1996.

Cummings, Owen F. *Eucharistic Doctors: A Theological History.* New York: Paulist Press, 2005.

Davage, William, ed. *In This Sign Conquer: A History of the Society of the Holy Cross.* London: Continuum, 2005.

Davison, John. *Discourses on Prophecy, in Which are Considered its Structure, Use, and Inspiration: Being the Substance of Twelve Sermons Preached in the Chapel of Lincoln's Inn, in the Lecture Founded by the Right Reverend William Warburton, Bishop of Gloucester.* London: Murray, 1824.

Dawson, Christopher. *The Spirit of the Oxford Movement.* 1933. Reprint, with an introduction by Peter Nockles. London: St Austin Press, 2001.

Denison, Keith. 'Dr Pusey as Confessor and Spiritual Director'. In *Pusey Rediscovered*, edited by Perry Butler, 210–30. London: SPCK, 1983.

Dodsworth, William. *Discourses on the Lord's Supper, Preached in Margaret Chapel, St Marylebone.* London: James Burns, 1835.

Edison, John Sibbald. *The Doctrine of Dr Pusey's Sermon, Considered: In Two Supplemental Chapters to an Essay on the Oxford Tracts, Published in 1839.* London: T. Cadell; Edinburgh: W. Blackwood and Sons, 1843.

Faber, Geoffrey. *Oxford Apostles: A Character Study of the Oxford Movement.* London: Faber & Faber, 1933.

Faussett, Geoffrey. *Jewish History Vindicated from the Unscriptural View of it Displayed in 'The History of the Jews' (by Henry Hart Milman), in a Sermon Preached before the University of Oxford (18 Febr. 1830).* Oxford: n.p., 1830.

Forbes, Alexander Penrose. *The Church of England and the Doctrine of Papal Infallibility.* Oxford: Parker, 1871.

Forbes, Alexander Penrose. *An Explanation of the Thirty-Nine Articles.* Volume One: *Articles I–XXI with an Epistle Dedicatory to the Rev. E. B. Pusey D. D.* Oxford: Parker, 1867. Volume Two: *Articles XXII–End.* Oxford: Parker, 1868.

Forbes, Alexander Penrose. *The Notes of Unity and Sanctity in Reference to Modern Scepticism: A Charge.* London: Masters, 1864.

Forbes of Brechin; An 'Unofficial Patron Saint' of the Scottish Episcopal Church. Stirling: CSG Publications, 1985.

Forrester, David. 'Dr Pusey's Marriage'. *Ampleforth Journal* 78 (Summer 1973): 33–47.

Forrester, David. 'The Intellectual Development of E. B. Pusey 1800–1850'. DPhil thesis, University of Oxford, 1967.

Forrester, David A. R. *Young Doctor Pusey: A Study in Development.* London: Mowbray, 1989.

Franklin, R. W. *Nineteenth-Century Churches: The History of a New Catholicism in Württemberg, England, and France.* New York: Garland, 1987.

Franklin, R. William. 'Tradition as a Point of Contact between Anglicans and Roman Catholics in the Nineteenth Century: The Case of Johann Adam Möhler and Edward Bouverie Pusey'. In *The Quadrilog: Essays in Honor of George H. Tavard*, edited by Kenneth Hagen, 147–61. Collegeville, MN: The Liturgical Press 1994.

Frappell, Leighton. '"Science" in the Service of Orthodoxy: The Early Intellectual Development of Edward Bouverie Pusey'. In *Pusey Rediscovered*, edited by Perry Butler, 1–33. London: SPCK, 1983.

Garbett, James. *A Review of Dr Pusey's Sermon; and the Doctrine of the Eucharist According to the Church of England*. London: J. Hatchard and Son; Brighton: Folthorp; Oxford: Parker, 1843.
Gardner, C. E. and Richard Meux Benson. *Life of Father Goreh*. London: Longmans, Green & Co., 1900.
Geck, Albrecht, ed. *Autorität und Glaube: Edward Bouverie Pusey und Friedrich August Gotttreu Tholuck im Briefwechsel (1825–1865)*. Göttingen: V&R-unipress, 2009.
Geck, Albrecht. 'The Concept of History in E. B. Pusey's First Enquiry into German Theology and Its German Background'. *Journal of Theological Studies* 38, no. 2 (1987): 387–408.
Geck, Albrecht. 'Edward Bouverie Pusey: Hochkirchliche Erweckung'. In *Theologen des 19. Jahrhunderts*, edited by Peter Neuner and Gunther Wenz, 108–26. Darmstadt: Wissenschaftliche Buchgesellschaft, 2002.
Geck, Albrecht. 'Pusey, Tholuck and the Reception of the Oxford Movement in Germany'. In *The Oxford Movement: Europe and the Wider World c. 1830–c. 1930*, edited by Stuart J. Brown and Peter Nockles, 168–84. Cambridge: Cambridge University Press, 2012.
Geck, Albrecht. *Schleiermacher als Kirchenpolitiker. Die Auseinandersetzungen um die Reform der Kirchenverfassung in Preußen (1799–1823)*. Bielefeld: Luther-Verlag, 1997.
Gill, Sean. *Women and the Church of England: From the Eighteenth Century to the Present*. London: SPCK, 1994.
Goode, William. *The Nature of Christ's Presence in the Eucharist: or, the True Doctrine of the Real Presence Vindicated in Opposition to the Fictitious Real Presence Asserted by Archdeacon Denison, Mr (Late Archdeacon) Wilberforce, and Dr Pusey: With Full Proof of the Real Character of the Attempt Made by Those Authors to Represent Their Doctrine as That of the Church of England and her Divines*. 2 vols. London: T. Hatchard, 1856.
Greaves, R. W. 'The Jerusalem Bishopric, 1841'. *English Historical Review* 64, no. 252 (July 1949): 328–52.
Greenfield, R. H. '"Such a Friend to the Pope"'. In *Pusey Rediscovered*, edited by Perry Butler, 162–84. London: SPCK, 1983.
Grueber, C[harles] S[tephen]. *The Presence, the Sacrifice, the Adoration: A Letter to the Right Reverend The Lord Bishop of Bath and Wells, on Certain Statements of His Lordship's Charge, in Reference to the Holy Eucharist, May, 1873*. 2nd ed. Oxford and London: James Parker and Co., 1873.
Hales, E. E. Y. *Pio Nono: A Study in European Politics and Religion in the Nineteenth Century*. London: Eyre and Spottiswood, 1956.
Härdelin, Alf. *The Tractarian Understanding of the Eucharist*. Uppsala: Uppsala University Press, 1965.
Hare, Julius. *Vindication of Luther Against his Recent English Assailants*. 2nd ed. London: John W. Parker and Son, 1855.
Harrison, John. *An Answer to Dr Pusey's Challenge Respecting the Doctrine of the Real Presence, in Which the Doctrines of the Lord's Supper, as Held by Him, Roman and Greek Catholics, Ritualists, and High Anglo-Catholics, are Examined and Shown to be Contrary to the Holy Scriptures, and to the Teaching of the Fathers of the First Eight Centuries, with the Testimony of an Ample Catena Patrum of the Same Period*. 2 vols. London: Longmans, Green & Co., 1871.
Harrison, John. *Letter to the Rev. E. B. Pusey, D. D., on his Unfair Treatment of the Testimony of the Fathers, concerning the Doctrine of the Real Presence: with a Refutation of That Doctrine*. London: The Religious Book Society, 1877.
Hengstenberg, Ernst Wilhelm. *Christologie des Alten Testaments, und Commentar über die Messianischen Weissagungen der Propheten I–III*. Berlin: Oehmigke, 1829–35.
Hilliard, David. 'Un-English and Un-Manly: Anglo-Catholicism and Homosexuality'. *Victorian Studies* 25, no. 2 (Winter 1982): 181–210.

Hoadly, Benjamin. *An Answer to the Reverend Dr Snape's Letter to the Bishop of Bangor*. 6th ed. London: James Knapton, 1717.

Hoadly, Benjamin. *The Common Rights of Subjects, Defended and the Nature of the Sacramental Test, Consider'd in Answer to the Dean of Chichester's Vindication of the Corporation and Test Acts*. London: J. Knapton, 1719.

Hoadly, Benjamin. *A Letter to a Clergy-Man in the Country, Concerning Votes of the Bishops in the Last Session of Parliament upon the Bill against Occasional Conformity*. London: John Nutt, 1704.

Hoadly, Benjamin. *The Nature of the Kingdom, or Church, of Christ: A Sermon Preach'd before the King, at the Royal Chapel at St James's on Sunday, March 31, 1717*. London: James Knapton, 1717.

Hoadly, Benjamin. *A Persuasion to Lay-Conformity: or the Reasonableness of Constant Communion with the Church of England, Represented to the Dissenting Laity*. London: Timothy Childs, 1704.

Hohenlohe-Schillingsfürst, Chlodwig zu. *Denkwürdigkeiten*. Edited by Friedrich Curtius. 2 vols. Stuttgart: Deutsche Verlags-Anstalt, 1907. Translated by George W. Chrystal as *Memoirs of Prince Chlodwig of Hohenlohe Schillingfuerst*. London: Heinemann, 1907.

Hook, Walter Farquhar. *The Eucharist: A Sacrament and a Sacrifice: A Sermon, Preached at Birch Church, on Sunday, the 5th of July, 1846, Being the Sunday Immediately Following the Consecration*. London: F. & J. Rivington; Oxford: Parker; Cambridge: I. & J. J. Deighton; Leeds: T. Harrison, 1847.

Hooker, Richard. *The Works of that Learned and Judicious Divine, Mr Richard Hooker: With an Account of his Life and Death by Isaac Walton*. Oxford: Clarendon, 1865.

Imberg, Rune. *In Quest of Authority: The 'Tracts for the Times' and the Development of the Tractarian Leaders (1833–1841)*. Bibliotheca historico-ecclesiastica Lundensis 16. Lund: Lund University Press, 1987.

Jasper, David. 'Pusey's *Lectures on Types and Prophecies*'. In *Pusey Rediscovered*, edited by Perry Butler, 51–70. London: SPCK, 1983.

Johnston, John Octavius. *Life and Letters of Henry Parry Liddon*. London: Longmans, Green & Co., 1904.

Jurich, James P., S. J. 'The Ecumenical Relations of Victor De Buck S. J. with Anglo-Catholic Leaders on the Eve of Vatican I, 1854–68'. Doctor of Sacred Theology diss., Université Catholique de Louvain, 1970.

Keble, John. *On Eucharistical Adoration*. Oxford and London: John Henry and James Parker, 1857.

Kilmartin, Edward J. *The Eucharist in the West: History and Theology*. Edited by Robert J. Daly. Collegeville, MN: Liturgical Press, 1998.

[Kingsley, Charles]. *Charles Kingsley: Letters and Memories of his Life*. Edited by Fanny Kingsley. London: Kegan Paul, 1877.

Larsen, Timothy. 'E. B. Pusey and Holy Scripture'. *Journal of Theological Studies* 60, no. 2 (October 2009): 490–526.

Lee, Samuel. *Some Remarks on the Sermon of the Rev. Dr Pusey Lately Preached and Published at Oxford, in a Letter Addressed to That Gentleman*. London: Seeley, Burnside, and Seeley, 1843.

Liddon, Henry Parry. *Life of Edward Bouverie Pusey*. Edited by J. O. Johnston, Robert J. Wilson and W. C. E. Newbolt. 4 vols. London: Longmans, Green & Co., 1893–97.

Livesley, Alan. 'Regius Professor of Hebrew'. In *Pusey Rediscovered*, edited by Perry Butler, 71–118. London: SPCK, 1983.

Lockhart, J. G. *Charles Lindley, Viscount Halifax*. London: Geoffrey Bless, 1936.

Lough, A. G. *Dr Pusey: Restorer of the Church*. Newton Abbot, Devon: privately published, 1981.

Lubenow, William C. *The Cambridge Apostles, 1820–1914: Liberalism, Imagination, and Friendship.* Cambridge: Cambridge University Press, 1998.
Lücke, Friedrich.'Erinnerungen an Dr Friedrich Schleiermacher'. *Theologische Studien und Kritiken* 7 (1834): 745–813.
MacCulloch, Diarmaid. 'The Myth of the English Reformation'. *Journal of British Studies* 30 (1991): 1–19.
Mackey, Donald J. *Bishop Forbes: A Memoir.* London: Kegan Paul, Trench, 1888.
Matthew, H. C. G. 'Edward Bouverie Pusey: From Scholar to Tractarian'. *Journal of Theological Studies* 32 (1981): 101–24.
McCormack, Ian. '"The Glory of the Indwelling God": The Pneumatology of E. B. Pusey'. MA essay, University of Leeds, 2009.
Meldrum, Patricia. *Conscience and Compromise: Forgotten Evangelicals of Nineteenth-Century Scotland.* Carlisle: Paternoster Press 2007.
Meller, T. W. *Dr Pusey and the Fathers; or, A Comparison of the Doctrine in the Sermon of the Former with the Writers of the First Five Centuries.* London: J. Hatchard and Son, 1843.
Michaelis, Johann David. *Introduction to the New Testament, Translated from the Fourth Edition of the German, Augmented with Notes, etc. (and a Dissertation on the Origin and Composition of the Three First Gospels), by Herbert Marsh.* 4 vols. Cambridge: J. Archdeacon, 1793–1801.
Middleton, R. A. *Dr Routh.* Oxford: Oxford University Press, 1938.
Milman, Henry Hart. *The History of the Jews.* Vols 1–3. London: John Murray, 1829.
Milner, John. *Remarks on the New Doctrine of the Real Objective Presence as Propounded by the Ritualists.* 2nd ed. London: Longmans, Green & Co., 1876.
Morgan, Nicholas and Richard Trainor. 'The Dominant Classes'. In *People and Society in Scotland 1803–1914*, edited by W. Hamish Fraser and R. J. Morris, 2:103–37. Edinburgh: John Donald, 1990.
Morris, R. J. 'Urbanisation and Scotland'. In *People and Society in Scotland 1803–1914*, edited by W. Hamish Fraser and R. J. Morris, 2:73–102. Edinburgh: John Donald 1990.
Mosig, Jörg Manfred. *The Birthpangs of Neo-Protestantism: Hugh James Rose, Ernst Hengstenberg and the Conservative Response to German Rationalism.* PhD thesis, Durham University, 2000.
Müller, Friedrich Max. *The Life and Letters of the Right Honourable Friedrich Max Müller.* Edited by his wife. 2 vols. London: Longmans, Green & Co., 1902.
Mumm, Susan. *Stolen Daughters, Virgin Mothers: Anglican Sisterhoods in Victorian Britain.* London: Leicester University Press, 1999.
Neale, J. M. *Sermons on the Blessed Sacrament: Preached in the Oratory of S. Margaret's, East Grinstead.* 7th ed. London: J. T. Hayes, n.d. [1871].
Nenadic, Stana. 'The Rise of the Urban Middle Classes'. In *People and Society in Scotland 1760–1830*, edited by T. M. Devine and Rosalind Mitchison, 1:109–26. Edinburgh: John Donald 1988.
[Newman, John Henry]. *Letters and Correspondence of John Henry Newman during His Life in the English Church, With a Brief Autobiography.* Edited by Anne Mozley. 2 vols. London: Longmans, Green & Co., 1891.
[Newman, John Henry]. *The Letters and Diaries of John Henry Newman.* Vol. 2: *Tutor of Oriel, January 1827 to December 1831.* Edited by I. Ker and T. Gornall. Oxford: Clarendon Press, 1979.
Newman, John Henry. *The Letters and Diaries of John Henry Newman.* Vol. 7: *Editing the British Critic, January 1839 to December 1840.* Edited by Gerald Tracey. Oxford: Clarendon Press, 1995.
Newman, John Henry. *The Letters and Diaries of John Henry Newman.* Vol. 8: *Tract 90 and the Jerusalem Bishopric.* Edited by Gerard Tracey. Oxford: Clarendon Press, 1999.

Newman, John Henry. *The Letters and Diaries of John Henry Newman.* Vol. 23: *Defeat at Oxford, Defence at Rome, January to December 1867.* Edited by Charles Stephen Dessain and Thomas Gornall. Oxford: Clarendon Press, 1973.

Newman, John Henry. *Letters and Diaries.* Vol. 24: *A Grammar of Assent, January 1868 to December 1869.* Edited by Charles Stephen Dessain and Thomas Gornall. London: Nelson and Oxford: Oxford University Press, for the Birmingham Oratory, 1973.

[Newman, John Henry]. *Tract 3: On the Introduction of Rationalistic Principles into Religion.* London: J. G. & F. Rivington, 1835/36.

Newman, J. H. *Tract XC on Certain Passages in the XXXIX Articles (1841) with a Historical Preface by Rev. E. B. Pusey and Catholic Subscription to the XXXIX Articles Considered in Reference to Tract XC by the Rev. John Keble, M. A.* 1841. Oxford: Parker; London: Rivington, 1866.

Nockles, Peter. 'Our Brethren of the North: The Scottish Episcopal Church and the Oxford Movement'. *Journal of Ecclesiastical History* 47 (1996): 655–82.

Nockles, Peter B. *The Oxford Movement in Context: Anglican High Churchmanship, 1760–1857.* Cambridge: Cambridge University Press, 1996.

Noether, Emiliana P. 'Vatican Council I: Its Political and Religious Setting'. *Journal of Modern History* 40, no. 2 (June 1968): 218–33.

O'Connell, Marvin R. *The Oxford Conspirators: A History of the Oxford Movement 1833–1845.* New York: Macmillan, 1969.

Overton, J. H. *The Anglican Revival.* London: Blackie and Son, 1897.

Paley, William. *Natural Theology: or, Evidences of the Existence and Attributes of the Deity, Collected from the Appearance of Nature.* London: R. Faulder, 1802.

Paley, William. *A View of the Evidences of Christianity.* 2 vols. London: R. Faulder, 1794.

Paulin, Roger. 'Julius Hare's German Books in Trinity College Library (Cambridge)'. *Transactions of the Cambridge Bibliographical Society* 9 (1987): 174–93.

Pawley, Bernard and Margaret. *Rome and Canterbury through Four Centuries.* 2nd ed. Oxford: Mowbrays, 1981.

Pereiro, James. *'Ethos' and the Oxford Movement: At the Heart of Tractarianism.* Oxford: Oxford University Press, 2008.

Perry, William. *Alexander Penrose Forbes, Bishop of Brechin, the Scottish Pusey.* London: SPCK, 1939.

Perry, W. *The Oxford Movement in Scotland.* Cambridge: Cambridge University Press, 1933.

Prestige, G. L. *Pusey.* London: Mowbray, 1982.

Pusey, Edward Bouverie. *The Articles Treated on in Tract 90 Reconsidered and Their Interpretation Vindicated in a Letter to the Rev. R. E. Jelf, D. D., Canon of Christ Church.* Oxford: John Henry Parker, 1841.

Pusey, Edward Bouverie. *Case as to the Legal Force of the Judgment of the Privy Council in Re. in Fendal v. Wilson; with the Opinion of the Attorney General & Sir Hugh Cairns, and a Preface to Those Who Love God and His Truth.* 2nd ed. Oxford: John Henry Parker, 1864.

Pusey, E. B. *'Christ in Us, and We in Him', the Bond of Catholic Unity.* Tracts on Catholic Unity, by Members of the Church of England. No. 5. London: James Darling, c. 1845.

Pusey, E. B. *The Church of England a Portion of Christ's One Holy Catholic Church, and a Means of Restoring Visible Unity: An Eirenicon, in a Letter to the Author of 'The Christian Year'.* Oxford: Parker; London: Rivingtons, 1865.

Pusey, Edward Bouverie. *Collegiate and Professorial Teaching and Discipline in Answer to Professor Vaughan's Strictures, Chiefly as to the Charges Against the Colleges of France and Germany.* Oxford and London: Parker, 1854.

Pusey, Edward Bouverie. *The Councils of the Church from the Council of Jerusalem A.D. 51 to the Council of Constantinople A.D. 381, Chiefly as to Their Constitution, but also as to Their Objectives and History.* Oxford: John Henry Parker, 1857.

Pusey, Edward Bouverie. *Dr Hampden's Theological Statements and the Thirty-Nine Articles Compared: by a Resident Member of Convocation, with a Preface, and Prepositions Extracted from his Works.* Oxford: Baxter, 1836.

Pusey, E. B. *The Doctrine of the Real Presence, as Contained in the Fathers from the Death of S. John the Evangelist to the Fourth General Council, Vindicated, in Notes on a Sermon, 'The Presence of Christ in the Holy Eucharist', Preached A.D. 1853, before the University of Oxford.* Oxford: John Henry Parker; London: F. & J. Rivington, 1855.

Pusey, E. B. 'The Entire Absolution of the Penitent'. In *Famous Sermons by English Preachers*, edited by Douglas Macleane, 257–79. London: Sir Isaac Pitman and Sons, 1911.

Pusey, E. B. *First Letter to the Very Rev. J. H. Newman in Explanation Chiefly in Regard to the Reverential Love due to the Ever-blessed Theotokos, and the Doctrine of her Immaculate Conception; with an Analysis of Cardinal de Turrecremata's Work on the Immaculate Conception.* Oxford: Parker; London: Rivingtons, 1869.

Pusey, E. B. *Healthful Reunion as Conceived Possible before the Vatican Council: The Second Letter to the Very Rev. J. H. Newman, D. D.* Oxford: J. Parker and Co., 1876.

Pusey, Edward Bouverie. *An Historical Enquiry into the Probable Causes of the Rationalist Character Lately Predominant in the Theology of Germany; To Which is Prefixed a Letter from Professor Sack, upon the Rev. H. J. Rose's Discourses on German Protestantism; Translated from the German.* London: C. & J. Rivington, 1828.

Pusey, Edward Bouverie. *An Historical Enquiry into the Probable Causes of the Rationalist Character Lately Predominant in the Theology of Germany; Part II: Containing an Explanation of the Views Misconceived by Mr Rose.* London: C. J. G. & F. Rivington, 1830.

Pusey, E. B. 'Holy Communion: Exceeding Danger in Careless Receiving, Death in Neglecting'. In [E. B. Pusey], *Plain Sermons, by Contributors to the 'Tracts for the Times'*, 3:87–104. London: J. G. F. & J. Rivington, 1841.

Pusey, E. B. 'Holy Communion: Privileges'. In [E. B. Pusey], *Plain Sermons, by Contributors to the 'Tracts for the Times'*, 3:105–20. London: J. G. F. & J. Rivington, 1841.

Pusey, E. B. *The Holy Eucharist a Comfort to the Penitent: A Sermon Preached before the University in the Cathedral Church of Christ, in Oxford, on the Fourth Sunday after Easter.* New York: D. Appleton, Philadelphia: George S. Appleton, 1843.

Pusey, E. B. *A Letter to His Grace the Archbishop of Canterbury, on Some Circumstances Connected with the Present Crisis in the English Church.* Oxford: John Henry Parker; London: J. G. F. & J. Rivington, 1874.

Pusey, E. B. *A Letter to the Right Hon. and Right Rev. The Lord Bishop of London, in Explanation of Some Statements Contained in a Letter by the Rev. W. Dodsworth.* Oxford and London: John Henry Parker, 1851.

Pusey, E. B. *A Letter to the Right Rev. Father in God, Richard Lord Bishop of Oxford, on the Tendency to Romanism imputed to Doctrines Held of Old, as Now, in the English Church; With an 'Appendix': Extracts from the Tracts for the Times, the Lyra Apostolica, and Other Publications, Showing that to Oppose Ultra-Protestantism is Not to Favour Popery.* Oxford: J. H. Parker, London, J. G.& F. Rivington, 1839.

Pusey, E. B. *Parochial Sermons.* Vol. 2. Plymouth: The Devenport Society, 1862.

Pusey, E. B. *The Presence of Christ in the Holy Eucharist: A Sermon, Preached before the University, in the Cathedral Church of Christ, in Oxford, on the Second Sunday after Epiphany, 1853.* Oxford and London: John Henry Parker; London: F. & J. Rivington, 1853.

Pusey, E. B. *The Real Presence of the Body and Blood of our Lord Jesus Christ the Doctrine of the English Church, with a Vindication of the Reception by the Wicked and of the Adoration of Our Lord Jesus Christ Truly Present.* Oxford: John Henry Parker, 1857.

Pusey, Edward Bouverie. *The Royal Supremacy Not an Arbitrary Authority but Limited by the Laws of the Church of which Kings are Members.* Oxford: John Henry Parker, 1850.

Pusey, Edward Bouverie. *Sermons during the Season from Advent to Whitsuntide.* Oxford: John Henry Parker, 1848.

[Pusey, E. B.] *Spiritual Letters of Edward Bouverie Pusey.* Edited by J. O. Johnston and W. C. E. Newbolt. London: Longmans, Green & Co., 1898.

Pusey, E. B. *This is My Body: A Sermon Preached before the University at S. Mary's, on the Fifth Sunday after Easter 1871.* Oxford: James Parker; London, Oxford, and Cambridge: Rivingtons, 1871.

P[usey,] Edward Bouverie. *Tract 28: Thoughts on the Benefits of the System of Fasting, Enjoined by our Church.* London: J. G. & F. Rivington, [1833/34].

Pusey, Edward Bouverie. *Tract 28: Thoughts on the Benefits of the System of Fasting Enjoined by Our Church.* 2nd ed. London: Parker, 1833.

Pusey, Edward Bouverie. *Tract 66: Supplement to Tract 28; On the Benefits of the System of Fasting Prescribed by Our Church.* London: J. G. & F. Rivington, 1835.

[Pusey,] Edward Bouverie. *Tracts 67–69: Scriptural Views of Holy Baptism.* Oxford: Palmer, 1835.

Pusey, Edward Bouverie. *Tracts 67–69. Scriptural Views of Holy Baptism.* 2nd ed. London: J. G. & F. Rivington, 1836.

Pusey, E. B. *Tract 81. Catena Patrum. No. 4. Testimony of Writers in the Later English Church to the Doctrine of the Eucharistic Sacrifice, With an Historical Account of the Changes Made in the Liturgy as to the Expression of that Doctrine.* London: J. G. & F. Rivington, 1836/37.

[Pusey, Edward Bouverie.] 'Ueber den Zustand der Neuern Englischen Theologie: Ein Schreiben von Einem Englischen Geistlichen'. *Litterarischer Anzeiger für Christliche Theologie und Wissenschaft überhaupt* 2 (1831): 348–52, 356–60.

Pusey, E. B. *Will Ye Also Go Away? A Sermon, Preached before the University of Oxford, on the Fourth Sunday after the Epiphany, 1867.* Oxford and London: James Parker; London, Oxford and Cambridge: Rivingtons, 1867.

Ralls, Walter. 'The Papal Aggression of 1850: A Study in Victorian Anti-Catholicism'. *Church History* 43, no. 2 (June 1974): 242–56.

Reed, John Shelton. *Glorious Battle: The Cultural Politics of Victorian Anglo-Catholicism.* Nashville: Vanderbilt University Press, 1996.

Remains of the Late Reverend Richard Hurrell Froude, M. A., Fellow of Oriel College, Oxford. London: Rivington, 1838.

Reynolds, Michael. *Martyr of Ritualism: Father Mackonochie of St Alban's, Holborn.* London: Faber & Faber, 1965.

Robinson, James Harvey. *Readings in European History.* New York: Ginn & Co., 1906.

Rogerson, John. *Old Testament Criticism in the Nineteenth Century: England and Germany.* London: SPCK, 1984.

Rose, Hugh James. *A Letter to the Lord Bishop of London, in Reply to Mr Pusey's Work on the Causes of Rationalism in Germany; Comprising Observations on Confessions of Faith, and Their Advantages.* London: C. J. G. & F. Rivington, 1829.

Rose, Hugh James. *The State of the Protestant Religion in Germany; in a Series of Discourses Preached before the University of Cambridge.* Cambridge: J. Deighton & Sons, 1825.

Rose, Hugh James. *The State of the Protestant Religion in Germany, Described; Being the Substance of Four Discourses Preached before the University of Cambridge in 1825: Second Edition, Enlarged,*

With an Appendix (A Reply to the German Critiques on the 'State of the Protestant Religion in Germany'). London: C. J. G. & F. Rivington, 1829.
Rowell, Geoffrey. *The Vision Glorious: Themes and Personalities of the Catholic Revival in Anglicanism*. Oxford: Oxford University Press, 1983.
Schleiermacher, Friedrich. *Brief Outline of the Study of Theology; Drawn up to Serve as the Basis of Introductory Lectures by Friedrich Schleiermacher; to which are Prefixed Reminiscences of Schleiermacher by Friedrich Lücke; Translated from the German by William Farrer.* Edinburgh: T&T Clark, 1850.
Schleiermacher, Friedrich Daniel Ernst. *Der Christliche Glaube nach den Grundsätzen der Evangelischen Kirche im Zusammenhange Dargestellt*. 1–2. Berlin: G. Reimer, 1821/22.
Schleiermacher, Friedrich Daniel Ernst. *A Critical Essay on the Gospel of St Luke, with an Introduction by the Translator Containing an Account of the Controversy Respecting the Origin of the Three First Gospels since Bishop Marsh's Dissertation*. Translated by Connop Thirlwall. London: Taylor, 1825.
Schleiermacher, Friedrich Daniel Ernst. *Kurze Darstellung des Theologischen Studiums zum Behuf einleitender Vorlesungen*. Berlin: Realschulbuchhandlung, 1811.
Schleiermacher, Friedrich Daniel Ernst. *Über die Religion: Reden an die Gebildeten unter ihren Verächtern*. Berlin: Johann Friedrich Unger, 1799.
Sherlock, Thomas. *An Answer to a Letter Sent to the Reverend Dr Sherlock, &c. Relating to his Sermon Preach'd before the Lord-Mayor, November the 5th 1712, to which are Added, Some Observations upon the Account the Lord Bishop of Bangor has Given of his Intended Answer to the Representation*. London: John Pauberton, 1717.
Skinner, Simon. 'History versus Historiography: The Reception of Turner's Newman'. *Journal of Ecclesiastical History* 61 (2010): 764–81.
Smollett, Tobias. *The Expedition of Humphry Clinker*. 1771. London: Penguin, 2008.
Stanley, Arthur Penrhyn. *The Life and Correspondence of Thomas Arnold*. London: B. Fellowes, 1858.
Strange, Roderick. 'Reflections on a Controversy: Newman and Pusey's *Eirenicon*'. In *Pusey Rediscovered*, edited by Perry Butler, 332–48. London: SPCK, 1983.
Straka, Gerald. 'The Final Phase of Divine Right Theory in England, 1688–1702'. *English Historical Review* 77, no. 305 (October 1962): 638–58.
Strong, Rowan. *Alexander Forbes of Brechin: The First Tractarian Bishop*. Oxford: Clarendon Press, 1995.
Strong, Rowan. *Anglicanism and the British Empire c. 1700–1850*. Oxford and New York: Oxford University Press, 2007.
Strong, Rowan. 'Coronets and Altars: Aristocratic Women's and Men's Support for the Oxford Movement in Scotland during the 1840s'. *Studies in Church History: Gender and the Christian Religion* 34 (1998): 391–403. Woodbridge, Suffolk: Boydell & Brewer.
Strong, Rowan. *Episcopalianism in Nineteenth-Century Scotland: Religious Responses to a Modernizing Society*. Oxford: Oxford University Press, 2002.
Strong, Rowan. 'High Churchmen and Anglo-Catholics: William Gladstone and the Eucharistic Controversy in the Scottish Episcopal Church 1856–1860'. *Journal of Religious History* 20, no. 2 (December 1996): 175–84.
Strong, Rowan. 'The Oxford Movement and the British Empire: Newman, Manning and the 1841 Jerusalem Bishopric'. In *The Oxford Movement in Europe and the Wider World*, edited by Stewart J. Brown and Peter Nockles, 78–98. Cambridge: Cambridge University Press, 2012.
Strong, Rowan. 'In Search of Certainty: Scottish Episcopalian Converts to Rome in the Mid-Nineteenth Century'. *Recusant History* 25 (2001): 511–29.

Stuart, Elizabeth Bridget. 'Roman Catholic Reactions to the Oxford Movement and Anglican Schemes for Reunion, from 1833 to the Condemnation of Anglican Orders in 1896'. DPhil thesis, University of Oxford, 1988.

Sumner, John Bird. *The Evidence of Christianity, Derived from its Nature and Reception*. London: Hatchard & Son, 1824.

Taylor, Stephen. 'William Warburton and the Alliance of Church and State'. *Journal of Ecclesiastical History* 43, no. 2 (1992): 271–86.

Teale, Ruth. 'Dr Pusey and the Church Overseas'. In *Pusey Rediscovered*, edited by Perry Butler, 185–209. London: SPCK, 1983.

Thirlwall, Connop. *Letters Literary and Theological of Connop Thirlwall, Late Lord Bishop of St David's*. Edited by J. J. S. Perowne and L. Stokes. London: R. Bentley & Son, 1881.

Tholuck, Friedrich August Gotttreu. 'Gespräche über die Vornehmsten Glaubensfragen der Zeit'. *Dr August Tholuck's Werke* 8: 93–280. Gotha: Perthes 1865.

Thompson, David M. *Cambridge Theology in the Nineteenth Century: Enquiry, Controversy and Truth*. Aldershot: Ashgate Publishing House, 2008.

Tjernagel, Neelak Serawlook. *Henry VIII and the Lutherans: A Study in Anglo-Lutheran Relations from 1521 to 1547*. Saint Louis, MO: Concordia Publishing House, 1965.

Tracts for the Times. 2 vols. London: J. G. F. & J. Rivington, 1840.

Trench, Maria Marcia Fanny. *The Story of Dr Pusey's Life*. London: Longmans, Green & Co., 1900.

Turner, Frank M. *John Henry Newman: The Challenge to Evangelical Religion*. New Haven and London: Yale University Press, 2002.

Vance, Norman. *The Sinews of the Spirit: The Ideal of Christian Manliness in Victorian Literature and Religious Thought*. Cambridge: Cambridge University Press, 1985.

Walsh, Walter. *The Secret History of the Oxford Movement*. London: Swan Sonnenschein & Co., 1897.

[Warburton, William]. *The Alliance between Church and State, or the Necessity and Equity of an Established Religion and a Test-Law Demonstrated, From the Essence and End of Civil Society, upon the Fundamental Principles of the Law of Nature and Nations in Three Parts: The First, Treating of a Civil and a Religious Society; the Second, of an Established Church; and the Third, of a Test-Law*. London: Fletcher Gyles, 1736.

Ward, Wilfrid. *Life of John Henry Cardinal Newman*. London: Longmans, Green & Co., 1912.

Webster, John. *Theological Theology: An Inaugural Lecture Delivered before the University of Oxford on 27 October 1997*. Oxford: Clarendon Press, 1998.

Wilberforce, Robert I. *The Doctrine of the Holy Eucharist*. 1853. New York: E. and J. B. Young, 1885.

Williams, Rowan. *On Christian Theology*. Oxford: Blackwell, 2000.

Williams, Thomas Jay. *Priscilla Lydia Sellon: The Restorer after Three Centuries of the Religious Life in the English Church*. Revised edition. London: SPCK, 1965.

INDEX

Acland, Henry Wentworth 26–7
Andrewes, Bishop Lancelot 99, 101, 103
Anglicanism: *see* Pusey, Church of England
Anglicization 140, 145
Anglo-Catholicism 6, 7, 11, 14, 26, 34, 37, 38, 40, 42, 43–5, 49, 50, 62, 63, 115, 116, 117, 118, 125, 126–7, 128, 133
Arnold, Thomas 68
Ascot Priory: *see* Pusey, sisterhoods and
Athanasian Creed 6
Atterbury, Bishop Francis 75–9, 81–2, 89n139

Bagot, Bishop Richard 50, 92
Bathurst, Bishop Henry 68
Bennett, William James Early 92
Bevis, Henry J. 102
biblical criticism: *see* Pusey, biblical criticism and
Bilio, Cardinal Luigi Maria 122–3
Blomfield, Charles James 37, 42, 55, 56, 92, 98
Book of Common Prayer 1637 and 1662 140, 141, 144
Bosanquet, Claude 102
Boyle, George, sixth Earl of Glasgow 136
Bramhall, Archbishop John 101
Broughton, Bishop William 146
Burke, Edmund 57

Calvin, John 94
Calvinism 34, 42, 43, 44, 75, 126, 142
Cambridge, University of 51, 52
Catholicism: *see* Pusey, Roman Catholicism and; Roman Catholicism

Catholic Emancipation Act 1829 38, 68, 69
Charles I, King 141
Church Association 92
Church Temporalities (Ireland) Act 68, 69
Close, Francis 36
Christ Church College, Oxford 1, 2, 3, 7, 14, 105
Church, Richard William 48n55, 133–4
church fathers 102, 117, 118, 122, 124, 125, 128; *see also* Pusey, church fathers and
convocations, of the Church of England 76, 77–8, 85; *see also* Pusey, convocation and
Conybeare, John Josias 52

Darboy, Archbishop Georges 119
de Buck, Victor 120–26
de Luca, Cardinal Antonio Saverio 125, 126
Denison, George Anthony 92, 137
Döllinger, Ignaz 63, 118, 120, 128
Dorner, Asaak August 63
Dupanloup, Bishop Felix Antoine Philibert 120, 125

Ecclesiastical Commission 68
Essays and Reviews 6
Evangelicalism 43, 44, 60, 88n120, 141, 145

Forbes, Bishop Alexander Penrose; *see also* Pusey, Forbes, Bishop Alexander Penrose and ecclesiology/church unity 116–18, 125–6

French Revolution 70
Freytag, Georg Wilhelm 35, 45
Froude, Richard Hurrell 69, 135, 136, 138, 144

Gladstone, William Ewart 62, 69, 109n7, 116
Glorious Revolution of 1688–89 67, 75
Golightly, Charles Portales 50, 69
Goode, William 103
Gore, Bishop Charles 26, 33, 45
Gorham Judgement 70, 85n58, 142
Gothic architecture 110n38
Guest, Bishop Edmund 100, 103

Hampden, Renn Dickson 61, 69, 70
Hare, Julius 51
Harrison, John 96, 102–3
Hawkins, Edward 2
Hengstenberg, Ernst Wilhelm 54, 55
High Church 6, 27, 44–5, 54, 56, 67, 69, 72, 75, 79, 80, 88n120, 122, 135–6, 137
Hoadly, Bishop Benjamin 75, 78–9, 80–82, 86n97, 87n100, 87n102, 89n138
Homilies, Book of 99
Hook, Walter Farquhar 5, 71–2, 84n40, 92
Hooker, Richard 56
Hughes, Marian 43

Islam 42, 50

Jacobitism 89n139, 140, 147n20
Jelf, Richard William 2
Jerusalem, Bishopric of 69, 70
Johnston, John Octavius 1, 27–8, 31, 32, 33, 34, 35, 36, 37–8, 42, 44, 45n1, 46n2, 46n12

Keble, John 1, 2, 4, 5, 6, 11, 17, 22, 25, 42, 69, 70, 87n117, 93, 106, 134, 135–6, 137, 138, 139–40, 141, 142–3, 144
Ketteler, Archbishop and Baron Wilhelm von 120
Kingsley, Charles 6
Kosegarten, Johann Gottfried Ludwig 35

Laud, Archbishop William 82n1
liberalism 11, 14, 53–4, 57, 60, 125
liberal Protestantism 10, 12, 50
Library of the Fathers 71
Liddon, Henry Parry 1, 3, 8, 9, 10, 13, 14, 15, 16, 26, 31–48, 52, 59, 63, 93, 105, 121, 122
Life of Pusey: *see* Liddon, Henry Parry
Lloyd, Bishop Charles 52, 143
Longley, Archbishop Charles Taylor 5
Lothian, Marchioness of 136
Lücke, Friedrich 57, 63
Luther, Martin 10, 37, 41, 51, 56, 61, 62
Lux Mundi 6, 45

Maltby, Edward 2
Manning, Henry Edward 5, 120, 121, 123, 125, 146
Marriott, Charles 116
Marsh, Herbert 51
Melbourne, Lord 68
Michaelis, Johann David 51
Milman, Henry Hart 59
Milner, John 102, 103
Milner, Maud 25
Müller, Friedrich Max 62

Neander, August 54, 56–7, 63
Newbolt, William Charles Edmund 1, 27, 28, 32, 33, 46n2
Newman, John Henry 1, 2, 3, 4, 5–6, 7, 8, 9, 11, 19, 20, 33, 35, 42, 43, 44, 52, 55, 60, 69, 87n117, 93, 105–6, 115, 116, 119, 120, 123, 124–5, 133–4, 135, 136, 144, 145
Nicoll, Alexander 50
Nitzsch, Karl Immanuel 36, 63
Non-Jurors 70–71, 75, 79, 147n20

occasional conformity 78, 79, 87n114
Oriel College 2, 35, 38, 50, 68
Orthodox (Chalcedonian) churches 71, 120
Overall, Bishop John 101
Oxford Movement, historiography of 7–8, 9, 15, 133–5, 145–6
Oxford, University of 1, 3, 13, 50, 52, 54, 59, 68, 145

Paget, Francis 33
Palmerston, Lord (Henry John Temple) 141
Paulus, Heinrich Eberhard Gottlob 51
Peel, Sir Robert 68, 69
Phillpotts, Bishop Henry 70, 82n3, 108n2
Pius IX, Pope 118, 120, 121, 127, 130n34
Powell, Clarissa (Sister Clara) 22, 25, 27, 30n61
Powell, Frederick York 13–14
Pusey, Edward
  asceticism of 17–19, 22–4, 25, 143
  biblical criticism and 6, 9, 36, 52, 58–9, 97, 104
  Church of England/Anglicanism and 70–72, 84n42, 98–104, 144–6
  church fathers and 19, 23, 58, 61, 69, 71, 76, 82, 83n28–9, 36, 84n42, 92, 95, 97, 98, 102, 117, 118
  convocation and 6, 70
  Forbes, Bishop Alexander Penrose and 11–12, 92, 115–32, 133–48
  Germany and 2–3, 10, 36, 40, 45, 69 (see also Pusey, Lutheranism and)
  historiography of 7–12, 13–30, 31–48, 92–3
  letters of 27–8
  life and career 1, 2–7
  Lutheranism and 35–6, 41, 49–66
  personality 25–8, 109n9, 143
  Presbyterianism and 39–40, 56
  publications 3, 5, 6, 19–20, 49–55, 58, 59, 91–2
  Roman Catholicism and 5–6, 35, 71–2, 83n28, 94, 115–32
  ritualism and 5, 91, 108n3
  Scottish Episcopal Church and 11–12, 39, 73, 91, 133–48
  sermons and preaching 3–4, 21–3, 83n32, 97, 137–8
  sex and 17–18, 106, 107
  sisterhoods and 4, 7, 17, 22, 23–4
  Society of the Holy Cross and 38–9, 106
  spiritual director 22

  theology of (see also Pusey, biblical criticism)
    early church and 70, 71, 83n29, 98
    ecclesiology/church unity 36–7, 62, 71–2, 74–82
    ecstatic 21–2, 24
    episcopacy 37, 56, 69, 71–4, 138–9
    Eucharist and 3–4, 11, 39–40, 42, 91–113, 137–8, 144–5
    pneumatology 19–21
    Royal Supremacy 73–82
    sacraments 62, 92, 103–5, 108n5
    sin 106–8
    Vatican Council I and 11
  wife and children 2, 105 (see also Pusey, Lucy; Pusey, Maria; Pusey, Mary; Pusey, Philip)
Pusey House 1, 10, 14, 16, 26, 31, 45
Pusey, Lucy 4, 15, 26, 105
Pusey, Maria 3, 4–5, 10, 15, 17, 18, 36, 38, 39, 49, 105, 106
Pusey, Mary 26
Pusey, Philip 6, 15–16

rationalism: see liberalism
Rattray, Bishop Thomas 141
Reformation 58, 62, 116, 117, 127
ritualism 5, 6–7, 92; see also Pusey, ritualism and
Roman Catholicism 4, 110n37; see also Pusey, Roman Catholicism and
Rose, Hugh James 40, 52–7
Rossetti, Christina 1
Routh, Martin 135

Sack, Karl Heinrich 54, 63
Schleiermacher, Friedrich 3, 35, 45, 51, 52, 54, 56–7, 60
Scotland 10, 39, 80, 137, 140, 145
Scottish Communion Office 140–45
Scottish Episcopal Church 135, 136, 140, 147n20; see also Pusey, Scottish Episcopal Church and
Sellon, Priscilla Lydia 4, 24–5, 43
Selwyn, Bishop George Augustus 146
Semler, Johan Salomo 53
Shaftesbury, Lord 141

sisterhoods (*see also* Pusey, sisterhoods and)
   Park Village 4, 23–4
   Holy Trinity 4, 24–5
Socinianism 75
Spener 41
Strossmeyer, Bishop Joseph Georg 126
Sumner, Archbishop John Bird 141

Tait, Archbishop Archibald Campbell 6
Test and Corporation Acts 1828 38, 69, 79
Thirlwall, Bishop Connop 51
Thirty-Nine Articles 99–101, 116, 118
Tholuck, Augustus 3, 33, 45, 49, 50, 51, 54, 55, 58, 61, 62, 63
Toleration Act 1689 75
Tories 68, 74, 75, 86n98, 136
Tractarianism 44, 51, 60–61, 66, 74, 110n49, 137, 146
Tracts for the Times 3
Trench, Maria 14, 15

United States of America 72–3, 148n55

Vatican Council I: *see* Pusey, Roman Catholicism and; Pusey, theology of, Vatican Council I and)
Victoria, Queen 17, 39

Walsh, Walter 15
Warburton, William 68, 75, 79–81
Wellington, Duke of 68
Whigs 68, 69, 70, 74–5, 76, 78, 81–2, 87n103
William III, King Frederick of Prussia 52
William III, King of England 75, 77, 85n70
Wilson, Robert John 1, 32, 46n2
Wilson, Bishop William 140
Wordsworth, Bishop Christopher 21

Zwingli, Ulrich 94

www.ingramcontent.com/pod-product-compliance
Lightning Source LLC
Chambersburg PA
CBHW021831300426
44114CB00009BA/401